book are from the archives of the U.S. Department of Defense.
tesy of Bob Rosenburgh.

kpole Books
obe Pequot, the trade division of
Littlefield Publishing Group, Inc.
d., Ste. 200
0706
Books.com

NATIONAL BOOK NETWORK

021 by Michael Lee Lanning

y Cataloguing in Publication Information available

ngress Cataloging-in-Publication Data

8117-3974-0 (cloth : alk. paper)
-8117-6972-3 (electronic)

er used in this publication meets the minimum requirements of American National
Information Sciences—Permanence of Paper for Printed Library Materials, ANSI/
48-1992.

D1212536

BLISTE

THE EXTRAORDINARY
AMERICAN AIRM
TO SAFETY IN

MICHAEL LE

STACKP(
BOOK

Guilford, Connec

All photos in this
The maps are cou

Published by Sta
An imprint of G
The Rowman &
4501 Forbes Blv
Lanham, MD 2(
www.Stackpole

Distributed by

Copyright © 2

British Librar

Library of C(

ISBN 978-0-
ISBN 978-0-

The pa
Standard fo
NISO Z39.

Books by Michael Lee Lanning

The Only War We Had: A Platoon Leader's Journal of Vietnam

Vietnam 1969-1970: A Company Commander's Journal

Inside the LRRPs: Rangers in Vietnam

Inside Force Recon: Recon Marines in Vietnam (with Ray W. Stubbe)

The Battles of Peace

Inside the VC and NVA: The Real Story of North Vietnam's Armed Forces
   (with Dan Cragg)

Vietnam at the Movies

*Senseless Secrets: The Failures of U. S. Military Intelligence from George Washington
   to the Present*

The Military 100: A Ranking of the Most Influential Military Leaders of All Time

The African-American Soldier: From Crispus Attucks to Colin Powell

Inside the Crosshairs: Snipers in Vietnam

Defenders of Liberty: African-Americans in the Revolutionary War

Blood Warriors: American Military Elites

The Battle 100: The Stories Behind History's Most Influential Battles

*Mercenaries: Soldiers of Fortune, from Ancient Greece to Today's Private
   Military Companies*

*The Civil War 100: The Stories Behind the Most Influential Battles, People, and Events
   in the War Between the States*

*The Revolutionary War 100: The Stories Behind the Most Influential Battles, People,
   and Events of the American Revolution*

Double T Double Cross Double Take: The Firing of Coach Mike Leach

At War With Cancer (with Linda Moore-Lanning)

Tours of Duty: Vietnam War Stories

Tony Buzbee: Defining Moments

Texas Aggies in Vietnam: War Stories

The Veterans Cemeteries of Texas

Dear Allyanna: An Old Soldiers Last Letter to His Granddaughter

*The Court Martial of Jackie Robinson: The Baseball Legend's Battle for Civil Rights
   During World War II*

Contents

Introduction

Book ideas come from a multitude of places. The initial spark for this work arose some twenty years ago but lay dormant before finally coming to life. In the late 1990s, I visited my parent's graves in a dusty, tumbleweed-strewn cemetery in West Texas. I made the trek every year or so out of respect and mostly fond memories of those who had bred and raised me.

The remote graveyard, some five miles from the nearest residence and twenty from a town of any size, lay surrounded by a low wire fence. A few cedar trees of green interrupted what was otherwise yellow and the gray coverage of dead vegetation intermingled with exposure of the red topsoil. I always placed a rock on their headstone—a Jewish tradition that I had picked up and appreciated. On previous visits, I had always had the cemetery to myself.

This time was different. A few plots away, an aged man dressed in the usual jeans, khaki shirt, and cowboy boots that make up the uniform of West Texas ranchers as well as farmers, used a garden hoe to remove a few weeds and rake the top of several graves.

I introduced myself and, on hearing his name, thought I recalled hearing it before. When I asked if he had been an airman in World War II, he responded in the affirmative. I told him that I remembered as a boy hearing he had been shot down over Europe. He nodded his head and laughed when I asked how many missions he flew. He responded, "Well, I guess none. Went down on first mission in Yugoslavia and used my feet to evade and walk to freedom."

In 2019, I recalled that conversation when I discovered the World War II archives that tell the stories of American airmen evaders. This book is the result of that long ago graveyard conversation and a year's worth of research.

The ranks of young men who earned admittance to the "Blister Club," those who walked out of German-occupied western Europe, have dwindled with the passage of decades. The old rancher I met in the cemetery long ago is now buried under a Veterans Administration headstone a few yards from my parents.

A few evaders left behind published and unpublished manuscripts about their experiences, but the primary source of material about their escapes is found in the US War Department, US Forces, European Theater, Military Intelligence Service (MIS) Escape and Evasion Section (MIS-X) and Interview Section, Collection and Administrative Branch individual debriefings and interviews conducted with each returnee at their London headquarters. These reports total some 43,000 pages in fifty-eight boxes. The documents include hand-written accounts, first-typed drafts, edited copies, and final reports. However, in many cases, only one or two of these reports have made their way into the archives. Also included in the thousands of pages are movement orders, authorization for rations, related materials, and pictures of helpers. In some instances, the spelling of the evader's name and his position aboard the aircraft differ from squadron and United States Army Air Forces records. Generally, the spelling and crew position as noted in the escape and evasion report (E&E) is used in this book. All quotations in this work are from these E&E reports unless otherwise noted. Spelling of villages and towns are also as written in the reports. Date style and rank abbreviations have been standardized for clarity.

First Evaders

SECRET—AMERICAN
MOST SECRET—BRITISH

HEADQUARTERS
EUROPEAN THEATER OF OPERATIONS
P/W and X Detachment
Military Intelligence Service

E&E Report No. 5
Evasion in France

January 27, 1943

Name:	Forrest D. Hartin
Rank:	2LT
Unit:	423rd Bomb Squadron, 306th Group (B-17)
Home Address:	Westfield, Mass.
Target:	Saint-Nazaire
MIA:	November 9, 1942
Arrived in UK:	January 18, 1943

Other members of the crew:

Pilot	1LT L. M. Felts
Co-Pilot	2LT Robert Jones
Navigator	Myself
Bombardier	2Lt Graham
Crew Chief	SGT Beers

Radio Operator	SGT Westcott
Tail Gunner	SGT Bogunill
Ball Turret Gunner	SGT Vonderleith
Waist Gunner	SGT Hague

We left Thurleich at 1000 hours, 9 November 1942, with Saint Nazaire as our target. At approximately 1440 hours we ran into very heavy flak, and I bailed out about 5 miles northwest of Saint Nazaire. The plane crashed and burned. After landing I saw two parachutes from our plane and think Graham and Bogunill bailed out at the same time as I. In getting out of the a/c I was caught under the bomb sight for a short time. When free, I was hit by small flak and was also shot at by the Germans while on my way down. I sprained both ankles in landing.

Immediately, I folded my parachute and hid in the brush which was growing along the side of the field. In coming down I lost the special purse containing money but did have my escape kit. I could not walk but managed to crawl along a ditch at the side of the field for 300 or 400 yards. I saw two French peasants walking to the spot where I had landed. I continued crawling until exhausted, then picked out a soft and muddy spot in the ditch and covered myself with leaves and mud.

At this time I heard rifle shots but don't know what they were. I heard someone running and two German soldiers passed within 5 or 6 feet of me. Shortly after this I saw 3 or 4 pairs of Germans searching in the immediate vicinity of where I had come down. I heard dogs barking and think they may have tried to put dogs on my trail but don't believe they were bloodhounds. The smoke from the St. Nazaire raid was drifting over my hiding place, obscuring the sun and making everything very hazy.

After waiting in the ditch until 1900 hours I crawled out and found two stout sticks to use as canes. I started walking in a northeasterly direction. Prior to this I had opened my escape kit and had taken two of the Benzedrine tablets. I had lost quite a lot of blood from my wound. I walked slowly for about half an hour and arrived at the top of the small mole. Looking back, I saw several flashlights near the spot where I had landed. I continued to walk slowly all night in a northeasterly direction until 0600 hours. Then I rested in a field for an hour. It was extremely cold and I was wearing only a light jacket. Setting off in the same direction again I soon came to a small farmhouse. Here, from a distance of about 200 yards, I watched the house. While doing this I ate several of the Horlicks tablets and took more of the Benzedrine tablets. I saw several people in the barnyard while watching the house. Finally I walked up to the rear of the house and listened at the back door. Not hearing any German spoken I knocked and a woman came to the door.

There were, with the woman, two young men in the house. I asked for help. They would not allow me to enter the house but they did bring me coffee. I went back to my hiding place and holed up all day.

At about 1600 hours two or three German military cars drove up to the farm house and about twenty German officers got out. Eight or ten mounted Germans also arrived at this time. They appeared to be holding a meeting at the front of the house and one officer reading from a book and apparently giving the others a pep talk. About an hour passed; the German group broke up and most of the mounted troops departed, but the officers came in the direction I was hiding. They walked past me and stopped about six or seven yards from my hiding-place. I was well hidden and was lying on my face. I thought they would surely see me. They stood very close for about half an hour and the one officer who had apparently been talking to the man at the front of the house continued his talk there. By this time it was getting dark. Finally all the Germans walked back to the house. They appeared to have had one sentry posted about fifteen feet from where I was hiding and one close to the road. They all returned, got into their cars and, after a short delay, drove off.

I waited in hiding for a short time and then started walking about 1900 hours in a northeasterly direction. I followed a muddy road about three miles, stopped several times to rest and finally came to a small village. I stayed on the outskirts of the town and heard German spoken in the streets. I left and retraced my steps.

11 November 1942
I came to a barn which I had previously passed. I slept there in the straw. Later I was awakened by voices. I got up, and, looking through a crack in the barn, I saw several German soldiers. There seemed to be a German billet a short distance away in the main farmhouse. I remained hidden in the barn for several hours until the Germans left, then I walked to some woods close by. I rested there and walked on to the Grande Briere, which is a large marsh. It was now 1700 hours and, after walking a short while, I saw three small villages and started for them. I estimated the distance to be about ten miles and that I could arrive there shortly after dark. On the way I passed two German anti-aircraft guns. The marsh, which was high, very thick grass made walking difficult. At about 2200 hours I was so tired that I picked out the driest spot I could find, gathered some dry reeds, and made a small fire. It was very cold and I kept a small fire going for most of the night. In spite of this my hands and feet became numb.

12 November 1942
About 0800 hours I left my hiding place and started walking again, finally coming to a peat bog and a canal. I turned left, walked for about a quarter of a mile and found three elderly Frenchmen who were cutting peat. I asked them, in broken French, for food. They gave me a cold potato and some sausage. After walking along the canal for about a mile I came to three small boats, two were dilapidated and the other half-full of water. I bailed out the third boat, cut the chain with the small file from my Escape Kit and crossed the canal.

There was another canal branching off from this one. I entered it and rowed for about two hours. I heard voices. I stopped and hid on the bank. A group of five or six Frenchmen and two boys came along. I approached them and told them, in French, I was an American flyer. They gave me food and wine and clothes consisting of pants, an old sweater and a beret. I spend most of the afternoon with these people. They were herding cattle. Finally we all set off together in a boat, poling upstream. We continued until within a mile of the three villages I had seen the evening before. We left the boat and started walking. They were afraid to take me into the village where they were going. They said there were Germans in their village, but told me to go to the center village, where they would meet me at 0900 hours the next day.

13 November 1942
I walked to the village, went to a house where I said I was an American airman. They took me in, gave me food, but refused to let me spend the night. I went to a nearby barn and spent that night and all of the next day in the straw until about 1600 hours. At this time the door suddenly opened and an old Frenchwoman started in. Seeing me, she became very frightened and started yelling. I tried to quiet her but could not, even getting down on my knees in front of her. Eventually the lady who had fed me the night before came out and explained to the old Frenchwoman who I was. They took me in, fed me again, gave me a pair of socks, and told me the Germans were very close. They advised me to go north.

I left, following a path. Coming to a fork I decided to take the left-hand one. This led to a house, where I stopped and knocked on the door. An old man refused to let me in until I said "American." He then took me in, gave me milk and food and one of his cigarettes. He told me that if I had taken the right-hand path, I would have gone to a house where five Germans were billeted. I stayed with the old man a short while, then started walking again in the northeasterly direction and came to a railroad. This I followed until I saw that it entered a village. I left it, walked around the village and along the side of a main road for about a mile.

14 November 1942
*I stopped at the farmhouse and asked if I could sleep in the barn. They refused. I
tried the next farmhouse, where they were very cordial, took me in, gave me food,
talked to me for some time, and finally hid me in their barn. I stayed there until
0500 hours the next morning, at which time a boy awakened me, gave me more
food, and showed me the way to go.*

*I walked to a small village, where I stopped and asked for food, but was refused
the first time. When I said, "American airman" and showed them my wounds, they
gave me food, also a shirt to replace the army shirt I was wearing. I asked for a
doctor to take care of my legs. They drew a rough sketch showing me where I could
find a doctor.*

*I set out again and finally came to St. Croix. On the way I passed a German
camp, which apparently contained about 3,000 men. I could not follow the diagram the people had drawn for me so I decided to ask again.*

*I stopped in a tailor's shop and was very startled on opening the door to see
that there was a German soldier having a button sewed on his blouse by a woman
tailor. I asked her as best I could where I could find a doctor and then departed
in a hurry. I went to the back of another house and asked a woman if she knew
where I could find a doctor. She took me to a doctor's house in the center of the town,
but found that the doctor would not be back for another two hours, so she took me
to a café and gave me an excellent meal. We then returned to the doctor's office.
He bandaged my legs and treated them with ether. I talked to him for some time.
While we were talking, St. Nazaire was bombed again and we noticed Germans
running around, apparently in great confusion. I showed the doctor my photos and
an identity card was prepared for me and I was given an overcoat and wooden
shoes, a bottle of cognac, and a supply of food and cigarettes, and started out on the
road to Nantes.*

*The shoes blistered my feet and I was walking along very slowly when a friend
of the doctor's and another man came along on bicycles and told me they would take
me to the first man's home. The second man was apparently very weary, but he
went on and made arrangements for a truck which was hauling several workmen.
I joined them and soon after arrived in Blain. I was taken into a stable and was
kept there for some time, then was taken to a house and placed upstairs, where I
stayed for one month. I was only allowed to leave the house at night. After two
days a woman came and replaced my bandages. She told me after several days
that she had written to a friend of hers in Paris. The man I was staying with had
been working on the coast but he quit work as soon as I arrived and spent most of
the time with me. He told me of a large munitions factory N.E. of Blain, which*

had been bombed, but was now practically idle. While there, I saw many training planes from Nantes. They went over the house where I was staying every day. After about 30 days a man came from Paris. He took me on the bus to Nantes and from there first-class on a train to Paris.

There we got on a subway and went to an apartment in the heart of the city. He left me with a man and woman in this apartment. They gave me clothes and food and took me for a walk. I stayed there two days. They then took me to a café, where I met several French people and the man who I had met in Blain furnished me a passport.

We left that evening for Bayonne, arriving there at about 11 a.m. On leaving the station we had to show our passes, but had no trouble. We were taken to a café where we split up, I went to a house, and slept until 5 p.m. Then we all met in the center of the town. One of the girls who had been with us departed in the direction from which we had come. We took the train and travelled for about a half-hour and then got out and went to a farmhouse where we were given food and rope sandals. We set out again and started over the mountains with a guide. My other clothes had been put in the packs which we and the guide carried. We crossed the mountains in about seven hours. We saw several German sentries but our guide was successful in getting us by them without our being seen.

We arrived at the outskirts of San Sebastian about 4.30 a.m., went to a farmhouse, were fed and then went to sleep. The following afternoon we were taken to another house and told to wait there for the British Consul. He came soon, bringing us cigarettes. We stayed in this house for three days. The Consul then took us in his car to Bilbao, where we stayed in an old seamen's club for two days. From there we were taken by the Consul to a place 120 kilometers from Madrid, where we met an Embassy Red Cross truck. Finally we were overtaken by a car with Mr. Criswell and several evaders. He put them in the truck and took several of us in his car and went to the Embassy in Madrid where we stayed for two weeks.

We were then taken by car to Seville; I stayed at the home of the Vice Consul there. We were then placed on a boat. They put us in the hold, down by the propeller, and we stayed there all night, being allowed to come up about noon the next day. This boat travelled down the river and finally arrived at Gibraltar at about 4.30 a.m. We were met at noon by an Englishman and I stayed in his home for two weeks. I left Gibraltar January 26 on a US Fortress, arriving at Port Reath, where I was not questioned, and left there a short time after arrival on a transport plane for Hendon and from there, by train, to London.

APPENDIX D:
Please answer carefully the questions below. Suggestions for improvement of escape equipment and training must come largely from those who make use of them. Your report and comments will help others to evade capture or to escape.

1. *AIDS BOX*
    a. *Did you use your aids box? Yes*
    b. *If not, had you one on you?*
    c. *If not, why had you no aids box?*
    d. *If you used it, which of the following items did you use? Put a tick (X) against each item used and state briefly the circumstances, e.g. "Lying up for 2 nights", etc.*
        i.   *Horlicks tablets. Yes. Ate several first day, several that night.*
        ii.   *Chocolate.*
        iii.   *Milk (tube).*
        iv.   *Benzedrine tablets (fatigue). Took several almost immediately after coming down and more later the first day.*
        v.   *Halazone tablets (water purifier).*
        vi.   *Matches. Yes. To light fire.*
        vii.   *Adhesive tape.*
        viii. *Water bottle.*
        ix.   *Chewing gum.*
        x.   *Compass. Yes*
    e. *Did any of the items prove unsatisfactory? If so, in what respect? No*
    f. *How did you dispose of the box? Yes*
    g. *Can you suggest any way in which the contents of the aid box might be changed to make it of greater use, bearing in mind that the size of it cannot be large? Add iodine and bandages*
2. *PURSE*
    a. *Did you carry a purse? If so, state color. If not state why not. No*
    b. *Did you use the purse?*
    c. *If so, which of the following items in the purse did you use? Put a tick (X) against each item used and state briefly the circumstance.*
        i.   *Maps. Which ones?*
        ii.   *Compass.*
        iii.   *File (hacksaw). Yes. Used to cut chain on boat I stole.*
        iv.   *Foreign Currency. State countries and amounts. How did you spend the money?*

   d. *How did you dispose of:*
      i.   *Maps.*
      ii.   *Compass.*
      iii.   *File (hacksaw).*
      iv.   *Surplus currency.*

3. AIDS TO ESCAPE – (GADGETS*)

(Issued separately from aids boxes and purses).

   a. *Did you carry or wear any of the following: If you used any of them, state briefly WHEN and WHERE. No*
      i.   *Round compass.*
      ii.   *Stud compass.*
      iii.   *Swinger compass.*
      iv.   *Fly-button compass.*
      v.   *Pencil clip compass.*
      vi.   *Tunic button compass.*
      vii.   *Pipe compass.*
      viii *Pouch.*
      ix   *Special flying boots (and knife).*
   b. *Were they satisfactory?*
   c. *Can you suggest any improvements, additions, or substitutions which would improve the above equipment?*

4. PASSPORT SIZE PHOTOGRAPHS

   a. *Did you carry passport-size photographs? If so, how many? Yes 3*
   b. *Did you use them? State how. Yes. Used for identity papers.*

5. LECTURES.

   a. *Were you lectured on evasion and escape? Yes.*
      State WHERE, WHEN and by WHOM. At field
   b. *Did you find the lectures of value? Yes.*

Hq ETOUSA
19 October 1942

SUBJECT: *Safeguarding of P/W Information.*
TO: *Personnel concerned.*

1. *It is the duty of all Americans to safeguard information which might, either directly or indirectly, be useful to the enemy.*
2. *It is an offense, carrying heavy penalties, to publish or to communicate to any unauthorized person any information which might be useful to the enemy.*

3. Information about your escape or your evasion from capture _would be useful to the enemy_ and a danger to your friends. It is therefore _SECRET_.

4. _a._ You must therefore not disclose, except to the first Military Attaché to whom you report, or to an officer designated by the Commanding General of the Theater of Operations:

   1. The name of those who helped you.
   2. The method by which you escaped or evaded.
   3. The route you followed.
   4. Any other facts concerning your experience.

   _b._ You must be particularly on your guard with persons representing the press.

   _c._ You must give no account of your experiences in books, newspapers, periodicals or in broadcasts or in lectures.

   _d._ You must give no information to anyone, irrespective of nationality, in letters or in conversation, except as specifically directed in Par. 4_a_.

   _e._ No lectures or reports are to be given to any unit without the permission of the War or Navy Department.

By command of Lieutenant General Eisenhower:

Ralph Pulsifer,
Colonel, AGD, Assit. Adj. Gen.

CERTIFICATE

I have read the above and certify that I will comply with it.

I understand that any information concerning my escape or evasion from capture is _SECRET_ and must not be disclosed to anyone other than the American Military Attache to whom I first report, or an officer designated by the Commanding General of the Theater of Operations. I understand that disclosure to anyone else will make me liable to disciplinary action.

Name (Print): Hartin, F.D.   Signed: Forrest D. Hartin
Rank: 2nd Lt.   Date: Jan 27, 1943
Unit: 306 Gr. 423rd Sqdn

Lieutenant Hartin was among some of the first American airmen flying missions over German-occupied territory to bail out of his aircraft and evade his way back to England. His escape and evasion (E&E) report, the earliest completed form in the MIS-X files, is an excellent example of the accounts of the 3,000 or so evaders who followed. Hartin's narrative covers the spectrum of challenges that evaders faced: exiting his bomber, landing in France, hiding from the Germans, receiving assistance from local peasants, crossing the Pyrenees Mountains into Spain, and eventually returning to the United Kingdom. The report also contains the various annexes and forms contained in most of the E&E reports. Hartin, like many of the evaders, did not include the full names of his crew members. Unlike most of the reports that followed, he did not list information about them being killed, captured, missing, or successfully evading.

More than 11,000 United States Army Air Force planes—bombers, fighters, and transports—went down in German-held territory during World War II. The causes for their departure from the skies included flak, Nazi fighter attacks, midair collisions, fuel depletion, and mechanical problems. Of the American aircraft crew members in those planes, approximately 26,000 died as a direct result of enemy fire. Another 30,000 crewmen survived their aircraft disasters by either crash-landing their planes or parachuting into enemy territory only to be captured and become prisoners of war.

Only about 3,000 of the almost 60,000 Americans shot down over Europe between 1942 and 1945 managed to evade the Germans and make their way to friendly territory. From there they were returned to Great Britain where they were interviewed and debriefed by Military Intelligence Services.

Each airman had his own story with events that were sometimes harrowing, often daring, frequently ingenious, at times incredulous, occasionally humorous, always unpredictable, and yet—as amazing as it may seem—routinely similar to the others. Each airman took off from his base in Great Britain or North Africa to fly a mission over enemy-occupied land; encountered insurmountable obstacles to returning back to base; found himself on the ground in a foreign environment, often injured and usually alone; evaded capture by hiding, traveling at night, blending in with locals, or finding helpers to aid and guide him; and worked his way across Europe, often including crossing the Pyrenees Mountains between France and Spain, with the assistance of escape line networks that returned him to Great Britain.

In part, the stories appear similar because they were solicited by American military debriefers and interviewers as soon as the airmen returned to Britain. Those staffers were interested in whatever immediate intelligence and firsthand details the airmen could provide about the enemy as well as local civilian circumstances. They needed to know what these men had seen, what they had heard about German movements and morale, and what methods they had used to survive and evade capture. Given that the military specializes in uniformity and form-driven information collection, it is understandable then that the recounted events fall within certain parameters. Even so, the stories—told in the airmen's own words—contain vivid details of their evasion experiences and insights into their individual personalities.

Because human intelligence is by far the most reliable of information that can be gathered on the enemy, the wealth of the data brought back by these airmen was critical to the strategies and tactics of war planners. The returnees reported on German defenses, movements, and capabilities that they had observed. They could assess and evaluate the morale of the Nazi occupiers and the local citizens and partisans they had encountered. The returning airmen were also the only ones who could provide information on the fate of other Americans who had also been shot down. They frequently knew the status of fellow crew members—whether they had gotten out of their aircraft, if they had escaped initial capture or immediately been apprehended, or if they had been killed. At times they could provide debriefers with information on the burial sites of airmen that were killed in action.

More importantly, the return of downed airmen was a huge morale boost for the thousands of aviators continuing their dangerous missions over occupied Europe. Crew members were well aware of the casualties taken in the skies over Europe. The idea that, even if shot down, they still had a chance to reach safety was compelling and reassuring. At that time, aerial combat was, after all, an evolving mode of warfare with only a short history of existence.

The field of aviation was essentially an innovation propelled by technology's new fighting machine—the airplane—being employed as the world went to war for a second time. While the US Army in World War I had had its flying aces and aerial reconnaissance components, it was not until World War II that the airplane became a crucial factor in winning a conflict.

Military officials realized that technological advances would allow aircraft to drop bombs, resupply units, and transport troops quickly and efficiently. The military reconfigured its World War I Army Air Service into the Army Air Corps in 1926 and again reorganized as the Army Air Forces in 1941 in anticipation of the United States becoming engaged in war.

Soldiers interested in aircraft and air operations had two choices: volunteer for army airborne units where they would parachute into enemy territory to take control on the terrain or volunteer for Army Air Forces services where they would man and maintain aircraft engaged in combat missions, aerial reconnaissance, or air resupply. The paths were divergent because the missions differed greatly. As a result, their training was quite dissimilar even though both involved aircraft, parachutes, and survival.

Using aircraft, army paratroopers were recruited to take the war to the enemy behind his own lines. The job of the paratrooper was to jump from his plane, safely parachute into enemy territory, and form up with his fellow paratroopers into combat or reconnaissance units to complete their mission. The preparation for this specialty focused on rigorous physical training, simulated jumps, and at least five actual practice jumps from airplanes before the new paratroopers joined airborne units. These recruits were issued sturdy lace-up leather jump boots and taught how to manipulate their chutes, judge impact speed, and land in a feet-together-knees-bent position to fall into a roll to prevent injury. They jumped at a prescribed altitude in a "stick" of dozens of other jumpers. The paratroopers were supervised by jumpmasters ensuring that their gear was properly in place, that their static lines from the individual parachute rip cords to the plane's overhead cable were securely attached, and that their exit from the aircraft was orderly and over the target precisely when they were least likely to be detected by the Germans. For the paratroopers, the airplane was no more than a mode of transportation to their mission.

By contrast, the training for aircrews focused on the performance of their jobs within the aircraft as part of a team—pilots on flying the planes, navigators on reading maps, gunners on firing weapons, bombardiers on dropping the payload. They were issued high-top rubber pull-on flying boots, aviation uniforms, "Mae West" flotation devices (so called because when inflated, they gave the appearance of a well-endowed woman), and parachutes. The only preflight survival support they received before taking off into "the wild blue yonder" was limited to evade and escape briefings and aids kits for use should they find themselves on the ground in a hostile environment. Whereas the paratroopers jumped from their planes in a systematic manner with equipment in place, the airmen bailed out of their aircraft only under chaotic conditions: their planes riddled with bullets and usually on fire, themselves often wounded. They had to attach their own parachutes to O-rings on their harnesses with D-clips—and hope they did it correctly—as they made their way to an exit with little or no warning. They jumped alone from whatever altitude they were when forced to bail out, pulled their own rip cords on their chutes, and held on for dear life as they descended into the unknown territory of the enemy who could watch them descend.

The evade and escape briefings did little to prepare downed airmen for what awaited them on the ground. Generally, the information offered procedure guidelines:

- Immediately unhook from parachute and hide it as well as all other identifying equipment.
- Get as far away from landing area as quickly as possible.
- Seek cover as fast as possible.
- Blend in with the locals whenever feasible.
- Head for friendly territory.
- Travel only at night.
- Circumvent cities with their high concentrations of German occupiers.

- Do not draw attention.
- Study phrase cards.
- Approach locals only when they are alone.
- Avoid approaching the wealthy and their residences.

The aids kits, which evolved over the years in accordance with the recommendations of returned evaders, typically contained sufficient food to sustain an airman—malted milk Horlicks tablets, condensed milk, chocolate, chewing gum, and a water bottle with halazone purification tablets—for a day or two. Each kit also provided Benzedrine pills for fatigue, matches, and first-aid adhesive tape. Some aids kits contained fishing hooks while others had a razor, soap, and a file or saw.

Before each mission airmen received a preflight briefing, and each was issued a purse. These custom-made purses came in red, yellow, khaki, and brown as well as with a combination of colors and stripes. They were color-coded to match the contents, which included a compass, maps, and local currency equivalent to about forty dollars ($590 today). Each airman carried photographs of themselves in European civilian clothes to make it easier for helpers to get them false identity papers. Phrase cards—known as "pointie talkies" that translated English into French, Italian, German, and Spanish—completed the purse's contents.

Maps in the early war purses were made of paper or tissue that proved to be unable to withstand the rigors of evasion. Later maps were printed on silk or rayon.

Beyond that, the airmen relied on their own wits and physical abilities —and as much luck as they could attract.

The United States Army Air Forces (USAAF) did not emphasize the odds for an airman being shot down for the obvious reasons that such emphasis would be a detriment to recruiting and a blow to crew morale.

While the Army Air Forces did not specifically focus major training efforts on teaching airmen what to do if they were shot down, the military had begun behind-the-scenes planning, implementing, and maintaining of a support system to help downed airmen get out of enemy territory if at all possible. By the time the first USAAF personnel arrived in England on February 20, 1942, to support Allied efforts in Europe, the Germans and their Axis allies had control of Belgium, Holland, France, Italy, and most of Eastern Europe. This meant that all targets required air missions that put Allied flyers over enemy territory.

In the following months, additional personnel—as well as bomber and fighter aircraft—joined their fellow American flyers to form the 8th Air Force. On March 25, Major Cecil P. Lessing of Ellsworth, Kansas, became the first USAAF pilot to fly a mission over occupied France when he flew with the Royal Air Force in a borrowed Spitfire fighter.

Even before American aircrews arrived in Britain to begin air attacks and resupply, Military Intelligence Services (MIS) had been organizing a special branch, designated as MIS-X, to deal with helping shot-down Americans evade the Germans. In accomplishing this assistance program, MIS relied on what the British had been successfully doing. The British War Department, based on experience from World War I, had, early in the second European war of the century, accepted that members of their armed forces would be shot down, captured, and imprisoned by the Axis powers. On December 23, 1939, the British established Military Intelligence Section 9 (MI9) with the responsibility of not only interrogating enemy prisoners of war but also providing escape assistance to British military personnel held by the enemy. The office also established a branch whose mission was to insert agents behind enemy lines to assist stranded soldiers in evading German forces, whether they had been captured during ground combat and escaped or had parachuted or crashed-landed. This office also established interview procedures for those who successfully returned to Britain in order to gather information about the fate of other evaders and to glean firsthand intelligence on enemy locations and numbers.

Officers of the 8th Air Force were so impressed with the operations of MI9 that they began efforts to form a similar operation. When Major General Carl Spaatz assumed command of the 8th Air Force in May 1942, he attached one of his staff officers to MI9 to learn their procedures.

Within months, MIS-X established an office in London and joined MI9 in supplying aids kits to aircrews, providing pre-mission E&E briefings, and creating and supporting escape route "lines" established by the

French, Belgium, and Dutch underground to assist downed aviators and other Allies caught behind enemy lines. The American MIS-X London office also followed the British lead and conducted detailed debriefings of successful evaders for insights on what led to their "shoot down"; how they had managed their subsequent escape; what they had observed about the fate of their fellow crew members; and whatever other observations of enemy positions, activity, and morale they could provide.

So began the collection of each returnee's story.

The first evaders arrived in the MIS-X London office for debriefing on November 17, 1942. That group included Captain Dal O. Hollingsworth and his three crew members who were logged in as E&E report numbers 1–4. The records of these four evaders are unfortunately sparse. Either the MIS-X staff was not yet adequately prepared, or perhaps not prepared at all, for their initial interviewees. Nevertheless, the reports, such as they are, eventually made their way into the National Archives and relate that the four men were aboard a C-46 transport assigned to the 17th Troop Carrier Squadron. Apparently, on November 11, 1942, their C-46 crashed into the sea after becoming lost in poor weather and running out of fuel. A Spanish freighter on its way from West Africa to Bilbao, Spain, picked them up and delivered them to Portugal where they were treated well. They were then flown from Lisbon to London, arriving on November 17.

It would be two months before another evader arrived in England and this time MIS-X was much better prepared for a detailed debriefing. The E&E report number 5 of Second Lieutenant Forrest D. Hartin, which opens this chapter, set the standard that MIS-X followed—with a few additions and adjustments—for the remainder of the war.

Always concerned with the possibility of German infiltrators, the London MIS-X required each returnee to first confirm that he was, in fact, who he claimed to be. This was usually accomplished by a sworn statement from a member of the man's unit or other personnel with whom he had previously served. A witness also signed an acknowledgment that the thumbprint on the document was that of the returnee.

After being verified, evaders hand wrote their reports, usually in pencil on notebook paper—sometimes lined, somethings not. Some evaders dictated their stories to a MIS-X staff member; reports often were a combination of the two in an attempt to capture the complete information the returnee could provide.

The final item in each file, and the only one that is found without exception in each, is an evader signed certificate titled "Instructions Concerning Publicity in Connection with Escaped Prisoners of War, to Include Evaders of Capture in Enemy or Enemy-Occupied Territory and Internees in Neutral Countries."

Some airmen were natural-born storytellers who recounted their tales verbosely in vivid and dramatic detail; others lacked literary skills to deliver spellbinding narratives. In the case of the former, the military format rewrite and editing often flattened or obscured much of the personality of the writer; in the case of the reticent writer, the staffer took down the particulars of dictated events, commented on aspects of the writer's notes, added supplemental detail, and combined these efforts in order to compile the most accurate rendition of the airmen's usable intelligence. The narratives were then transcribed so that the gleaned information could be distributed and analyzed by Military Intelligence as well as frontline units. The results were an assorted 43,000 pages of drafts, polished reports, notes, commentary, and observations.

Because warfare is a young man's game, the airmen of World War II, like their counterparts on the ground and at sea, were males barely out of high school led by officers only a few years older, possibly with some college. Including their training time in the United States, most enlisted airmen had less than two years in uniform before they boarded their aircraft and flew into enemy skies.

Nearly all the enlisted men who served as air crew members held the rank of sergeant or higher. The USAAF promoted all enlisted airmen to this rank when they qualified as crew members for two reasons: First, the higher pay of the rank added an incentive to attract volunteers. Second, captured noncommissioned officers received better treatment than enlisted men at the German Luftwaffe-run prisoner of war camps. When a roster of a downed crew included a private or corporal, it is likely that the individual was a ground support person pressed into last-minute flight duty or that he was a former sergeant who had lost his stripes for some disciplinary reason.

Officers in the air corps were a bit older and generally had more time in service because training them as pilots, bombardiers, and navigators took additional months. Most of the planes were commanded by first or second lieutenants, occasionally by captains. It was not unusual for an entire officer crew to wear only the gold bars of second lieutenants. Few senior officers flew missions.

Other items in the E&E numbered files that made their way to the National Archives include orders temporarily assigning evaders to the US offices in neutral countries to which they escaped, transfer orders back to England, financial documents and per diem authorizations, and letters from helpers. A few E&Es contain medical reports on the health of the returnees or accounts of their hospitalizations prior to being debriefed.

Overall, the E&E reports show a tremendous effort by the MIS-X staff to record the narratives of evaders accurately and completely. Some files reveal four or more edits and rewrites before being typed on mimeograph sheets, printed, and distributed to various headquarters and intelligence organizations. Penmanship and the proper use and spelling of the English language are remarkable in their clarity and accuracy throughout.

CHAPTER 2

Pat O'Leary Line

SECRET—AMERICAN
MOST SECRET—BRITISH

HEADQUARTERS
EUROPEAN THEATER OF OPERATIONS
P/W and X Detachment
Military Intelligence Service

E&E Report No. 503
Evasion in France

23 March 1944

Name:	George Anthony Collins
Rank:	2LT
Unit:	332nd Bomb Squadron, 94th Bomb Group (B-17)
Home address:	Swansea, Mass.
Target:	Merignac
MIA:	5 January 1944
Arrived in UK:	23 March 1944

Other members of the crew:

Pilot	2LT	Harold Keller Lockwood	E&E #510
Co-Pilot	2LT	Charles Eugene Adcock	E&E #449
Navigator	2LT	Harry J. Wiener	MIA
Bombardier	2LT	George A. Collins	Narrator
Radio Operator	TSGT	Floyd L. Stevens	MIA

Top Turret Gunner	*SSGT*	*Robert H. Martin*	*E&E #512*
Ball Turret Gunner	*SGT*	*Floyd E. Saunders*	*MIA*
Waist Gunner	*SGT*	*Bennie E. Livesay*	*MIA*
Waist Gunner	*SSGT*	*Horace S. Mann*	*MIA*
Tail Gunner	*SGT*	*George M. Bertholdt*	*E&E #511*

Our ship was heavily armored and tended to have less speed than the others in the group. On our 5 January mission we flew the briefed course to the target area without incident, except for a little flak over St. Nazaire, but we had to push the engines to keep up with the formation. We let our bombs go over the target at Merignac but met heavy and concentrated flak soon after. I could hear the flak rattle off the fuselage. The stabilizers were hit and would not respond. We soon fell behind the formation. Two FW 190's came at us from 3 o'clock. A 20mm shell hit the top turret, injuring the gunner and putting the gun out of commission. The oxygen system was also knocked out.

At about 16,000 ft another fighter dove right under us. The right nose gun went out and wouldn't fire. No 4 engine was out. I thought I heard the pilot call "All bail out" over the intercom, but suddenly the attack stopped just afterwards, though the fighters continued to circle about in plain sight. When we had dropped to about 7,000 ft I looked around and found everybody gone, so I put on my Mae West (we appeared to be over the water at the time) and went out the bomb bay.

On the way down I saw 4 chutes open below me. I opened mine at about 1,000 ft and landed in a small pine tree, unhurt. Our plane was burning nearby. It was about 1130. A German plane buzzed us but did not fire. I left my chute and hid in the underbrush. About a quarter of a mile to the west I could see a lake where there was a seaplane base, so I started off in the opposite direction to find help. I met an old woman walking along the road and called to her, but she did not reply and went on. Then I ran across a man on a bicycle. "Je suis un aviateur Americain." I said to him. Then I saw he was in uniform so I went on hastily.

I came to the main highway and started towards a house. A boy on a bicycle came up behind me and said "Suivez-moi, vite, vite!" He took me on along the road several kilometers to an abandoned house in the woods, where I hid while he fetched his father, who brought some food and civilian clothes for me, and a good pair of French GI shoes. That evening they took me on to their house on a bicycle. They gave me a long saw to carry and told me to pretend to be deaf and dumb if we were stopped.

I stayed with them that night and all the next day. Two older men came and asked me to identify myself. I showed them my dog tags but did not give them to them.

The following day they came again and took me in a truck to a nearby town where my journey was arranged.

APPENDIX B

List all military information which you observed or were told while evading. Give fullest possible details. (Airfields, troop encampments, coastal and interior defenses, AA batteries, radar installations, troop movements, results of allied bombing, location of enemy factories and ammunition dumps, enemy and civilian morale, etc., etc.,...)

Troops concentrated at Le Verdun where Germans expect Allied invasion moving down river to Bordeaux. All public parks in Bordeaux are being heavily fortified with machine gun emplacements and underground defenses. On Jan 30, 1944 there were 8 submarines in the locks at Bordeaux.

German troops in southeastern France are largely made up of a mixture of young boys (15) and older men up to the age of 60. There are also a good many Hindu troops in eastern France. I tried to get an approximation of the number and was given the figure of 100,000. I doubt the reliability of this figure.

In Bordeuax at foot of rue d'Orleans was large dock handling 10,000 ton ship —8 ships in harbor—fisheries no longer running.

Saw many trains coming up from Spain with gasoline.

AA guns in church steeples this part of France—taken over schools.

2 RR bridges NE of Bordeaux have AA guns.

Block houses on coast about 1-2 km apart (concrete with machine guns) mines around block houses only—space between generally without wire

APPENDIX C

The first town to which I was taken was Hourtin. I stayed with Paul Henri Baguet, who ran a garage there. The postmaster and doctor there were also in touch with the Bordeaux organization.

I met Taddeo at a farmhouse north of Hourtin where Marcel Andron and his family lived. After being given food and wine, we were taken to a small brick house in the woods about 500 yards away where we stayed for 16 days. We were joined by Sgts Morris and Leonard two days later. We had a wood fire, and breakfast was sent out to us. We went in to the farmhouse for other meals. There were several false alarms while we were there, and we were told we would leave any day by plane from Bordeaux, but nothing happened. Finally we were told the Bordeaux organization was being broken up by the Germans, and we'd have to wait a while. A woman came and took our photos for false identity cards, which were given us just before we left.

Finally on 23 January we left by truck for Bordeaux, hidden by bags of charcoal piled in the back of the truck. We were taken to a house where there was a woman who spoke English. We took baths and had dinner, but were told the agents who were to take us out had been picked up by the Germans, so we'd have to wait again. We went to another house about ½ a mile away, where we stayed during the next week. This woman did not give her name. Several members of the organization came to see us, and I was taken out for a ride by one of them, a Canadian who had been a General in the World War. He said "G.O.C., C.M.G.C" would identify him, and that he was a friend of Sir John Dill's. He was a man of 65 or so, and of course spoke perfect English. We saw the Merignac airfield, the submarine pens, and the parks and squares of the city, where the Germans and Hindu troops were working on fortifications.

I was also shown a letter from an operative called "XP4" of the French Secret Service (Deuxieme Bureau) asking us to tell the British Intelligence that the British and American aviators should wear some civilian clothes under their flying suits or coveralls, as it was becoming difficult for the French to find such clothes for evaders. They also asked that at least 10,000 franks be put in each purse, as money was not coming through to this organization in sufficient quantities to finance operations.

During this time we had to be careful and did not go out, as the Gestapo chief was supposed to be living in the next house. We were told that 110 persons had been arrested shortly before we arrived, and most of them had been shot.

On the 30th all four of us were taken to the RR yards, where the engineer of a large electric locomotive hid us in the machinery compartment of his engine. A German guard came aboard to inspect it just before we were due to leave, but the engineer started the motors, making a terrific racket, and the German got off. We were then taken back to a freight car in the middle of the train and hidden in the small guard's compartment. The train was a fast freight, loaded with automobiles which were to be taken to Spain. We were told that only a few Frenchmen had been smuggled through in this way, and that we must keep the whole thing dark, even after reaching Spain.

We reached St. Jean de Luz safely and spent the day in a small house on the beach south of the town where a smuggler lived. He was to take us across the frontier that night. A Belgian, a former Major, also turned up to join the party. He was an older man and we later had some trouble getting him across. We went about halfway to the frontier by car, then at 2100 that evening started to walk across the frontier. It took about six hours. The guide left us at the frontier. (I understood he had already received 30,000 frs. from the man who had brought us from Bordeaux.) It was hilly and fairly hard going and we had to give the Belgian a shot of cognac to get him through, but we reached Vera de Bridasoa safely and went straight to the Spanish police.

They asked our nationality, names, and whether we had been prisoners of war. We said we had, and we all said we were officers. The Belgian was extremely talkative. The police took our identity cards, money, and knives, but were extremely friendly and pleasant. We were fed and taken to sleep in the barracks. In a café where we went the next day we met S/Sgt Gassaway (E&E 519) who had been there several days.

Next day the border police came and took us on the tram to Irun where we reported to the Commandante of the town. We stayed at the Hotel Norte, which was full of refugees, spies, and evaders. We telephoned to the US Consul at Bilbao, but he said there was nothing he could do until the Spanish Air Ministry released us. He never came to see us, but the British Consul brought us some clothes and money, and Mrs. Stevens, wife of one of the Military Attaches in Madrid, came over from San Sebastian and we went there one day and had lunch with her. There was plenty to drink and we charged everything at the hotel to the US Consul. There was a German officer in the building with the Commandante who glowered at us, but we were not molested, though we heard that some Allied flyers who had gone out alone had been kidnapped and taken across the border into France.

We heard that there were two girls at the Café Espana who were paid by the Germans to try to get information about organization methods and personnel out of evaders.

We stayed there from 31 January until 4 March, when a representative of the Spanish Air Ministry came and took us to Alhama de Aragon, by way of Saragossa. One of our Military Attaches came and interviewed us, and we left there on the 19th for Madrid, and went on next day to Gibraltar.

The escape and evasion (E&E) report of Lieutenant Collins is typical of those evaders who received help from the Pat O'Leary Line in central and eastern France to reach Barcelona, Spain. Its appendix C, like those of others assisted by the Pat O'Leary Line, details the names and places of those who provided assistance.

From November 1942, when the American aerial units arrived in Britain, until June 1944, when the Allies invaded France on D-Day, US airmen shot down over continental Europe had to evade their way through enemy territory to reach neutral or friendly countries for their extraction back to Britain or remain hidden for extended periods if they were unable to travel. After D-Day, the Allies progressively liberated more of the occupied countries from Nazi control, allowing downed airmen closer access to safety. Where they had once had to cross vast distances and even scale the Pyrenees Mountains to find friendly reception, after June 1944, they could head for the north of France or hold in place until the Allies reached them.

During those nineteen months, however, downed airmen were on their own until and unless they could seek assistance from Dutch, Belgian, and French civilians or connect with Resistance personnel organized into formal "escape lines" who would help them reach Spain, Sweden, Switzerland, or directly back to the United Kingdom.

While the names of these escape lines were never written down in the debriefing materials of evaders, more than 80 percent of the documents conclude with the statement, "[F]rom there my journey was arranged," meaning they had made contact with "helpers" from one of the lines who would guide them to freedom.

Neither the exact number of escape lines nor the number of helpers is known. The Pat O'Leary, Comet, and Shelburne are the best known of these lines. However, there is evidence that more than seventy other escape routes functioned, operating as either independent or "feeder" organizations that linked with the major lines. An undated two-page document in the National Archives, with the typed letterhead reading "Research Section 6801 MIS-X Detachment," lists sixty-five Lines "D'evasion." Many, if not most, of these lines were not formalized organizations but rather merely consisted of lists of contacts of sympathetic partisans.

An estimated 14,000 French, Belgian, Dutch, and other nationalities acted as helpers and guides within these organizations, more than half of the organizers and leaders being female. They, along with countless teenagers, assisted in hiding the evaders and in getting them from place to place, setting aside personal conflicts and old grudges among themselves in order to help the stranded evaders. Helpers shared their meager possessions of clothing, medical supplies, food, and, at times, even gave up their own beds to exhausted airmen. They provided identity cards, and they arranged transportation that included foot guides, bicycles, automobiles, and train tickets.

The primary motivation of the helpers on the lines was simple: they resented the Germans who had defeated their own armies, occupied their lands, impressed many of their fellow citizens as workers in war production plants, and confiscated their properties and agricultural products. Many of the helpers also simply felt compassion for the men and believed they were doing what was right. Downed airmen needed food, clothing, lodging, disguises, identification cards, and transportation, and these people were willing to take great risks to do what they did.

British and American agents parachuted into the occupied zones with cash to assist the lines with expenses involved in helping the evaders. Most helpers expected no compensation, but, of course, there was a minority who provided assistance for their own personal gain. Still others, particularly the paid guides who led evaders over the Pyrenees into Spain, came from long lines of smugglers who had earned their livings for generations transiting the treacherous mountain passes.

The Pat O'Leary Line was the first and best established escape route, originally running from Paris to Limoges, Toulouse, and—over the Pyrenees—to Barcelona. Like all the others, the Pat O'Leary, or simply the Pat Line, developed from necessity earlier in the war when Lieutenant Ian Grant Garrow of the British Highland 51st Division missed the Allies' evacuation from Dunkirk in May and June 1940. Rather than surrender to the advancing Germans, Garrow evaded his way from the Normandy coast to Marseilles while the French were negotiating an armistice with the Germans that divided the country: the Nazis to take control of northwestern France and the "free French" government, relocated to Vichy, to retain authority of the southeastern portion. Garrow and his fellow evaders found the Vichy French fairly lenient, allowing Brits freedom to move around Marseilles, but he was anxious to return home.

In October of that year, Garrow led the evaders over an escape route he had planned that took them across southern France, over the Pyrenees

Mountains, and into Spain. The timing was fortuitous because in November the Germans disregarded the armistice and occupied the whole of France.

In the meantime, Albert Guerisse, a Brussels-born cavalry officer, successfully evacuated from Dunkirk with the British and made his way to England. In England, he accepted a commission in the British navy under the alias of Patrick Albert (Pat) O'Leary, a French Canadian name that protected his family who still resided in occupied Belgium and explained his odd French-British accent. After six weeks of training with Naval Intelligence, Guerisse began escorting agents into southern France by small boat from a mother ship.

On April 25, 1941, O'Leary and three crewmen were captured by Vichy French coastguardsmen who were not as hospitable as the authorities in Marseilles. Imprisoned at Saint-Hippolyte-du-Fort near Nimes for two months, O'Leary escaped and made his way to Marseilles where he soon contacted Garrow. Because Garrow neither spoke French nor had any intelligence training, he persuaded O'Leary to stay and help run the evasion line. Via clandestine radio communications on July 2, 1941, O'Leary received permission from England to remain in France. He immediately began assisting in the escape of prisoners from regional POW camps and helping evaders who had been hiding in Marseilles. In his first four months on the line, O'Leary assisted more than fifty men cross the Pyrenees into Spain from where they made their way to London.

O'Leary expanded the route from Paris to include travel through Dijon, Lyons, Avignon, Marseille, to Nimes, and Perpignan before the hike over the mountains to Barcelona. Both routes then took the evaders from Spain to Gibraltar and then back to England.

Vichy French police took Garrow into custody in October 1941 and imprisoned him in the Mauzac concentration camp. O'Leary and his team smuggled a German uniform into the prison and Garrow used it to escape on December 6. Because he was a known entity and could not speak French, Garrow was ordered to return to London and leave the command of the line to O'Leary in whose honor it was ultimately named.

A typical example of the evaders who benefitted from the line is when flak and enemy fighters shot down B-17 navigator Second Lieutenant James D. McElroy from Farwell, Texas, on October 20, 1943. He parachuted and landed safely near Soignies, Belgium. He began walking south. During the next six days, he encountered Belgium farmers who provided him clothing and then Frenchmen who gave him food and directions. After a final walk of sixty kilometers in a single day, he reached Paris where a bartender recognized him as an American and linked him up with the helpers from the Pat O'Leary Line. In his E&E narrative, McElroy ends his story by writing, "The rest of my journey was arranged."

McElroy's appendix D, like that of Lieutenant Collins, contains the specifics of the airman's arranged journey. His debriefer noted,

> In Paris McElroy entered a cafe owned by Maurice Lorion, 119 Jean Jaures, who had been a member of the crew of *S. S. Paris*. Mc-Elroy stayed with Maurice from 26 through 28 October. Then on 28 October, Maurice took McElroy to meet a woman who took him to the apartment of another man who had been a member of the crew of the *S. S. Paris*. The next day Maurice's wife brought an English-speaking man (sandy hair, moustache) and a woman (gold teeth and horn-rimmed glasses). This English-speaking man took McElroy to an apartment in the market district. In this apartment there were many escape kits and identity cards.

The report continues with the details of McElroy's movement to a series of houses where he received new clothes and identity papers. In each instance the helpers were identified by name and description. A series of helpers then moved McElroy by bicycle and train to Bayonne and then over the mountains to Spain on November 7. McElroy arrived back in the United Kingdom on November 16, less than a month after being shot down over Belgium.

Flak and enemy fighters also brought down Waist Gunner Technical Sergeant Kenneth A. Morrison's B-17 on December 30, 1943. The Phoenix, Arizona, native immediately received assistance from a French farmer who took him in and gave him clothing and food. According to his appendix C, "On December 31 while I was at the house of the French couple in St. Just en Chausee, the Polish lad who had taken me there came to the house and showed me a paper on which was written in English, 'This is a friend. We understand your circumstances and will get you out as soon as possible.'" Over the next five months helpers working with the Pat Line moved Morrison by train, motorcycle, automobile, and on foot to Paris and then Toulouse with frequent stays at safe houses in-between before crossing the mountains into Spain. Morrison arrived back in the United Kingdom on May 30 after a journey that took five months.

Other than first names, Morrison identified his Pat Line helpers in his report mostly by physical descriptions. He wrote of his first helper, "Louis, a heavy-set man with very ruddy cheeks and about thirty-seven years old." He described another named Rollo as "a tall Frenchman about thirty-four years old." Still another was, he wrote, "A very large man whom we knew as Joe." Still others he described only as "a girl of about twenty-nine" and "a very frightened boy."

Major Leon W. Blythe from Columbus, Georgia, was copilot of a B-17 that crash-landed in France on January 7, 1944. Initially hidden by farmers, Blythe became the charge of two sisters—Monique and Genevieve Fabry—who arranged his journey on the Pat Line. The girls' mother and father had previously both been arrested by the Germans and sent to concentration camps for their help on the line.

Waist Gunner Sergeant Thomas J. Glennan from Lawton, Oklahoma, was wounded in the foot when Nazi fighters shot down his B-17 over France on February 11, 1944. French farmers met him when he parachuted in and initially hid him in a barn before moving him to a house owned, he wrote in his narrative, "by a wounded and much decorated machine gunner of 1914–1918." There he received medical treatment for his wounded foot.

After four weeks, Glennan had sufficiently recovered and was moved by train to Paris. After a brief stay there, helpers took him on another train to the Pyrenees where he crossed on foot into Spain. He arrived back in the United Kingdom on March 24. Appendix D of his E&E report does not make clear just where or when Glennan came under the control of the O'Leary Line but likely it was during the four-week period of recovery from his wound.

In his narrative, Glennan concluded, "The care and kindness which I everywhere received from the French, in spite of the great risks involved in handling a wounded and helpless man, have deeply impressed me with the duty of evaders to give these helpers implicit obedience and considerate cooperation."

Comet Line

HEADQUARTERS
EUROPEAN THEATER OF OPERATIONS
P/W and X Detachment
Military Intelligence Service

E&E Report No. 648
Evasion in Belgium and France

May 18, 1944

Name:	Omar M. Patterson, Jr.
Rank:	2LT
Unit:	334th Bomb Squadron, 95th Bomb Group (B-17)
Home address:	Roanoke, Virginia
Target:	Frankfurt
MIA:	January 29, 1944
Arrived in UK:	May 18, 1944

Other members of the crew:

Pilot	1LT	Andy Roznetinsky	MIA
Co-Pilot	2LT	Philip B. Warner	E&E #667
Navigator	2LT	Jennings B. Beck	E&E #649
Bombardier	2LT	Omar M. Patterson, Jr.	Narrator

Radio Operator	*TSGT*	*Robert B. Buchanan*	*KIA*
Top Turret Gunner	*SSGT*	*Frank W. Vandan*	*MIA*
Ball Turret Gunner	*SSGT*	*Charles T. Staudt*	*KIA*
Waist Gunner	*SSGT*	*Ragner A. Kvickstrom*	*KIA*
Waist Gunner	*SGT*	*Larry R. Esala*	*KIA*
Tail Gunner	*SGT*	*Larry R. Kiner*	*KIA*

Were you wounded: Twisted knee bad on landing and tore right hand in several places (minor wound).

Returning on January 29th from our target at Frankfurt, flying at about 25,000 feet near the Belgian border, two superchargers went out, forcing us out of formation. We lost altitude to about 20,000 feet and were attacked by five ME 109's and one Folks-Wulfe. We fought for fifteen minutes, diving the ship straight down most of the time. From 12,000 to 3,500 we were firing steadily on the enemy. As we reached 3,500 the bell rang, and I dove headfirst out through the nose. I pulled my ripcord and it came away in my hands, so I had to pull the chute out with my hands. A ME 109 came straight at us. I stood up in my chute and saluted. The pilot saluted back, swerved away and flew off. I landed in a plowed field in Belgium, north of Courtrai at 1235 hours, with Lt Beck about 100 yards away. I saw the ship burning and a hundred or more people about.

Getting out of my chute very fast, I sprinted straight away from the plane. A crowd of Belgians formed a lane through which I ran. For fifteen minutes I continued running fast, vaulting fences and hedges. I became sick, vomited, and slowed down to a dog trot, when a boy of about 16 made motions to me, pointing to his clothes. In about four minutes I changed clothes with him behind a haystack, giving him my greens and OD sweater, but retaining the GI shoes I was wearing. He wanted to go with me, but I refused and went on. A Belgian riding a bicycle saw me and came up. He gave me his cap and pointed toward a canal near which I should wait for him at dusk. I walked on about a mile to the canal and hid in a stone house. Several people passed along the canal. I picked out the poorest, a farmer, and he came into the stone hut with me. Using my language card, I asked him, "How do I cross this river?" He took me to his house nearby, fed me and hid me. From there on my journey was arranged.

APPENDIX C

I landed at Hulste, Belgium at 1235 hours January 29th. A boy of 16 gave me his clothing ten minutes later as I was running away. A man in farmer's clothes rode up on a bicycle and gave me his cap. He told me to go to a canal and wait for him.

He had lived in the US, was about 50, and had means. He asked me to write to M. Paul Roecheck, 324 S Scholum St, South Bend, Indiana (his daughter's husband). Waiting by the canal, I stopped another man, farmer, 35, who took me to his house and fed me. His name was Gerome, with him lived his mother, 60, and sister, 24. A flax dealer came in, dark, 29, medium build, called "Little Jock." He asked me to write his friends Mr. and Mrs. John Houston, Elgon, Lisburn, Northern Ireland. He left with Gerome, and brought back four bicyclists and five bicycles. These young men were armed and took me into Courtrai, one riding each side of me, one far ahead and one far behind. I understood they were in the White Brigade. One boy, 22, blonde, 5-7, 140 lbs spoke fluent English and seemed to be the leader.

We went to the home of Mrs. Nasseons, 40, about 3 blocks from the station. She had a daughter 15 from 1st husband, another 3 from present husband, Belgian Major picked up by the Germans 18 months ago. I stayed with her until the evening of Feb 1st.

On the night of the 1st we went nearby to M. Weedelsmitt, map maker and surveyor, an older man, with wife and daughters 24 and 27. He and elder daughter work in furniture factory in Courtrai.

At 2100 Feb 4th I moved nearby to the house of Mrs. Delporter, where Lt Beck joined me at 2200. She is Dutch, with a husband a Belgian manufacturer, then away, and daughter 15. She had money, worked as nurse in German hospital, had car, gas, and ration stamps, and bought food on the Black Market, was very intelligent, good organizer and had helped others. Miss Peel came, 35; her brother was in prison for having a radio. She took us out to have pictures made. Mr. Depoorter (no relation to Mrs Delporter) came, owner of tapestry factories all over Europe and one near London. Son in English Army. Other son, 24, Frank Depoorter helped us with suggestions.

Feb 15th after dark Mrs. Delporter and Frank Depoorter drove us to within 500 yards of Belgian border. Mrs. D took us on foot through the 1st barrier, led us to restaurant on left. We went out back door, followed an old woman with black shawl, then another old woman with white shawl, zigzagging for about 500 yards. We entered back of house where two old Frenchwomen, with two old men, smoking and laughing at us. We followed woman with white shawl again out of this house and met Mrs. D on corner in car with Frank and drove to house in Tourcoing, spending night with French war veteran, postman. On Feb 16th Frank took us to train, bought tickets for Paris, he took 1st class ticket, Beck and I rode 2nd class. We had identity cards and passports but were not asked for them. Our luggage was inspected. There was no German control on this train. Changed train at Paris; by bribery Frank got 1st class carriage for the three of us alone to St. Sulpice on Tarn.

Next morning to house of Mr. and Mrs. Paul Decone, St. Sulpice, close friends of Mrs Delporter, about 50, Mr. D rich, Nylon brush manufacturer. Girl, cousin from Courtai, there for three weeks. We were there for nearby 6 weeks. Lived next door with Mr. Fauvel, with wife and three small children. Maid and gardener of Mrs. D suspicious. About March 1st moved to house of Mr. and Mrs. Pichon, baker, rich, active in underground, listened to BBC with great attention, had secret conferences.

Also stayed with Gorce, shoemaker, former French colonial official in Africa, very large, 230 lbs, 6-3, about 5 days.

One night to avoid Gestapo, stayed with Mr. Furrier, 30, dark, pretty wife, 7 miles out of St Sulpice.

Also 5 days with Ernest Cambon, 55, gray, wife, daughter.

Back to Pichon's again. Met two students from U of Toulouse, about 18, working with Maquis. One called Lavignotte Hertrich (father Dr. H in Algeria). They took us by train to Toulouse. Pichon, Gorce, and Mrs. Decone saw us off. There met Dutch organization Francoise (Francoise Henri-French organization-Beck). Sat., March 25 on train with ticket for St. Laurent St. Paul (Toulous-Motabiau line) and got off before station, between St. Gaudens and Montrejeau. Met by Maquis and tall blonde Californian called "San Francisco," presumably veteran Abraham Lincoln Brigade in Spain. Took us to large house where we totaled 15 Americans, 22 Dutch, 1 RACF. Actions very bold. Town seemed to belong to Maquis. At dusk by truck into hills to sawmill. Four Maquis guards and one guide, all armed with sten guns. Walked, crossing creek many times, until 0200 hrs, stopped at shepherd's house. Sun 26th, 1030 hrs walked on with three new guards, new guide, until 0400 on 27th. Hid in cabin all day (P-51 pilot seen by Patterson in Spain got away from ambush here in next party to come; many lost). Left at dusk and walked until 0700 on 28th when were at border. Guards left us here. Patterson delirious from fatigue, no food, helped over last hours by Charles E. Yeager of West Virginia, P-51 pilot.

Arrested 1700 by Spanish Guardia Civile while eating at farm near Les. Taken to Vielda, where called Mr. Forsythe at Consulate, Barcelona. On 31st walked 42 km to Esterri de Aneu. Then to Sort and Lerida by bus. Stayed Hotel Palacia, Lerida 3 weeks. Train to Alhama 22nd April. Stayed until May 14th, when Col Clark took us to Madrid. Sleeper to Gibraltar arriving 16th. Left by plane on 17th arriving UK May 18th.

Lieutenant Patterson's E&E report is an excellent example of those airmen who were assisted by the Comet Line to reach San Sebastian, Spain, from Belgium via Brussels, Paris, and Bayonne. Similar to the other reports, he acknowledges his helpers in appendix C and also mentions interaction with other, smaller lines.

In August 1941, Andree de Jongh, known to her family as Little Cyclone because of her energy and tenacity, walked into the British consulate office in Bilbao, Spain, with two fellow members of the Belgium Resistance and a young Scottish soldier left behind when the British evacuated mainland Europe. The twenty-four-year old de Jongh, nicknamed "Dedee," requested assistance. Inspired by her heroine Edith Cavell—a British nurse executed by a World War I German firing squad in 1915 for helping Allied soldiers escape from occupied Belgium to the neutral Netherlands—de Jongh wanted help moving British soldiers left behind in the Dunkirk evacuation and downed Allied aviators from Belgium through Paris to Bayonne and then over the Pyrenees into Spain.

After some skeptic deliberation, the British agreed to help de Jongh, authorizing funds and placing the responsibility for the evasion route under MI9. This route of escape would eventually become known as the Comet Line.

The starting point of the original Comet Line, *le Reseau Comete*, was Brussels where helpers assembled aviators downed over Holland and Belgium. From there they followed several routes south, mostly by rail, through occupied France into the western Pyrenees Mountains and then into Spain. Along the way evaders stopped at a series of safe houses and ultimately ended up at the "last house" in the Basque village of Urrugne where guides, often led by a giant of a man named Florentino Goicoechea, accompanied them over the mountains. The Basque smuggler paired his desire for money with his deep hatred for fascism to repeatedly lead evaders over the mountains. More than a few evaders later commented on the Basque smuggler's frequent stops during the climb to take a drink from bottles of cognac that he had previously hidden under rocks or in hollow trees.

Dedee did not shy from leading evaders over the mountains herself. In addition to her original trek to coordinate with the British, she guided airmen over the Pyrenees a total of thirty-two times.

To move downed airmen from Belgium to Spain along the Comet Line required a network of 2,000–3,000 helpers—all amateurs at espionage and clandestine operations—from different nationalities, religions, and lifestyles. The exact number of helpers cannot be calculated for several reasons: some provided minimal and sporadic assistance; others helped when they could but not consistently; a few dedicated their entire lives to the Comet. Line leader Jean-Francois Nothomb described the helpers, saying, "In their efforts to rescue others and in the strength of their love, the members of the Comete were armed only with their courage and their belief in the value of freedom."

Dedee was constantly at odds with the exiled Belgian government and MI9 over the Comet Line remaining independent. She insisted that only she and the internal line network regulars know its operational processes. Dedee believed that outsiders could not understand the individual situations of all involved or the overall spirit of its helpers. Neither she nor any other members of her organization accepted financial compensation except funds to pay for transportation, food, and clothing for the evaders.

De Jongh did, however, encourage coordination between the Comet Line and other smaller groups who were also aiding downed airmen. For example, partisans in the Netherlands established the Smit-van der Heijden Line in early 1942 initially to aid escaped French prisoners of war and then expanded to help Dutch Jews and Allied airmen make their way to England. Its agents worked closely with Comet Line helpers and other escape lines to accomplish their mission.

Other ancillary lines contributed to the Comet's line success as well as their own independent triumphs. On July 15, 1943, MI9 agents parachuted into southeast Belgium to establish another direct mean of repatriating downed aviators. This Possum Line made three successful extractions before being compromised. The Brandy and Burgundy Lines were also briefly in operation to support the Comet Line or to evacuate evaders on their own.

B-17 ball turret gunner Staff Sergeant Joseph J. Walters from Pittsburgh, Pennsylvania, was shot down over Belgium while returning from a bombing run on the Schweinfurt Ball Bearing Works on August 17, 1943. As part of Walters's E&E report, his interviewer wrote, "SGT Walters landed near Boirs, Belgium. He was immediately hidden by several Belgians and then taken to the house of Joseph Godin Peters, 4 Rue D'Etat, Boirs. He stayed there overnight and the next afternoon was taken away in a truck driven by a Belgian who had formerly been a taxi driver in New York City."

The next day Walters joined another evader and the two gave their photographs for identification papers to helpers who accompanied them for their entire journey. Three weeks later they walked across the border into France by bribing a guard to let them pass. They took a bus to Lille and then a train to Paris where, according to Walters, they "were taken to the home of Mme. Germaine Bajpai, whose brother-in-law is Indian commissioner in Washington." On October 2, the evaders went by rail to Dax and then by bicycle to Bayonne. Walters's interviewer continued with details in Walters's notations, writing, "The next day (October 3) they walked ten miles into the woods, met some guides, and at 0500 on October 4 crossed the frontier." Walters arrived back in the United Kingdom on November 20, just three months after being shot down.

The journey of First Lieutenant Roy F. Claytor, a B-17 pilot from Birmingham, Alabama, was similar to that of Walters's. Shot down by fighters on the same day as Walters, Claytor evaded for a day on his own before hiding in a grist mill where he met helpers, including "an organization chief" who took him to Liege where he was hidden in a florist shop until September 3. From there helpers moved him to Brussels where he received an identity card. They took him on a train to the French border, walked him across, and met more helpers who provided French papers for Claytor. He boarded trains that then took him to Paris, Bordeaux, and then to Dax. Helpers led him to Bayonne on bicycles and then turned him over to guides who escorted him over the Pyrenees. He arrived in Spain on October 6. Claytor was then returned to the United Kingdom on October 18, a mere two months after being shot down over Belgium.

Still another airman shot down by enemy fighters and flak on August 17, 1943, was Staff Sergeant Joseph M. Aquino, a B-17 tail gunner from Beaver Falls, Pennsylvania, who landed near Antwerp, Belgium. Belgian peasants hid him for two days before moving him by bicycle into Antwerp where he met line helpers who were assisted by a British intelligence officer. From there Aquino began his train journey south, escorted by "a man who had red hair, freckles, and a scarred nose." Aquino arrived in Spain on October 5 and returned to the United Kingdom on November 20.

As a result of evacuations such as these, the Comet Line went on to become one of the most successful escape routes of World War II.

CHAPTER 4

Shelburne and Other Lines

SECRET—AMERICAN
MOST SECRET—BRITISH

HEADQUARTERS
EUROPEAN THEATER OF OPERATIONS
P/W and X Detachment
Military Intelligence Service

E&E Report No. 530
Evasion in France

March 25, 1944

Name:	*William A Hoffman*
Rank:	*2LT*
Unit:	*326th Bomb Squadron, 92nd Bomb Group (B-17)*
Home address:	*Alexandria, Virginia*
Target:	*Frankfurt*
MIA:	*February 8, 1944*
Arrived in UK:	*March 24, 1944*

Other members of the crew:

Pilot	*1LT*	*Warren E. McMurray*	*MIA*
Co-Pilot	*2LT*	*Clayton F. Fitzgerald*	*MIA*
Navigator	*2LT*	*William A. Hoffman*	*Narrator*
Bombardier	*2LT*	*Sidney Scheiman*	*MIA*
Radio Operator	*SSGT*	*Harold H. Barnett*	*MIA*

Top Turret Gunner	SSGT	*George Buckner*	*E&E #539*
Ball Turret Gunner	SGT	*Leburn W. Merritt*	*MIA*
Waist Gunner	SGT	*David Warner*	*E&E #540*
Waist Gunner	SGT	*Robert A. Herber*	*MIA*
Tail Gunner	SGT	*Marion Knight*	*MIA*

After we reached Luxemburg on the way to Frankfurt on 8 February about twenty ME 109's made a pass at us, head on, and put two 20mm shells into our motors. We turned back with the rest of our formation, but lost altitude rapidly. Flak went through the left wing and fuselage. The interphone was out, so the co-pilot went through the ship telling us to bail out. We threw the engineer out and saw his chute open. I went out at 1,000 ft and pulled the cord at once. I was in the air only about 15 seconds.

It was 1130 when I landed on my back in a plowed field NW of a large village. There was a lot of wind and I was dragged half way across the field before I could get up. Two German planes were flying around but did not fire at me. I could see a farmer nearby at the edge of the woods.

I got my chute and harness off, and carried it towards the woods. The farmer waved at me so I went up to him. He helped me hide my chute, Mae West, and flying boots in the woods. Then a girl came up, followed by four or five other people. I followed the girl off to the SW, away from the burning plane.

After walking about 2 miles we came to a small village on the edge of the woods. They took me to a house where I was given cognac and some food, and a slight wound on my hand was dressed. Many people came and stared at me. One woman brought a French-English dictionary and wrote out some questions on a piece of paper. They asked what nationality I was, what I wanted to do, and whether I knew of any helpers in the vicinity. (This last question may have been meant to test me, as I later found out that this woman knew all about helpers in this district.) I told them I wanted to get to Spain.

I spent that night there. Next day my helpers told me they could arrange to have me sent back to England. That night three men in a closed truck came and took me to the larger village nearby where my journey was arranged.

APPENDIX C

I stayed the second night at Crevecoeur le Grand, in the house of Justin LeFranc and his wife. He was a bookkeeper in the textile factory and was 1st Sgt of the Resistance group in the town. I was taken to see Shevchik, Thorson, Wall and Scanlon (see E&E reports 527, 528, 529, 501), all of whom had been in the same raid and were being hidden in the town. I also saw S/Sgt Sidders and Sgt Higgins, who were in safe hands but did not make the rest of the journey with us.

There was a German garrison in Crevecoeur and some artillery in the neighborhood on maneuvers. The garrison was quartered in a big two-story building said to have been a sanatorium. These troops had been in Russia and were resting. They seemed to be in good condition, however. AA guns were mounted on the roof of the building where they lived.

I was told by LeFranc that several German sentries had been killed by the French, one knifed by a boy of 16. I saw several big guns being towed through the town by trucks on their way to the coast. The Germans seemed to expect the invasion at any time, and the troops in Crevecoeur were on the alert.

The last two days of my stay in the town were spent in the house of the organization chief, a man called Acuelle who ran the local garage. He asked me for my dog tags, but I kept one of them. He said that our insignia would be taken and buried, so we could get them after the war.

On the 18th two men picked up Shevchik, Thorson, Wall, and myself in a truck. We were given blue denim jackets and told to pretend we were foreign workers who had thumbed a ride in the truck if we were stopped. We stayed for a week with an old couple named Rousse, then Sgt Wall and I went to stay in a house 3 kms out of town, near St. Just les Marais. It belonged to an old farmer named Lesueur. He was 84 and lived with his wife and a younger couple whose relationship never was made clear to us.

We stayed there 24 days. We had lots of good food, sat in the sun, and chopped wood for the farmer. They were poor people and appreciated anything we did for them. The old man hated the English and the Germans equally but liked Americans. Lts Shevchik and Thorson came out to see us one day, also Sgts Cutino and Hamilton from Lt Laux's crew (see E&E Reports 525-526). A man came and took some pictures but we got no identity papers until just before we left. We managed to get haircuts.

We expected to leave much sooner than we did. An English speaking intelligence officer came and asked questions about baseball, etc. so we could prove our identities. He was dark, heavy set man about 5'10" who went by the name of Jacques. As he was leaving I heard him tell the farmer "Demain a trois heures" though he would not tell us when we would leave.

Next day we went to Paris, four Americans and two guides in one compartment. We went through Creil and Montargis, where there had been raids a few days before. The lines were still torn up and many wrecked freight cars were visible. We were late getting to Paris as a result, and the people who had been waiting for us had left, so we milled around in front of the station for some time until the man known as Jacques came up. We walked some distance and then took the Metro to Levallois-Perret, where after dinner at an apartment where there were a lot of Americans and organization people, we were taken to stay in an apartment 7 flights up in the Rue Baudin. Sgts Buckner and Warner (see E&E 539–540) were also there.

Pictures were taken again of those of us who had no passport photos. We were told next day we could not leave because there was trouble in Brittany and a boat had been fired on. So we stayed another night there. We did not go out. The following morning (23 March) we were taken to the Montparnasse station and given tickets and identity cards. A young woman called Comtesse Bertrand Lagestel and a young French doctor went with us in the train, where we had reserved seats. They spoke English. Lt Rosenblatt (E&E 520) and Sgts Cutino and Hamilton were with us. We saw the damage at Trappes as we went through, but the electric lines were working and we did not have to change engines. We were not asked for our papers and the change of trains at St. Brieus took place without incident.

At Guingamp, P/O Daniels of the RCAF and I were taken some distance outside the town where we stayed in a house belonging to a miller. A young girl took care of us. A truck came that night and we were taken some distance to the north where we met other members of the party who had left Paris the day before. We headed down towards the beach through ditches full of briars, guided by the girl, who seemed to know her way very well.

Finally we arrive at a house near the beach, where a French Canadian representative of the organization gave us a pep talk and collected our money. We went down a steep cliff where there were said to be some mines and waited two hours in the rocks at the foot before the boats came to take us off. The small boats were full, so four of us had to wait for a second trip.

We reached Dartmouth on 24 March without further incident.

The Shelburne Line, a name designed by British intelligence, was smaller but longer lasting than the Pat and Comet Lines. Lieutenant Hoffman's E&E report mirrors those of other airmen who escaped on the Shelburne Line from Northern France to the United Kingdom.

The Shelburne Line rescued evaders by boat, taking them directly from the French coast across the English Channel to Great Britain. It was the last major escape line formed by MI9 and the only one never compromised by the Germans. It replaced, by necessity, its predecessor, the Oaktree Line, when it was infiltrated and destroyed by Gestapo agents posing as Allied evaders in late 1943.

Helpers, as well as surviving airmen, were left in limbo when the Oaktree Line ceased to exist. Raymond Labrosse, a French Canadian radio operator, stepped into the void and gathered a group of evaders to lead them south across the Pyrenees to Spain. Back in England, Labrosse joined fellow Canadian Lucien Dumais and, after further training from MI9, the two returned to Brittany to replace the Oaktree Line route in what was to be known as the Shelburne Line.

Labrosse, disguised as a medical equipment salesman, and Dumais, presenting himself as a mortician, recruited helpers, established safe houses, and identified extraction points. They carried escape aids including compasses and French currency as well as blank identity papers to be forged with evader information. The two agents gathered evaders; hid them in safe houses in Paris and surrounding towns; and moved them by foot, trucks, and train to the Brittany coast. A small stone farmhouse near the village of Plouha, belonging to a member of the Resistance, served as a final assembly point before movement to the beach. Always in danger of detection by German land and sea patrols, extractions occurred only on moonless nights. On the night of January 28–29, 1944, the first evaders on the Shelburne Line were evacuated from Bonaparte Beach by vessels from the Royal Navy's 15th Motor Gun Boat Flotilla.

Over the next eight months, an additional seven extractions were conducted. Operations ceased with the Allied invasion of mainland France in 1944. In its short duration, the Shelburne Line returned 136 Allied evaders—including 94 Americans—to the United Kingdom.

One evader who benefitted from the Shelburne Line was Staff Sergeant Sabastian L. Vogel from Fargo, North Dakota, who was a B-17 radio operator until his plane was shot down on January 23, 1943. French farmers hid and fed Vogel for three days before helpers moved him to Plouha where he stayed one night. In his report Vogel wrote,

They then moved us out under a load of straw, but after about a 15-minute ride we were put into a truck behind a load of oyster baskets on the road to Carentec. On the journey we were stopped four times by German soldiers and the driver was questioned, but they did not find us. At Carentec we were taken into a house for one day and two nights. We found there that food was very scarce in that entire vicinity. While there we found that two Germans in civilian clothes had been looking for us and had begun questioning children. We were taken on bicycles to a house on the seashore, which was about a mile from the house where we had been staying. We stayed there one day before getting on a boat to return to England.

First Lieutenant Milton V. Shevchik, a B-17 pilot from Ambridge, Pennsylvania, bailed out after his plane was shot by German fighters on February 8, 1944. He landed near Domeliers, France, where farmers immediately assisted him. The next day he was taken by line helpers and, on February 23, moved to a house in Beauvais. He wrote in his report, "We were told that 40 Americans had passed through this house. The food was not very good and our host complained he got only 100 francs a day from his job and could not feed us, so we gave him some money. It was dirty and there were a lot of flies there, too."

On March 18, Shevchik was finally taken to Paris by train and then on the twenty-second on to a house near the beach at Paimpol. He described what happened next, writing, "We stayed there that night and next day. A girl of about 24 took us out after dark on the 23rd to the beach at Plouha. We had a scare when we met some people in a ravine near the beach, but got there safely after stopping in a house where we were given a security talk and asked for our money. After a half hour walk and a slide down a cliff, we waited two hours in the rocks before our boats came for us."

After fighters downed his B-17 near Bouvillers, France, on December 30, 1943, bombardier Second Lieutenant Edward J. Donaldson from Dumont, New Jersey, was told by local farmers that a car would come for him and that he would be in England within two days. Their estimate was a bit optimistic. The next morning helpers moved Donaldson on the back of a motorcycle to Clermont where he was hidden in a back room for three weeks. Helpers then took him and several others by train to Chatelaudren and then by truck to near the coastal pickup point. Donaldson wrote in his E&E report, "About 2330 hours we started across country in single file to the beach where we waited until 0200 hours when we were picked up by boats." Donaldson arrived back in the United Kingdom on March 17, 1944, two and a half months after he was shot down.

CHAPTER 5

Chutes

SECRET—AMERICAN
MOST SECRET—BRITISH

HEADQUARTERS
EUROPEAN THEATER OF OPERATIONS
P/W and X Detachment
Military Intelligence Service

E&E Report No. 325
Evasion in France

January 17, 1944

Name:	Trafford L. Curry
Rank:	TSGT
Unit:	351st Bomb Squadron, 100th Bomb Group (B-17)
Home address:	Hugo, Oklahoma
Target:	Paris
MIA:	3 September 1943
Arrived in UK:	17 January 1944

Other members of the crew:

Pilot	1LT Richard Clinton King	MIA
Co-Pilot	FO George Donald Brykalski	MIA
Navigator	2LT Ernest (NMI) Anderson	MIA
Bombardier	2LT Edward Harold Hoyde	MIA
Radio Operator	TSGT Robert L. McKnight	MIA

Top Turret Gunner	TSGT Trafford Leon Curry	Narrator
Ball Turret Gunner	SSGT Rudolph H. Harms	MIA
Waist Gunner	SSGT Heber (NMI) Hogge, Jr.	MIA
Waist Gunner	SGT James Marshall Sides, Jr.	MIA
Tail Gunner	SSGT Donald Earl Wise	MIA

I know nothing about my crew—except what French told me—There were 4 parachutes—including mine and the other three were taken prisoner immediately.

Were you wounded? A slight flak wound on left leg.

We crossed the Channel uneventfully, picked up our escort of P-47's, and met no fighters before they left. We came in at 22,000 feet. Shortly before the IP four fighters made head on attacks but did no damage. Then the flak started. The lead bombardier turned on the IP and never varied his direction or his altitude a foot. About three minutes after we turned on the IP, the first burst of flak hit the ship on our right wing. I think we got a few holes in our plane. About five seconds later we took a direct hit from a burst behind and under number two engine. The whole electrical system of the plane was knocked out. I tried to feather number two, but the mechanism did not work. I knew a fire was coming, so I cut the ignition switch on number two. When I stepped down from the turret to adjust the clutches, flak came right through the place where my head had been. Everything seemed to be all right, but we were losing altitude. The co-pilot was doing a marvelous job of flying. The nose was full of smoke, and the bomb bay was on fire. Twelve 500 pound bombs were lying there in the fire. I grabbed the fire extinguisher, but it could do nothing with the fire. I saw that we were over a forest and jettisoned the bombs. Fire from the left wing was reaching back to the bomb bay. I crawled back and told the pilot that the left wing was on fire and that I was getting out. I snapped on my parachute and started back to see how the rest of the crew was, but I got stuck, and my trousers caught on fire. I jumped out the bomb bay right through the fire. My face was covered, but I got blister burns on my hands, probably from an oil fire.

I fell free for about five minutes, it seemed. For some reason I remembered the P/W lectures I had heard about delaying one's jump. I did not delay my jump quite enough, however, for I opened the chute between 5,000 and 4,000 feet, which is too high. But the trees seemed to be getting awfully big when I did pull the cord. I was on my back when the chute opened, and it gave me a powerful jolt. I saw that the whole left wing of our plane was on fire; pieces of the wing kept falling past me. I saw one more parachute. An FW 190 coming up for an attack passed me; I went through its prop wash and was almost spilled. About 100 feet from the ground a twin engine trainer circled me until I hit, so I knew [that] I was well spotted for a search.

I landed near a creek about four kilometers from a German airdrome and hit hard and rolled over. I pulled off my Mae West and flying boots, rolled them up in the parachute, and hid the whole thing in some bushes. I knew I did not have much time. I hid while a plane circled above. A lady yelled to me to follow her. When a man asked me where my parachute was, I pointed it out to him. We walked down the creek around the edge of a village. The woman walked into the village; the man and I walked on. I hid in the woods. Soon the woman brought some civilian clothes. The man pointed to my watch and indicated that he would come back for me later. I slept. At the time he indicated another woman came for me. I was hesitant about going with her, but she kept motioning for me to come, so I followed her. I went to another woods where I received some wonderful food: eggs, rum, wine, tea, milk—everything.

When it was almost dark, a man came to see me. I pulled out my escape maps and told him that I wanted to go to Spain. He and his friends started making plans to help me. They brought me civilian clothes which I put on over my uniform.

I was taken to a place from which my journey was arranged.

Technical Sergeant Curry is the single crew member of his Flying Fortress not to be listed as missing in action. His E&E report details the difficulties and dangers in exiting a damaged aircraft experienced by many of his fellow aviators.

Before an evader could evade, he had to first reach the ground safely after his plane had been disabled. The first step in the process was to separate himself from his aircraft, a feat that was occasionally orderly but more often shocking because no one ever expected to actually be shot down; chaotic because of fires, missing engines, and other plane parts, wounds, and dead crew members; terrifying because he was thousands of feet above the ground; and obstacle-riddled because he had to free himself from his limited space inside the aircraft and attach his parachute while finding his way through the wreckage to an exit. This marked only the beginning of his escape and evasion experience.

Successfully getting out of a damaged plane did not guarantee airmen safety. When they had to jump at their normal flying altitudes, the men faced dangers of passing out from a lack of oxygen and of getting frostbite on exposed skin. A MIS-X interrogator commented on one of the reports of high-altitude jumpers, writing, "There is great danger of passing out and freezing at 24,000 feet, to say nothing of having all the Germans within five miles watch you come down for fifteen minutes."

Aircrews used one of two types of chutes—the AN-6513 front-mounted kind that bomber crew members preferred because they could detach it for easy movement inside the aircraft, or the smaller B-8 back-mounted type that pilots liked because they could wear them even in their cramped cockpits. Both styles of chutes attached with D-rings to their harnesses. The harnesses also had D-rings for essentials such as oxygen masks, goggles, first-aid kits with bandages, tourniquets, and morphine syrettes.

With little to no training on parachute jumping, airmen were often reluctant to leave their aircraft, damaged as they were. Technical Sergeant Harold B. Maddox, a radio operator from Lakeland, Florida, was aboard a B-17 over France on October 5, 1943, when a fellow crew member asked over the intercom if they were bailing out. Maddox reported in his E&E report that he heard an unknown voice replying, "Let's not." Orders came to do so nevertheless.

Evaders who had survived the ordeal of leaving their planes in midair offered advice for their fellow airmen in their postevasion interviews. One of those was Technical Sergeant Oscar K. Hamblin, a B-17 top turret gunner from Kennewick, Washington, who had bailed out over France on September 6, 1943. He wrote, "Anyone who has to bail out would do well not to look at the ground before he leaves his plane; otherwise he won't want to leave."

Some crewmen did indeed require encouragement to jump from their planes. Staff Sergeant Lloyd G. Wilson, a B-17 tail gunner from Belleville, Illinois, got the bail out warning on October 14, 1943. He wrote upon his return to England, "I did not want to jump, so I asked the pilot whether he was going to crash land. He told me to go ahead and jump. I straddled the bomb bay, but I just waited. I saw the pilot going to the bombardier's escape hatch, motioning for me to jump. I still waited. The pilot motioned for me to jump, and I finally went out."

Some crewmen needed more than oral commands. Major Edgar B. Cole of Nyssa, Georgia, who had crash-landed in friendly territory after his B-17 experienced engine failure on April 5, 1943, was aboard another B-17 as an observer the following month when the pilot gave the bail out. Cole wrote, "I pulled the emergency release on the escape hatch and our navigator pushed me out. I had not finished adjusting my chute and had only the right side hooked. I left the plane at about 18,000 feet and as soon as I got my breath hooked the left side of my chute. I pulled the rip cord at about 5,000 feet." Cole was the only crewman to successfully evade.

Whether a crewman was willing to jump or not, he often faced challenges just getting out of the aircraft. Staff Sergeant William M. Quinn, a Canadian from Malakwa, British Columbia, serving in the United States Army Air Forces, was the radio operator aboard a B-17 on August 17, 1943, when flak knocked out two engines. He wrote,

> I was firing at an ME-109 when the bail out order was given. I thought it was going to crash into us, but when it got really close, it veered left and I heard on the inter-phone: 'For God's sake bail out.' I picked up my chute off the floor of the radio room. When it would not go on after three or four jabs, I looked and saw that I was holding it upside down. I took off my gloves and attached each hook separately, because the harness rings were so loose they would not meet. I disconnected my intercom and opened the bomb bay doors. I had not disconnected the cord to my heating unit, and this caught me as I tried to go out the bomb bay. As I pulled it out I saw sheets of flame through the window. Thinking the plane was about to explode, I dove head first through the bomb bay, as the plane went into its final dive.

Fighter pilots also had difficulties getting out of their planes. Second Lieutenant John W. Herrick of Metuchen, Pennsylvania, lost a dogfight in his P-47 fighter to a ME-109 on November 26, 1943. He wrote in his report, "I released my safety belt and opened the canopy. I tried to climb out of the ship while it was in level flight. I got my head outside the cockpit, but the slipstream pinned me back. I slipped back and turned the ship upside down. I pushed the stick forward, and this threw me well out of the plane. I dropped 5,000 feet, to approximately 15,000 feet, before pulling the ripcord. I had been told to wait longer, but I got anxious."

In some instances crewmen did not get the opportunity to decide to jump. First Lieutenant Charles A. Bennett of Santa Cruz, California, was the pilot of a B-17 over France on August 17, 1943, and had to leave formation when German fighters knocked out two of his engines and set a third afire. He detailed what happened in his report, writing,

> The entire aircraft was in bad shape, the controls were sloppy, wings full of holes, AFCE shot out. With some aileron control the plane was held straight and level for bailing out. When the copilot and I got into the nose, the aircraft went into a spin and we were pinned to the roof. A few seconds after that the plane blew up and I must have been blown through the nose hatch. The last glimpse I had of the copilot was when we were trying to get down to the floor of the nose compartment. I was knocked unconscious and must have pulled my ripcord when recovering around 2,000 feet.

Sergeant Robert W. Sweatt of Lovington, New Mexico, the waist gunner on a B-24, on January 7, 1944, made a similar exit. Attacked by a German fighter flown by ace Eron Mayer, his Liberator exploded in midair, blowing Sweatt out his waist window. He wrote in his debrief, "The next thing I recall is falling through the air. I pulled my rip cord and then saw pieces of our ship all about me and a fully inflated dinghy floating above me." Sweatt was the only survivor of his crew.

Wounds also contributed to difficulties in bailing out of damaged planes. German fighters attacked the B-17 of waist gunner Staff Sergeant Elton F. Kevil from Ballinger, Texas, above France on October 14, 1943. He recorded the plight of the crew in this way: "Pilot, bombardier, and tail gunner were wounded. Pilot had .30 caliber bullet in stomach.

Bombardier was hit by 20 mm in left leg pretty badly. Tail gunner was wounded in neck by 20 mm."

Most aircraft were on fire when the pilot gave the bail out order. Second Lieutenant Manuel M. Rogoff from Ambridge, Pennsylvania, was a B-24 bombardier on a January 7, 1944, mission. Before he jumped, he was "burned severely about the eyes, face, neck. Burns on palm of left hand and back of both hands."

Staff Sergeant Eugene F. Hively, a B-17 ball turret gunner from Tracy, California, who had survived the crash-landing in England of his Fortress upon its return from a previous bombing mission, was badly wounded by 20 mm fire over Holland on February 22, 1945. According to his report, he delayed bailing out, writing, "I stayed in the plane to let my leg freeze so that I would not bleed to death."

At least one evader had a reason to pull his rip cord as soon as he exited his aircraft. A ME-109 shot down Second Lieutenant H. V. Stevens of Rush, New York, in his P-47 over France on July 4, 1944. He recorded his experience, writing, "I bailed out at about 9,000 feet but I had no time to contact my flight leader. I opened my chute almost immediately on leaving the air craft. My brother was flying in this formation and I wanted to let him know that I was OK."

Other than to delay pulling their rip cord, few airmen had any idea of what to do or what to expect once their parachute opened. One of the few who did get some instruction was Sergeant Carl W. Meilke, a B-17 tail gunner from Baltimore, Maryland, who was shot down by fighters over France on February 8, 1944. He included in his report how the information had helped, writing, "The day before we had a lecture by a paratrooper on jumping; so I did the right things. How to stop swinging, how to drop more rapidly, how to guide the chute, etc."

Parachutes did not always open as designed; and occasionally the crewman never pulled the rip cord, causing airmen to plunge to their deaths. First Lieutenant James S. Munday, a B-17 pilot from Benton, Illinois, had to work to get his chute open. He wrote, "The chute failed to open when I pulled the ripcord. I had to pull the silk out of the case."

Enemy flak and fighters also damaged parachutes before they could be deployed. On May 17, 1943, B-17 navigator Second Lieutenant Homer

Contopidis from the Bronx, New York, bailed out over France to find cannon fire had "destroyed half of parachute before jumping," causing him to land hard enough "to tear the heels off" his boots.

An airman's troubles were not necessarily over once his chute opened. Technical Sergeant John T. Ashcraft from Mineola, Texas, bailed out of his B-17 over France on December 31, 1943. In his account, he wrote,

> I followed the co-pilot out and pulled my rip-cord immediately because I had been off oxygen. The chute opened about 18,000 feet and I discovered that I had forgotten to fasten the leg straps. My arms flew out to my sides at ninety-degree angles and the chest strap fixed itself firmly over my eyes. After two attempts to do something about the situation I gave up because I was slipping through the harness every time I moved. With 18,000 feet to descend I thought I didn't have a chance, and must have passed out because it seemed like as if I had gotten to the ground in a few minutes. I landed in a cabbage patch, injuring my legs as I hit because I could not see when I was going to hit the ground.

For Staff Sergeant Jacob J. Dalinsky, a B-17 waist gunner from Hazleton, Pennsylvania, the descent was perilous. He bailed out over Belgium on August 17, 1943, and reported about his trip down, writing, "I think I left the plane around 18,000 feet. Counting three after clearing the aircraft, I pulled the ripcord and a few seconds later the plane blew up. The concussion of the explosion started a violent swing in my chute. Looking up, I saw a large piece of aluminum floating down above the canopy of my chute. I managed to get away from it by swinging my chute."

Second Lieutenant Merlyn Rutherford, a B-17 copilot from Tonganoxie, Kansas, shot down on February 11, 1944, reported being shot at by rifle fire from the ground while still in the air. Early in the war German fighters did not engage American airmen while in their parachutes. Technical Sergeant Bernard H. Koenig, the top turret gunner on a B-17 from Spencer, Nebraska, shot down over France on July 4, 1943, reported, "On the way down I was circled by FW's. They did not bother me but the 'wash' from their planes threw me so violently that I was sick before hitting the ground."

Second Lieutenant John C. Vollmuth, a B-17 bombardier from Richmond Hill, New York, shot down on February 25, 1944, over France noted that, after his parachute opened, a German plane circled him during his descent but did not shoot at him.

This nonengagement of airmen in parachutes apparently changed on March 5, 1944, when an enemy fighter shot at Second Lieutenant Herman I. Seidel, a B-24 navigator from Chicago, Illinois, while he was in the air in his parachute. His MIS-X interrogator commented at the end of Seidel's evasion report, writing, "Experience of being attacked by an enemy fighter is worth noting, as it may indicate an end of the traditional chivalry of German airmen toward flyers who have bailed out." Although the German fighter pilot could not know it, Seidel was a practicing Jew.

Safely reaching the ground by parachute was also often complicated by the landing itself. With no training in how to perform what airborne infantrymen called a parachute landing fall, airmen often turned ankles or broke legs as they crashed into the ground. They faced other difficulties as well, as noted by Second Lieutenant Frank H. Jacobson, a B-24 navigator from Philadelphia, Pennsylvania, who parachuted from his plane when it ran out of gas east of Brussels on April 1, 1944. Jacobson wrote in his report, "I landed in a tall tree not far from a road. My chute caught on the top branch leaving me suspended about 60 feet above the ground." Even with the help of two Frenchmen, it took nearly two hours for Jacobson to safely reach the ground and begin his evasion.

Despite the odds against having crew members survive crash-landings, some airmen did ride their aircraft all the way down rather than parachute into the sky. Crews received instructions on what to do in such an event. The main priority was to be sure their aircraft, along with classified bomb sights and communications equipment, was destroyed before they abandoned the wreckage. Second Lieutenant Jesse M. Hamby, a B-24 copilot from Fairfield, Alabama, bailed out over France on April 1, 1944, only to have his mostly-still-whole plane crash nearby. Concerned that the plane did not explode and destroy its secret equipment, Hamby and crew members went to the downed Liberator, neutralized German guards, and destroyed the plane.

Second Lieutenant Bernard W. Rawlings, a B-17 copilot from Kansas City, Missouri, was one of those who crash-landed in France on January 29, 1944. He wrote in his debrief,

> About 30 minutes from the IP number three engine starting throwing oil and had to be feathered. About 20 minutes before the target, when we were pretty well behind the formation, we saw German fighters knock a Fortress out of the squadron ahead of us. Then they came for us, but we did not see them until they had almost begun their dead level attacks and hit us heavily, apparently with rocket shells. Our oxygen system was knocked out. We went down to the deck to fly in the overcast, but our instruments were out so that we could not stay in the overcast continuously. We dodged the fighters pretty well until our cloud cover gave out over Luxembourg and the fighters were still chasing us. An attack from above knocked out the top turret. Suddenly the tail gunner called out a 6 o'clock attack. Number three burst into flames and the rudder controls were shot away. Some men were so badly wounded that they could not bail out, so I decided that we had better crash. We brought the plane down all right, jumped out of windows, and took the injured men out.

Rawlings was the only crew member to successfully evade.

Mechanical problems brought down B-17 pilot Second Lieutenant James A. Grumbles from Sumter, South Carolina, on December 31, 1943. In his report he wrote, "We were over the Bay of Biscay on our way to the target when number three oil line burst and I had to feather the engine. We dropped a bit back of the formation, and I never could catch up. I finally aborted and started back. As we made the turn number one prop ran away. I decided to get off the water and head into France, as I did not think we could make England. The engineer opened his chute by accident in the aircraft, so it was decided to crash land as the crew wanted to stay together." Grumbles safely crash-landed the plane, but he was the only member of his crew to make it to Spain.

Pilot First Lieutenant Leonard Keller from Portland, Oregon, crashed-landed his C-47 cargo plane in France on October 30, 1944. Keller, a veteran of seventy-five previous missions, got lost in overcast skies after delivering a resupply of antitank mines to an airfield north of St. Quentin and was shot down by fighters. He and his three-man crew all successfully evaded.

First Lieutenant John H. Oliphint, from Shreveport, Louisiana, crashed-landed his P-51 in France on June 8, 1944. Oliphint, very nearly an ace with 4.5 kills, was pinned in the gas-drenched wreckage for four hours before Germans arrived and freed him—breaking his arm in the process. He was taken to a French hospital from which, with help of hospital staff, he escaped and joined the Maquis until he could link up with advancing Allies.

In at least one instance, a plane continued to kill Germans even as it crashed. Second Lieutenant Ernest V. Lindell, a B-17 navigator from Grandview, Washington, bailed out after being hit by flak in Northern France on January 14, 1944. As the only one of his ten-man crew to successfully evade while the other nine became POWs, Lindell wrote in his report, "I landed between two haystacks and ran to the nearest one to hide my parachute. I heard shooting and thought it was at me. I saw a German flak position in an old building shooting at our plane which was headed right for it. Our plane crashed into the gun position and exploded."

For some crew members, it was not so much the act of getting to the ground that impressed them as it was realizing where they had landed. Although most airmen had at least a general idea of their location when they bailed out, they had little control of their destination once they left their aircraft. Most landed in fields and forests, but a few ended up in unexpected places. Second Lieutenant Melvin L. Heinke, from Wausau, Wisconsin, copilot of a B-24, was shot down on March 2, 1944. He reported his surprise, writing, "I landed in a plowed field in the vicinity of a cemetery north of Fricourt Somme where WWI dead of the Battle of Somme are buried."

Sergeant Charles M. Nekvasil, a B-17 radio operator from Cleveland, Ohio, bailed out over France on August 11, 1944, and landed on a plot of ground near the Eiffel Tower in Paris. Captured by the Germans, he was hospitalized for his wounds and later liberated by advancing Allied forces.

Shot down over Belgium on January 29, 1944, B-24 radio operator Technical Sargeant James R. Dykes of Clayton, Alabama, landed "in the vicinity of Waterloo."

Airmen were instructed to hide their parachutes as soon as they landed and before they began their evading techniques. Many parachutes, found by the locals where evaders had hidden and stashed them away, were adapted to new purposes. Due to fabric shortages during the war, many a bride went to the alter wearing a wedding dress made of parachute silk. The same parachutes that had saved a life played a role in the beginnings of new ones.

CHAPTER 6

Walkers

HEADQUARTERS
EUROPEAN THEATER OF OPERATIONS
P/W and X Detachment
Military Intelligence Service

E&E Report No. 753
Evasion in France

June 15, 1944

Name:	*John J. Carroll*
Rank:	*2d Lt*
Unit:	*561st Bomb Squadron, 388th Bomb Group (B-17)*
Home address:	*Rochester, New York*
Target:	*Bordeaux*
MIA:	*March 27, 1944*
Arrived in UK:	*June 15, 1944*

Other members of the crew:

Pilot	*2LT*	*Julius Lederman*	*P/W*
Co-Pilot	*2LT*	*Waite D. Law*	*P/W*
Navigator	*2LT*	*John J. Carroll*	*Narrator*
Bombardier	*2LT*	*John N. Luzell*	*P/W*
Radio Operator	*SGT*	*Blair H. Harman*	*MIA*

Top Turret Gunner	*SGT*	*Herman F. Hermanson*	*E&E #751*
Ball Turret Gunner	*TSGT*	*Louis Mizera*	*MIA*
Waist Gunner	*SSGT*	*Joseph J. Kapec*	*MIA*
Waist Gunner	*SSGT*	*George M. Schwarzkopf*	*MIA*
Tail Gunner	*SGT*	*George W. Hewett*	*MIA*

I heard bombardier say the bomb-bay was on fire. I jumped at around 15,000 feet and must have passed out, because upon coming to I had no recollection of pulling the rip-cord.

I landed hard and was surrounded by a crowd before I could get to my feet. They buried my chute and from their gestures I understood that I should start running and it was not until then that I discovered I had several bad burns. I hid under a fence, because in my dazed state I kept running into stone walls every few hundred feet. Later I realized that my confusion was due to shock.

I hadn't yet decided which way to go when I saw a gendarme walking through a field several hundred feet away. I crawled along the stone fence until out of his line of vision and ran almost steadily for two hours. Some peasants who had followed me brought food and said that I should stay hidden and they would get clothing. During the afternoon I saw German soldiers going to houses in the neighborhood. At dusk a young Frenchman rushed up to me with a note stating that the Germans were watching my helpers and that I should walk south where I would find everyone friendly.

I walked southeast by compass all night. My burned hand was useless and my sprained ankle made the going very slow. At daybreak I crawled into some berry bushes and hid there all day. . . . to dry my clothes and shoes in the sun and made plans for rationing the food in my aids box. My purse had been lost, probably during my flight from the gendarme.

The second night I got caught in a swamp and spent the last hours before daylight looking for high ground. I had to dry my clothes again and during the whole of this day I saw no one. Twice a day I ate a malted milk tablet and a piece of caramel; in the middle of the night I ate another ration and took a Benzedrine tablet.

The third night I felt desperate. My burned hand seemed infected. I felt that I had been walking in circles. I knew I must look for a place to stay the next morning.

I started early and soon found a large farm which I watched from a safe distance, but the farmer's dog found me and made such a racket that the farmer came out. I told him I was an American, after I showed my injuries and asked for help. I was given some food and wine and though I thought my helper cool in his attitude I had no suspicion of him at the time. At any rate he did not object when I asked to sleep in his barn. Three hours later I was awakened by a man and woman who told me I should leave immediately because the police knew I was in the area. I went back to my original hiding place in the fields and several hours later I awoke to see a gendarme patrol passing. When they were out of sight I walked about four kilometers southeast. Thinking I had gone far enough I crawled into high grass in a field and was awakened by someone yelling, "Hello!" This was repeated over and over again, and as I was about to get up I remembered that the Group S-2 had warned us of this German trick, so I waited a few minutes, and, raising my head quietly, I saw a German soldier searching the field. He passed very near me.

At dusk I started north, hoping by this change of direction to get away from the search. I made good time and in the morning went into hiding again in briar bushes. I had not been asleep long before a dog found me and brought two Frenchmen. I motioned for them to keep quiet and asked for a piece of paper and pencil. I wrote I was an American parachutist trying to reach Spain and asked for food. They told me not to be afraid, but after my other experiences I wasn't very trusting. They did not return to me, but later in the day sent another man into the brush looking for me. I didn't show myself at once but waited and looked the man over, until I decided he was friendly.

He had brought me food and drink and said that I could come over to his house, that he made me a bed in his barn. He tried without much success to get clothing. I spent all of the next day and following night resting in the barn. During the day I repaired an old pitchfork and was given it to carry with me. I had my green electric jacket turned inside out by a Frenchwoman who sewed a secret pocket in the center of the back for my maps and my aids box. I studied the maps on the backs of the French calendars until I had the layout of the district memorized. I found these maps easy to get at any farmhouse and they were of the greatest help to me. They show secondary roads and woods and the locations of chiefs of police and telegraph offices of villages. I was ready to leave on the eighth day, but a friend of my helpers came to the house and insisted that I have a better disguise. He found me some blue jeans and old shoes, so that with my pitchfork and a sack of food I started out looking very much like a local peasant.

I left in the morning hours, walking SE on secondary roads. I was told to stay away from large villages. When people spoke to me I muttered a greeting indistinctly. I found that it was best to speak to old people first and that young people could be ignored. I watched what other people did and imitated them in everything. I travelled about fifty kilometers this day. My burns were healing though I still had no use of my right hand, and my shoes were beginning to blister my feet. I slept this night in a wood.

The next day I talked to no one. Occasionally I had to mutter a casual "Bon jour." In the evening I went up to an old farmer and explained my situation. He took me to his home where I spent two days resting and waiting for my feet to heal. I was asked to stay until the invasion and work on the farm, but I explained that I must return to England as soon as possible. Before leaving I was given a pair of wooden shoes. They were more comfortable and in better condition than my first pair of shoes, but I regretted them later.

On the tenth day I continued my journey uneventfully except for the agony I suffered with my feet. I was not attracting much attention. I had to force myself to walk naturally through villages, for along the roads I could hobble slowly. By the end of the twelfth day I had to throw away my wooden shoes. Fortunately I had saved the felt lining of my electric shoes to wear at night but now with only these for foot gear.

I asked practically every one I met for shoes, but people just didn't have extra ones. I was managing to get all the food I needed. Each time I was refused help of any sort I either changed my direction or got quickly away from the place.

In the evening of this day I went to a farmer working in the fields near one of the richest-looking farmhouses I had approached. In general I had avoided this type of house. He was very friendly. He did not have extra shoes, but he wrote a note to a friend of his and pointed out where the friend lived. Upon producing the note to the friend I was shown a stack of old shoes and given my choice. The Frenchman refused to accept any money for them and, before I left, filled my sack with food.

This night I slept in the open as I was refused at the few places where I asked permission to sleep in barns. I was finding excellent hiding and sleeping places along fence rows in the back of briar patches. The briar patches were easy to see out of but difficult to see into. I kept my water bottle filled always before going into hiding so I wouldn't have to move around too much.

On the 13th day, late in the evening, I came across a small, isolated farm as the farmer was carrying tools in from the fields. I walked beside him and motioned towards a stone barn. I thought he nodded agreeably; at least he said nothing, and I went ahead of him into the barn. Once inside the old man dropped his tools and slammed the door, bolting it before I realized what he had done. I heard him running toward the house and yelling. He was like a wild man and I couldn't get him quiet long enough to listen to me. A woman came out of the house, and I heard the old man yelling something about gendarmes.

I tried to break through a small window at the rear, but the old man was watching carefully and beat me back inside with a pitchfork. I pleaded with him to let me out and told him that I was an American airman. I shoved my dog tags and escape equipment through the window to him and when he stopped yelling long enough to look it over I did some fast talking. By this time his wife had returned and I went to work on her. For some reason they began to believe me and after a long discussion let me out. I was so glad to get out that I kissed both of them. By this time they were in tears and telling me to run because the gendarmes would arrive in fifteen minutes, so I took off through the fields and woods.

The next morning I hid my pitchfork, for I was afraid that a description of me might have been given out. I had been walking all night and part of the next day after the barn episode when I thought from studying my map that I must be getting near the Line of Demarcation (between Occupied and Vichy France). I began asking people who were working alone in the fields, and one old man told me there was no such thing. I didn't believe him and wasted a couple of days moving cautiously around bends in the roads so that I would not come upon a sentry unawares. I stopped at no houses during these two days and finally knew I must have crossed the Line if one existed. The morning of the 17th day I began to reconnoiter a farmhouse to get food and rest. Before I could get to the house I aroused a dog, bringing the people to the door. They took me in at once, and gave me blankets, and a bed in the barn. I told them I knew there were good friends in France who would help if I could find them. I was careful to avoid mention of organization or underground. I stayed with them two days. On my last night the family had some visitors in to see me and I asked them for help. I was told to stay another day while they looked around to see what could be done. I was given an identity card and told to walk into a nearby town and get a train to a town near the Spanish border. I asked about clothing, for it was obvious I could not travel by rail in my peasant outfit. My helpers had only one suit of clothes each and could not get another, so the train plan was given up.

The next morning I set out toward Conflans. I passed through small villages with confidence now because of my identity card. In the evening I was taken in at a small farm where very few questions were asked. The next morning, I walked through Conflans, the largest town I had entered. I had given up the idea of going by rail, because my feet were now in better shape.

By this time the bread and wine diet I had been on for days had given me a bad case of diarrhea, and I suffered spells of dizziness. My progress was very slow, as I had to stop frequently and rest.

I walked through Nontron, worried because I needed a shave. Until now, I had not gone more than two days without shaving. I found that the most approachable of Frenchmen was usually about 45–50 years old, mustached, a farmer, and also invariably a war veteran. I located one in the fields before dark and told him that

I was American aviator. He took me to his house where I was allowed just enough time to shave and eat.

I had set a course for Perigueux but after passing through Brantome I was warned to avoid Perigueux because of the large number of Germans stationed there. I took the road to St. Astier and spent some time in that town window-shopping to learn the value of the 700 francs I had been given by two different helpers. In the afternoon I started a conversation with a farmer who was plowing and let me make an omelet for myself and rest a few hours until I felt like moving on. More and more often during the day I suffered from dizziness and nausea and was forced to rest.

My luck ran out in the days that followed. It rained continuously, and I had to go at least two days without food. The people around Vergt were cold and suspicious; one farmer asked me if I thought he was running a restaurant when I asked for food.

About the 23rd day I took shelter from the rain under the canopy of a small roadside café. There were very few people inside, so I went in and asked a woman for an omelet. She began to pump me about where I had come from, and, when she continued her questioning I said thanks but that I thought I had better leave. There were several men in the café who were listening, and as I started out the door one of them told the woman sharply to leave me alone and get the food. I ate at a table near the door and sat with my back to the wall. One of the men sat at a table near me and while I ate we watched each other closely. When I had finished eating they asked me to have a drink in the back room. The woman was still nosey but the men slammed the door in her face after she had served our drink, and then they asked me for my story.

I showed my dog tags and French identity card, my maps and escape equipment. They grew very excited at the idea of helping me, and from then on I was a "comrade." While we were discussing plans an English-speaking man came in and arrangements were made for me to leave with him. The French said that the nosey woman was not pro-German but that she talked too much and occasionally Germans stopped by the café just to hear what she had to say.

I stayed two days and nights with my helper. By that time I felt well enough to continue my journey and, although I wanted to rest a few days longer, it was not thought advisable because the area was under careful watch by the Gestapo. I was well fed and given extra food for my journey. I was taught how to make a sailor's pack and given a toothbrush, soap, comb, and complete new outfit of civilian clothing. I wanted to ride on trains from there, but they pointed out that two papers were needed: identity card and work papers. I was warned of guards on the bridges *over the Dordogne, but my helpers said that boats would be plentiful and that no one would notice if I rowed across, because the French often did so.*

The morning of my departure I was taken to a road and the route south was pointed out. That evening I slept in an open field. The next morning I asked a woman for food. She fed me and insisted that I go to a certain village where I was sure to find help. Because of her insistence and friendliness I followed her directions until I was out of her sight, but then I turned off into the fields. I had no sooner done so then a patrol of mounted gendarmes passed in the direction I would have been travelling. I thought the woman must have sent them after me but I cannot be sure of it. At any rate I hid in a small wood for the rest of the day.

That night—about the 26th or 27th night—I walked through St. Sylvestre and on through Penne, feeling very confident and making very good time. I walked a day, a night and another day at a steady pace, resting as little as possible.

I had reached the bottom of a plateau late in the evening and decided to go on to the top before resting. I was halfway there when I heard a car approaching and just in time hopped over a fence to wait for it to pass. I awoke four hours later, freezing, and realized I had passed out. I was afraid it would happen again while I was on a road, so I knew I must rest. I found an isolated farmhouse in the early hours of the morning and sat down to wait, but I fell asleep and it was almost mid-morning before I awoke.

I watched the house for a few minutes before going up. Several dogs announced my arrival, and I came upon a woman working in the barn. I tried a new approach this time and asked the woman if I could speak to the man of the house. She replied that she was the man of the house. I explained that I was a refugee in need of food and rest so that I could leave her with the impression that I was either Spanish or Italian in case she should turn me down. Previous helpers had told me there were many of these refugees on the roads.

After the woman had looked me over carefully and smiled I asked her if she was "Good French." She insisted she was, so I told her I was an American soldier and she laughed and said that she had guessed as much. I was fed in the house and a bed was made in the barn. I slept almost two days and a night without a break. At the end of two days I asked if I might rest there longer and was told I could stay as long as I liked. The third day a man who spoke English visited me, bringing clothing and shoes, and he suggested that I make part of the trip by train now that I had good clothes. The fourth morning, with a package of food, I set off for a nearby village to catch a train to Agen and Toulouse. I missed it because I had not remembered the trains were running on German time instead of French time.

65

Because I could write French better than speak it I had been given a pad and pencil, and I was to pretend to be mute.

The next train left in the late afternoon, so I went to a woods on the outskirts of town to wait until the next morning. While I was resting and studying my maps it occurred to me to go toward the Mediterranean where the mountains might be easier to cross. I caught the afternoon train and reached Agen without any difficulty. The station was packed with German troops. There was so much saluting going on that twice I almost raised my hand automatically.

After I had gotten aboard the train to Toulose I discovered I was on the Bordeaux-Marseilles Express. At first this worried me, but I got to Toulouse so fast that I determined to go on to the Mediterranean. I rushed off the train into the station, bought a ticket to Narbonne, ran back to the train through a no-entry gate and got back the seat I had vacated. The people in my compartment watched me closely. One man offered me a cigarette but I refused it and made a motion to show that I was mute. I feigned sleep and did not look at any of the passengers.

At Narbonne I started to get off the train but a Frenchman near the door raised his hand and indicated that I should not. He kept repeating, "Non, non!" The station was filled with German troops and not a Frenchman that I could see had gotten off the train. I didn't know what to do or why I should not get off, so at the last moment I swung off because I thought this would be better than travelling on to Marseilles. There was a soldier on the gate but he did not stop me. My ticket was not taken.

In the waiting room I found all the space taken by sleeping troops. I walked out of Narbonne into the fields and slept until 0630 hours when I came back to the station. From my maps I decided on Perpignan as the next stop and bought a ticket, making use of my pad and pencil. The ticket seller didn't glance at me during the transaction. The first train was scheduled for 1000 hours, but it was late. I stayed in the station rather than chance missing the train. I bought a razor and studied a posted timetable of an electric train that ran up into the Pyrenees from Perpignan. It was my intention to look for friendly sailors is Perpignan and ask them to help me get to Spain by boat. I memorized information about the electric train into the Pyrenees in case I had to use that way out. During the ride from Narbonne to Perpignan I saw rows and rows of barracks housing bombed-out refugees from all over France. I did not expect an Allied airman to find much help in this part of the country.

I got off the train in Perpignan, and too late to do anything about it, saw a double line of gendarmes at the gate through which all passengers had to pass. There were about 15 of them in different uniforms watching the passengers' faces *as if searching for particular people. No checks were being made on identity cards. I tried to show no hesitancy or fear and walked through at a normal pace, looking neither to the right nor left.*

I bought a paper and pretended to be reading it, though I actually was watching the ticket windows to see how tickets were being bought. I noticed that identity cards were automatically produced at the ticket windows when tickets were purchased. Then I saw that the ticket sellers were not examining the cards carefully. So I waited for an opportunity to approach the window alone and with my identity card in my left hand and money, pad and pencil in my right hand, I went up to the window and wrote down Err, which I chose because it was not far from the frontier and not at the end of the line. The ticket seller glanced at my paper and handed out my ticket. To be sure that I caught the right train I made a trainman near the gate look at my ticket and he nodded an impatient "Oui."

During the first part of the ride I slept, but after that I was afraid I might miss my station stop. There was a gendarme among the train passengers and a man who must have been Gestapo because he checked the gendarme's papers. One danger I knew I faced was showing any unfamiliarity with the country and the station at which I intended leaving the train. I watched carefully for signs when I knew we must be near my destination and saw one that read Err–1 Km. I made ready to get off and handed my ticket to the conductor when the train stopped. It was a small platform and there was a German soldier watching the train when it pulled in.

I walked out into the road without looking at him and turned into a lane that led away from the village, as if I knew where I was going. Out of sight of the village I took to the fields and headed into the mountains. In the dense brush of a hollow I hid until dark, changed to my rope sandals and began the climb. In 2½ hours I had reached snow. There was a bright moon and I climbed on until the snow was so deep and I was making so little progress that I knew I couldn't make it and had to turn back.

The next morning I was trying to shave at a small mountain stream and wondering what I should do next, when a woodsman approached. I told him I was an American and asked for a guide over the mountains. He insisted that he was only a woodsman and knew nothing about guiding. I asked if it was possible to cross the frontier, and he thought it was, because it was not well guarded. He said that I was only four miles from the border and that the best thing to do was take off and walk across, and he finally pointed out a direction. I took a compass course and climbed all day. Above the timberline I was in the open and in snow about two feet deep. I watched for tracks in case there were patrols, but I saw none.

At dark I reached a road in a valley and felt sure I had reached Spain, because late in the afternoon I listened to a farmer yelling in Spanish at his oxen while he plowed. I wanted to take no chances though and walked down the road until midnight. As I passed a house a man came out with a flashlight and I spoke to him. I had had very little to eat during the past five days, so I asked for food and a place to sleep. He assured me I had reached Spain. After three hours' sleep I walked to Ripoll, 17 km inside the frontier. I wanted to reach the American Consulate without being arrested so I used all the caution I could. I picked out a friendly-looking Spaniard in Ripoll and asked him to change my francs to pesetas so that I could ride the train into Barcelona. He did this for me only after I had convinced him I would not tell where I gotten the pesetas. I had an escape story ready in case I was picked up, but I thought too that if I could get the train to Barcelona and was caught, then, at least I would be taken on to Barcelona where it would be easier to make contact with the Consul.

For my 400 francs I was given 15 pesetas. My ticket to Barcelona cost 10 pesetas and I got into train without being stopped. Fifteen minutes later the conductor asked for my ticket and identity card. I had no card, of course, and he immediately hauled me into the aisle and searched me. I told him who I was and, much to the amusement of the other passengers, pointed out that he had not found the secret pocket in the back of my coat. He left all equipment with me to turn over to the police, but though I had him in a good humor he would not let me go on to Barcelona under arrest. I was taken back to Ripoll, questioned and searched again, thrown into jail for two days, and then moved to Figueras. I couldn't get authorities to call or let me call the Consul, but after four days a representative of the Consul appeared and asked about me. The Spanish interrogated me to find out how he had known I was there. I didn't tell them but had achieved this through a man who brought some food into the prison to another prisoner.

I was moved quickly after that to Alhama de Aragon and returned to UK 11 June 1944.

Every successfully evader had to hit the ground running. Lieutenant Carroll's story of challenges along the way, including problems with blistered feet, is similar to those of his fellow airmen.

Once on the ground, the airman, who had just minutes before been the hunter, became the hunted. He almost always arrived alone. If he was lucky, the locals on the ground who watched him descend into their domain were willing to help him. French, Dutch, and Belgian civilians frequently spotted parachutes and met the airman as soon as he was on the ground. A downed airman fortunate enough to be spotted by a member of one of the escape lines received immediate assistance in securing false identification papers and guides for his evasion. Most of those who came to the aid of the arriving airmen, however, were not members of any of the escape lines. They nevertheless frequently provided civilian clothing, food, initial hiding places from the Germans, and directions to additional help. Otherwise, the airman was on his own, dependent on his wits and what he could remember from the escape and evasion briefings.

As the months of the war proceeded and the E&E debriefers collected more and more details from returned airmen who made it back to England, they had additional information to pass along to crews in training and at their pre-mission briefings. In particular, the outbound crew members paid attention to advice on what immediate actions to take and how to decide whom they could trust as helpers. Second Lieutenant Robert O. Lorenzi, a B-17 pilot from Spokane, Washington, went down after bombing Frankfurt on February 8, 1944. He noted in his report, "I learned that you can count on the Frenchmen. I also realized that the first three minutes and the first three days are the most important. At first you don't know what to do or are inclined to do nothing. You must hide your equipment and get away at once. Frenchmen wearing a thin ribbon in the lapel are ex-soldiers. Most of them will help evaders. Most French gendarmes will also help. Whatever happens to you, don't give up. Do your upmost to make it easy for the French helpers. Be extremely cooperative, and show your understanding."

Additional advice about helpers came from First Lieutenant Neil H. Lathrop, a B-17 pilot from Los Angeles, California, shot down on January 7, 1944. He reported that elderly French were more likely to assist than young ones and that "the airman must not look for organized help, but only let it find him."

For those landing in Belgium, Second Lieutenant Arnold E. Frantz—a B-17 bombardier from Colden, New York, shot down on March 4, 1944—recommended evaders "keep out of sight" because many poor in the country would turn in airmen to Germans for ransom money offered by the Gestapo or in exchange for the release of relatives held in Germany. He added, "Middle and upper classes safe to contact."

First Lieutenant Milton L. Rosenblatt, a B-24 copilot from Miami Beach, Florida, bailed out over France after fighters attacked his plane on January 21, 1944. When he made his report, he offered advice, emphasizing, "Don't travel in France at night. Avoid large towns. Speak only to people alone. Approach only isolated houses. It was good to learn that most Frenchmen will help you. You must wear your dog tags. Put escape kit where you won't lose it—you will need it. I lost mine from open pocket. Wear shoes under flying boots."

More advice about shoes came from Second Lieutenant Carl T. Nall, a B-24 copilot from San Angelo, Texas, shot down by fighters on March 5, 1944. In his report he described himself when he wrote that he had been "one of many who brought along the indispensable GI shoes, only to leave them in plane during the excitement of bailing out." He emphasized his hard-earned wisdom, writing, "Shoes should be attached to the parachute harness or otherwise not left kicking about the fuselage."

B-17 copilot Second Lieutenant Clayton C. David from Topeka, Kansas, who went down in Holland on January 11, 1944, also had comments for those forced down into hostile territory when he wrote, "Shoes must be black in Holland. You can paint your GI boots with shoe polish. If in France your GI shoes look worn so much better. English shoes with leather soles are dangerous in the mountains because they are too slick. GI rubber soles and heels, or cleats driven into GI shoes give the best footing."

Airmen also acknowledged the advice given by previous evaders on other matters as well. Technical Sergeant Morris Elisco from Chicago, the top turret gunner on a B-24, bailed out over France on March 18, 1944, and landed in a tree, finding himself suspended off ground. He acknowledged his advantage when he wrote, "On the advice of an earlier evader who had found himself in a similar situation, I had made it a practice to carry a knife on operations so that I was able to cut my shrouds quickly and move away."

Other evaders were not so fortunate even after they rejoined invading Americans. Captain Weston M. Lennox from Akron, Ohio, a P-47 pilot, was shot down on June 11, 1944, near Vernix, France. French helpers hid him until an advancing American armor unit arrived on August 1. He described his fate, writing, "Since I knew the area well, and was in civilian clothes, I went out to reconnoiter ahead of the tanks. I ran into three Germans in a field, and there was a fight in which they stabbed me six times and kicked out my teeth."

Lennox managed to escape back to US lines. In large handwritten letters at the end of his E&E report he advised, "Never volunteer for anything."

P-38 pilot Second Lieutenant Jack W. Holton from Winston Salem, North Carolina, went down in France on May 7, 1944. He offered the simple advice in his report, advising, "Play all hunches and don't make the same mistake once."

The occasional evader made his way to Spain or other neutral territory with minimal assistance from local civilians. Sergeant Herve A. Leroux, a B-17 ball turret gunner from Hebronville, Massachusetts, after being shot down on January 5, 1944, walked for a month across France to Spain. He never encountered any members of the escape lines or the Resistance, but he did receive what he called "generous" assistance from ordinary civilians.

Staff Sergeant Peter Seniawsky, a B-17 waist gunner from Brooklyn, New York, bailed out over France on October 14, 1943, after Nazi fighters hit his Fortress. During the next few nights, he headed south by using his compass and hid in barns and haystacks during the day, drinking from outdoor well pumps. Finally, he approached a farmer, who spoke only French, and used his phrase card to identify himself as an American airman. The farmer told him he was sixty-five kilometers east of Metz—meaning he was inside Germany. After Seniawsky managed to bypass the city, he overheard a girl speaking Polish, a language he had spoken at home in America. Exhausted, he approached the girl whom he hoped would help him. His risk paid off when she and her father provided food and clothing and helped him reach France.

Between walking and purchasing rail tickets with money from his purse, Seniawsky crossed France to Nancy. He reported his experience there in his debrief, writing, "I walked through side streets until sunup. After that I looked for churches and spent the morning in them at different services. The town was full of Germans and I wanted to stay off the streets as much as possible. At 1430, I found a picture show and saw that a matinee was starting soon. Before going in the show I went to a bakery and bought some cakes by pointing at what I wanted and putting down a franc note. I bought my theater ticket in much the same way. Because of exhaustion I slept during the picture and stayed until it was over."

Seniawsky continued to walk and take trains until he reached Perpignan on the French coast from where he crossed the mountains into Spain. With no assistance from line helpers, he made it from Germany back to the United Kingdom in only a month, arriving back in Britain on November 10.

Second Lieutenant John J. Maiorca, a B-17 bombardier from Manchester, Connecticut, faced all kinds of challenges after being shot down by flak over Belgium on November 5, 1943. After hiding his chute in bushes, he threw his flying boots in a nearby pond. They floated, so he had to retrieve and "hide them properly." He gave chewing gum from his aid box to Belgium children but they "did not seem to know what to do with it." His purse had French francs but no Belgium money. Maiorca provided more details, reporting, "By 1400 I was completely soaked and pretty miserable. It was still raining hard, and it was cold, so I began to figure that it was a question of pneumonia or of giving up if I did not find some help pretty soon." Finally, two young girls led him to a café.

Evaders often walked long distances before making contact with line helpers. Technical Sergeant Howard J. Turlington, a B-17 top turret gunner from Dunn, North Carolina, walked for 140 miles on his own starting on September 16, 1943, until meeting line helpers in Central France who arranged the remainder of his journey.

B-17 pilot First Lieutenant Ralph M. Saville from Hanging Rock, North Carolina, after being shot down in occupied France on December 31, 1943, evaded and walked for eleven days before his journey was arranged.

B-17 pilot First Lieutenant Dennis P. Carlson, from Mitchell, South Dakota, received no help for eight days after landing in France on October 4, 1943. He avoided civilians and German soldiers by walking along a railroad track in his flight overalls. He reported that the railway bed made it easy to hear and avoid approaching people.

B-17 copilot First Lieutenant Norman C. Schroeder from Harbor City, New Jersey—who parachuted into France on September 16, 1943—recorded the value of local maps that augmented the one from his aid kit, writing, "I found that in nearly every farmhouse, there is a small map on one of the pages of a small calendar almanac. Each map shows just the right area for a day's walking (23 miles). All main roads, side roads, paths and trails are shown. After making this discovery, I would study these maps with my compass at night and plan the next day's journey."

Obviously, downed airmen needed food and water within hours for survival. Equally important in terms of their evasion techniques was the need to blend in with the locals by adopting disguises so as not to come to the attention of the Germans. In this respect, wits and assistance worked in tandem. For example, a woman approached Technical Sergeant Otto Bruzewski, a B-17 waist gunner from Bay City, Michigan, shortly after he landed in Belgium on August 17, 1943. He reported in his debriefing, "In twenty minutes she was back with civilian clothes, and a pick and shovel. She handed me a note which said, 'Dress—take these tools and follow this woman.'" He did as instructed, and she led him to members of the underground who arranged his evasion to Spain from where he arrived back in the United Kingdom on January 17, 1944.

P-38 pilot Major William A. Jones from Ontario, California, received a similar welcome from farmers when he landed in France on May 24, 1944. They gave him clothes and a fishing pole to carry as a disguise.

Second Lieutenant Morton B. Shapiro, a B-24 navigator from the Bronx, New York, set out walking at the instant he reached the ground on December 30, 1943. He soon met a woman on the road carrying a large bundle. He took the bundle and walked beside her until they reached the next town.

First Lieutenant H. E. Moebius, a P-51 pilot form Milwaukee, Wisconsin, was shot down while supporting Operation Market Garden in

Holland on November 1, 1944. He went into a field, put a halter rope on a cow and led it down a major road for five days until he reached advancing Allied units.

First Lieutenant Elwood D. Arp, a B-17 pilot from Sumner, Nebraska, bailed out over France on September 6, 1943. He and two crew members hid in a field for most of the day. He recalled his experience, writing in his E&E report, "At sunset two peasants came to us, one carrying a pitchfork, the other a hoe. We were given the tools to carry and followed the peasants across the fields to a farmhouse."

While Lieutenant Arp's disguise came easily to him, he learned other lessons about the difficulties of being on the ground and unprepared for his circumstances, particularly about footwear. Shoes played a critical role in successful evasions. In their E&E reports many evaders mentioned shoes—and especially the blisters that resulted from their lack of proper shoes. Arp wrote when debriefed back in England, "Evaders especially missed their GI shoes in the climb over the Pyrenees to neutral Spain. I had foolishly given up my GI shoes, which I had thought made me conspicuous. During the crossing I would gladly have given a hundred dollars for a pair. The French shoes I wore had pasteboard soles and my heels were frostbitten."

B-24 pilot First Lieutenant Donald J. Heskett, from Junction City, Kansas, went down on December 30, 1943. He noted, "During my journey I was glad I wore my GI shoes. They proved extremely useful for me."

Sargeant Kenneth R. Moore, a B-17 tail gunner from Dunellen, New Jersey, understood the importance of shoes and taking care of his feet after landing in France on September 6, 1943. He explained, "I found a stream and washed my feet. I had heard a lecture by a pilot who had evaded and he emphasized that one should take special care of his feet, so I washed mine every day that I was walking. It proved to be excellent advice. I was wearing one pair of cotton socks and one of wool. I started out down the road, wearing my GI shoes which I had had right along. If an evader has to do much walking, GI shoes are certainly the thing for him to wear."

B-17 tail gunner Staff Sergeant William C. Howell from Goldsboro, North Carolina, found himself on the ground in France on July 4, 1943.

In his report he wrote, "I had no shoes but my flying boots, and I certainly missed a good pair of shoes."

Staff Sergeant John Semach, a B-17 tail gunner, from Youngstown, Ohio, was shot down over France on September 16, 1943. "I had GI shoes with me in the tail but had to leave too fast to take them with me. I wished I had them when I was given shoes that were too large and blistered my feet."

German fighters shot down First Lieutenant Robert E. Biggs from Gordon, Texas, copilot of a B-17, on March 5, 1943, after their bombing run on submarine pens at Lorient, France. Biggs detailed his experience when debriefed, writing,

> I landed in a field near a large irrigation ditch. My shoes had fallen off when the chute opened so that I was in stocking feet. Walking along I could distinguish in the failing light a man some distance from the road. When within a hundred yards of him I saw that he was a German sentry. I turned to walk away and saw four German soldiers coming toward me from the direction I had followed. I walked very casually off the road, through a hedgerow, into the fields. Fortunately the field was thick with scrub trees and they could not get a good view of me. I had no shoes or hat and was dressed in overalls. The soldiers paid no attention to me as I walked away, and I could hear them laughing and talking.

Biggs continued to walk. "By evening of the next day I arrived at a river where a dam was under construction. The laborers were just leaving and in the confusion I walked across the dam unnoticed." He eventually found a helper about whom he wrote, "The woman of the house gave me a pair of wooden shoes. I walked all day but was not able to cover more than ten miles. The wooden shoes had not helped my feet."

Flak and enemy fighters brought down B-17 waist gunner Technical Sargeant Erwin D. Wissenback from Klamath Falls, Oregon, on October 9, 1943. He and one other crewman were the only ones not killed or captured. Given wooden shoes by helpers, he wrote in his report, "I could not keep the wooden shoes on my feet and had to walk in my socks. Later I was given a pair of old rubber shoes."

Second Lieutenant Elmo H. Berglind, a P-47 pilot from Seattle, Washington, was shot down over France on March 18, 1944. In his report he wrote that, while crossing the mountains into Spain, "I would have given my right arm for a pair of GI boots."

Staff Sargeant Lloyd E. Frazer, a B-26 waist gunner from Forgette, Ohio, who went down in France on September 27, 1943, wrote, "When I walked over the Pyrenees, I would have given anything to have my GI shoes on."

So once on the ground the downed airmen were faced with the immediate challenges of accessing whom they could trust, disguising themselves to blend into their surroundings, and struggling with service-able footwear. As if that were not enough, their intermediate problems included sources for food and water, inclement weather, and distances to safety.

Technical Sergeant Anthony R. Paladino, a B-24 top turret gunner from Albany, New York, shot down on March 2, 1944, was greeted on the ground by rain and snow. He wrote in his report, "I tried to sleep but it was too cold."

B-17 waist gunner Staff Sergeant Leonard J. Kelly from Everett, Washington, and fellow crewmen parachuted into France on September 23, 1943. In his E&E documents he recounted, "It started to rain. Before long we were soaking and knew we would have to find cover. By daybreak we were too cold and wet to stay any longer in the fields." The airmen made their way to the nearest farmhouse and "slept in a haystack."

Staff Sergeant William C. Howell, a B-17 tail gunner from Golds-boro, North Carolina, landed in France on July 4, 1943. "It rained all day, and I was wet and miserable," he recorded.

Illness added to weather miseries and vice versa. German fighters shot down Major Ivan W. Eveland, a B-17 copilot from Missoula, Montana, over France on December 31, 1943. He reported, "The third night I started to get sick. By the next afternoon I had a fever and terrific cold. I had only been released from the hospital the day before the mission. It rained harder the night of January 3. I got much worse and vomited continually. The next night it poured. By now I had dysentery and was weak, wet, and smelled badly."

While those who reached the ground with their aids kits intact had sufficient sustenance for a couple of days, the downed airmen still needed to find food and water sources as they made their moves toward friendly territory. Frequently, civilians offered food, including bread, cheese, and wine, to the airmen. Evaders also found local sources for themselves. Sergeant Kenneth R. Moore, a nineteen-year-old tail gunner from Dunellen, New Jersey, bailed out of his B-17 on September 6, 1943. In his debrief report, he wrote, "When I came to a town, I stuck a straw in my mouth and tried to amble along, looking as rustic as I could. When I passed a tomato patch, I took about 20 tomatoes. I walked along toward the south, eating tomatoes as I went. All that day I walked through the fields, keeping off the main roads. I ate apples, blackberries, and even some peaches along the way."

After his B-17 crash-landed in France on August 17, 1943, radio operator Technical Sergeant John M. Des Roches from Huntingdon, Pennsylvania, ran and hid in a briar patch when it got dark. It "turned out the next morning to be loaded with ripe blackberries."

Flak shot down Sergeant Kenneth N. Davis, turret gunner from Beaver Dam, Virginia, aboard an A-20 near Frankfurt on March 14, 1945. He and a crewmate walked about fifty miles toward American lines in six days, living off their escape kits and cabbage, potatoes, and turnips from the surrounding fields. About 0100 on March 20 near the Moselle River, the two were challenged by a sentry they initially thought might be German because he spoke broken English. In turn, the sentry was suspicious that the pair might be the enemy because they did not know the current password and they refused to tell him their unit's designation. Finally, the evaders produced dog tags that the sentry, a French Canadian who had not spoken English before joining the army, accepted.

One evader took a more direct approach to securing food. Second Lieutenant Eugene Sydlowski, a B-17 bombardier from St. Louis, Missouri, landed in France on September 5, 1944. While hiding, he and helpers raided a German supply dump and took three hundred pounds of potatoes that they lived on until Allies reached them several weeks later.

American airmen who safely reached the ground, avoided immediate capture, and acquired clothing, disguises, food, and water still faced hundreds of miles of enemy occupied territory between themselves and safety in friendly countries. Walking and running alone were not sufficient for most to successfully evade. Reaching safety required the exposure of travel by all transportation means available: by foot, by bicycles, aboard trains, in automobiles.

Bicycles provided an attractive alternative to walking. First Lieutenant French M. Russell, a B-24 copilot from Stillwater, Oklahoma, landed in France on May 6, 1944. He wrote in his debrief, "A bicycle is an excellent means of travel and to get one it is almost necessary to steal one. An evader must either meet an extremely good patriot who will sacrifice his own main means of travel or else steal one."

For Staff Sergeant Charles K. Bailey, a waist gunner from Wynnewood, Oklahoma, securing a bike came easy when he landed in Belgium after fighters shot down his B-17 on August 17, 1943. In his report he simply noted, "Provided a bicycle by villagers."

An evader could cover many miles on a bicycle. When Second Lieutenant Harry E. Roach Jr., a B-17 navigator from Philadelphia, Pennsylvania, parachuted into France on May 1, 1943, he was the only member of his ten-man crew in need of transportation because six had died in the plane and three were captured on the ground. Two farmers came to Roach's aid. They took him and his parachute, which became a communion dress for a relative, to the rectory of the village Catholic church. After spending three days there, one of the Frenchmen gave Roach a bicycle and an address of a safe house to the south. Roach apparently made good time with his bicycle. In his debrief report, he commented about his final day of the trip, "I had been averaging about 90 kilometers a day but this day I pedaled 140 kilometers to an address I had been given. I made the trip in thirteen hours."

Technical Sergeant Charles S. Bowman, a B-24 waist gunner from Marshalltown, Iowa, evaded on a bicycle after being shot down on April 12, 1944. He wrote in his report, "When my bicycle broke down I walked 38 kilometers to get it fixed. In all I rode over 150 kilometers."

Because of fuel shortages everywhere, few automobiles traveled the roads, limiting the opportunities for evaders to hitch rides. Among the few who were able to drive were medical doctors who made house calls across large areas. Several E&E reports indicate that the physicians were more likely than most to give the Americans lifts.

Rides on trucks were generally limited to referrals from sympathetic civilians. Staff Sergeant Joseph L. Kirkner, a B-17 top turret gunner from Radnor, Pennsylvania, went down in France on December 31, 1943. He asked a farmer for a place to spend the night and advice on transportation. In his report Kirkner wrote, "He said, 'Oh, that is very simple. We just flag a truck to the next city and you can get a room there.' He did stop a truck, and the driver consented to take me. As soon as the truck was moving, the driver turned to me and said, 'So you're an American.' I jumped. He had been with the Americans in the last war and spoke excellent English."

The fastest, yet often the most hazardous, means of evading capture were the trains. Helpers often bought tickets for evaders, many times accompanying them on the journeys. At other times, evaders had to take measures on their own. Sergeant Herman F. Hermanson, a B-17 top turret gunner from Austin, Texas, was assisted by line helpers after being shot down in France on March 27, 1944. He made his way to Bordeaux, where he had expected to be met by other helpers. When those helpers did not appear, he took care of his own travel. He wrote in his debriefing report, "Finally, I bought a ticket to Langon. This I did by writing the name of the city on a piece of paper, handing it to the ticket agent, and pretending to be deaf and dumb. I got my ticket and boarded my train without difficulty."

Technical Sergeant Bertil E. Erickson, a B-17 bombardier from Grassbelt, Pennsylvania, went down in France on August 27, 1943. French civilians helped Erickson and other evaders. In describing the events in his debrief, Erickson wrote,

> Later in our journey we were waiting in a railway station for our guide, and he never showed up. After we had waited about nine hours; we began to get pretty uncomfortable. A station workman started talking to me, and I could not understand what he

said. I replied, "Oui, oui" and that was evidently exactly the wrong answer, for he then began a near tirade. Finally he walked away, but everyone around the waiting room had been watching us. I expected to get picked up any minute. When evening came, and no one still showed up for us, we decided that we had better head for the country. We thought that we might have to make the rest of the journey on our own. I no longer had any compasses from escape kits, but fortunately I still had a pencil clip compass which had been given at my group. Using this compass we started south on our own.

To no one's surprise, some airmen evaders sought aircraft to make their escape. None were successful, but their efforts demonstrate the ingenuity of the evaders. P-51 pilot Second Lieutenant Elmo H. Berglind from Seattle, Washington, was shot down over France on March 18, 1944. He managed to evade capture for a month. In his report, he detailed his unorthodox attempt to get back to England, writing, "I heard that there were two single engine aircraft on a field nearby. I decided to steal one and persuaded a French friend to help me. While he was distracting the guards with the aid of a bottle of champagne, I got into the hanger unobserved. Instead of a ME or FW, I found, to my disgust, two Frieseland Storchs without the necessary fuel capacity. We returned home without arousing the guards' suspicions." Berglind went back to relying on his feet and successfully crossed the Pyrenees into Spain one day before the D-Day invasion.

B-17 copilot Second Lieutenant Howard W. Kelly, from Richmond, Indiana, went down in France after being hit by flak on February 16, 1943. After evading capture for a day, he came across a German airfield and attempted to sneak onto the field to steal a plane. His intent was to fly back to England, but he could not get past security. Kelly made his way to Spain on foot, the only crew member on his plane to successfully evade.

Every E&E report represented a successful evasion story. Still, some airmen were more descriptive and detailed in their writings than others. To compensate for omitted particulars, the MIS-X interrogators often made comments on the reports about the various escapes. Staff Sergeant

George R. Miller, a B-24 tail gunner from Woodbine, Pennsylvania, came down in France after bombing Mannheim on December 30, 1944. A 20mm shell from a German fighter had blown part of his turret out and wounded him badly. When he reached the ground, Miller could only crawl. French peasants took him to a civilian doctor and hospital. In his report Miller wrote, "I was taken right to the operating room. In the several months that I was there I had five operations which necessitated four blood transfusions. The nurses could not possibly have taken better care of me." Never detected in the hospital by the Germans as an evader, Miller recovered sufficiently to make his way to Spain and back to the United Kingdom. A comment added to his E&E report stated, "Some evasions can only be explained by the simple word 'guts.'"

The MIS-X interrogators also commented on how airmen could successfully evade from Germany itself. On April 7, 1945, west of Ludwigslust, German fighters shot down Staff Sergeant Francis Carman, a B-17 bombardier from Costa Mesa, California. During the next three days, he used his aids kit compass to walk westward where he met Allies nineteen miles east of Hannover. His E&E report included a comment from his interrogator who wrote, "The evasion of Sgt. Francis demonstrated again that it is possible to evade capture in Germany if airmen bailing out are not captured immediately upon hitting the ground. Avoiding all people, civilians and soldiers, escape can be accomplished if the evader will take advantage of wooded areas and travel by night. It takes determined walking and the will to get back."

Comments also included critiques of evader techniques and destination choices. Technical Sergeant Ray P. Reeves from Allenreed, Texas, was a cameraman aboard a B-24 that went down in Northern France on January 21, 1944. With six hundred miles separating him from freedom in Spain, Reeves decided to take a route through Paris. His MIS-X debriefer was apparently amazed that Reeves would make such a choice. The debriefer added his own sarcastic conclusions to Reeves's report, writing, "It seems incredible at this late date that an evader should even think he had been briefed to make for Paris. Why not Berlin?"

An occasional evader violated most, if not all, recommended evasion procedures and yet still made his way back to freedom. MIS-X officers, although pleased about the evader's success, nevertheless condemned their methods of escape. First Lieutenant Robert V. Krengle from Houston, Texas, a bombardier aboard a B-24, went down in France on December 30, 1943. After Krengle had written his story in his debrief in the United Kingdom on May 18, his interviewer added his own commentary of the tale. Referring to Krengle by his E&E 646 number in the comment section of the report, the interviewer wrote,

> This story is such an amazing jumble of good evasion practice, lucky breaks, and cool action in the pinches, that it is hard to know where to seize hold of it. By any reasonable standard, 646 should now be in Stalag Luft III cooling his heels. His first phase—hiding under difficult conditions—was excellently done, with coolness and presence of mind. Then, having safely landed in the hands of helpers, 646 committed two crimes; he abandoned his helpers without cause, and he went to Paris. Luck and coolness, and a friendly workman saved 646 in Paris. But then 646 made his capture almost certain by going to Bourges, another large town, contrary to his briefing and against common sense. There he betrayed himself carelessly to a stranger by speaking English, and then he declared himself to a boy in the street. 646's career on the railway runs in the same pattern. He declared himself first to a ticket seller at a station and then to a stranger in a car. At the very end of this incredible run of luck 646 partially redeemed himself by persuading a scared helper to carry on. In short, this is a cock-eyed story which proves only that the ways of God are obscure.

Some airmen were too injured to endure the long journey to Spain while others, on the advice of their helpers, determined their best course of action was to wait for the advancing Allies. Second Lieutenant Erwin J. Bevins Jr., a B-24 copilot from Watervliet, New York, crash-landed into a cemetery near Friesland, Holland, on December 22, 1943. Hidden by the Dutch until liberated on April 9, 1945, Bevins evaded for 472 days, the longest of any American airman in the war.

Staff Sergeant Roy A. Cheek, a B-17 tail gunner from Lawson, Missouri, also went down in Holland on February 22, 1944. He remained hidden for 314 days until joining advancing British infantry.

B-17 tail gunner Staff Sergeant Stuart E. Bouley from Champion, Michigan, was shot down over Holland on June 29, 1944. His Dutch helpers hid him for more than ten months before the arrival of the Allies.

After coming down in Holland on August 17, 1943, B-17 pilot First Lieutenant Hamden L. Forkner of New York City, remained hidden in a Dutch home for eleven months before being liberated. "I went outside three times during my stay—on Christmas Day, New Year's Eve, and on April 18th."

CHAPTER 7

Helpers and Hides

SECRET—AMERICAN
MOST SECRET—BRITISH

HEADQUARTERS
EUROPEAN THEATER OF OPERATIONS
P/W and X Detachment
Military Intelligence Service

E&E Report No. 759
Evasion in France

June 18, 1944

Name:	*Jack M. Ilfrey*
Rank:	*CPT*
Unit:	*79th Fighter Squadron 20th Fighter Group (P-38)*
Hometown:	*Houston, Texas*
Target:	*Bridge south of Angers*
MIA:	*June 13, 1944*
Arrived in UK:	*June 17, 1944*

On 13 June 1944 I led my squad down to attack a train in the vicinity of Angers. My P-38 was hit during the first pass. The cockpit filled with smoke and as I pulled up to 1,200 ft. I saw the right engine blazing. I went out over the supercharger on the right side as the plane veered off to the left. I pulled the ripcord and landed almost at the same moment in the backyard of a farmhouse.

Unbuckling my chute and leaving it on the ground I ran around the house and up to the French family standing in the yard watching me. I didn't want to hide there because my plane was burning in the next field and it was obvious the Frenchman didn't want me to stop. I asked the direction north and ran along hedgerows following a small country lane about four kilometers before stopping to rest in a ditch. I still was wearing my summer flying suit, helmet, goggles, and flying boots and GI shoes.

During this 20 minutes rest I took off my coveralls, insignia, and tie, took the things out of my aids box, ate candy bar, I looked over my maps and set out north on the dirt road. It was 2230 hrs. Now I was wearing my gray sweater, dark green trousers and GI shoes. My shirt was open at the neck and I had no cap.

I had been walking for ten minutes in the dusk when a young Frenchman rode up behind me on a bicycle and asked me in broken English, if I was the American who had crashed. I admitted my identity and asked where the Germans were. He had just come from my plane. Two or three Germans had reached the plane a few minutes after the crash and were searching the neighborhood for me. He estimated the Allied lines to be about 200 km north and assured me there were plenty of Germans about. I asked if I could buy his bicycle. He wanted to sell it, but he thought he had better ask his family. He gave me his beret and took me to his home.

The family greeted me cordially and said I could stay that night. They didn't know much about the fighting area to the north but they thought my idea of cycling to the lines was a good one. I asked the head of the family to write a note, as if he were a doctor, stating that I was deaf and dumb and on my way to visit my parents. I carried the note but never found any use for it. There was some argument in the family about selling the bicycle. Several members thought it would endanger them if I were caught and if the Germans used pressure to learn where I had gotten the bicycle. The head of the family overruled this objection, and I paid all the money from my escape purse and five francs from my pocket for it. I compared my maps with the Michelin road map, memorizing the route I meant to follow because I did not want to carry anything British or American with me. I planned to follow highway N 162 almost all the way to Caen. Before going to bed that night I left all my escape aids and purse, my crash brace, watch and fountain pen, my maps and GI shoes, in short, everything that would identify me, behind as souvenirs. I had not taken dog tags on my mission with me so now I had no means of identification if captured.

I started early the next morning so I would not be seen leaving the house. I was dressed in beret, old French slippers, a kind of Dutch trousers that buttoned up the sides, a green shirt and a dark blue coat. The family was pleased with my disguise and assured me that the Germans paid no attention to French cyclists. I was given food in an old musette bag. I pedaled without incident to the main road (N162) and turned north.

About mid-morning I was passed by a small German convoy of three trucks and two staff cars which I in turn passed ten minutes later when it had stopped because Allied aircraft were in the vicinity. On down the road I came to a single parked staff car and was stopped by a German soldier. I was ready to play deaf and dumb but he spoke in German gesturing, to ask if I had just passed three trucks and two staff cars. I answered, "Oui" and cycled on. Soon after this the convoy passed me again and I was never far behind them all the way into Laval. North of this town I stopped to rest and eat lunch.

In the afternoon, about half way to Mayenne, a German soldier called me to a halt. He wanted my bicycle and meant to have it. I began protesting by holding on to the bike and pointing down the road, saying "mama" and "papa" in French and he seemed to get the idea. At just this moment a German truck came along and he hitched a ride on it or I would probably have lost my bicycle.

I continued on through Mayenne and stopped at a farmhouse where I saw a man alone in the yard. I asked him in French for water and got it. The man began asking questions but I pointed to my ears and said "sourd (deaf)."

I pedaled without stopping to within 10 km of Domfront. I stopped again for water at an isolated farmhouse. Because it was getting dark and I wanted to get off the road before the curfew, I told them I was an American and asked if they would hide me. I got the water, but they refused to let me sleep there because the neighborhood was full of Germans. Not far from their house I found a small barn off the highway and slept in it that night.

It was daylight when I awakened. I pedaled all morning and into the afternoon without stopping except for a short rest and without speaking to anyone. I was seeing more Germans on the roads and signs of evacuees from the fighting areas, but no one paid me any attention. By mid-afternoon I was thirsty and hungry enough to look for help. I examined the houses carefully and chose one where I could not easily be seen approaching and where a woman was working alone in the yard. She gave me water and began asking questions while I drank it. I started to tell her I was deaf, but I changed my mind because of her friendly attitude, admitted to being American, and asked for food. She was still not frightened and asked me into the house. I had decided it was best always to leave quickly when anyone showed signs of nervousness at hearing I was an American. I left the woman as soon as I had eaten, cycled through Conde, and found a barn before dark.

The next morning the front tire on my bicycle was flat. I pushed it out to the highway and stopped a man whose cycle had a pump. I managed to borrow his pump without having to speak. However, before I finished, he started talking to me and I discovered he could speak some English. He was friendly, so I told him my story and asked what he thought of my chances. He was not too encouraging but thought them fair. We travelled together until he had to turn off. I could hear the guns now, though they were twenty miles away.

At Thury I turned northwest away from Caen, and zigzagged over country roads to Fontenay. This took about two hours, and I arrived around 0930 hours. I started north on a road out of Fontenay and had ridden about fifteen minutes when I was stopped by two Germans who were carrying a soldier whose leg had been shot off. They paid no attention to my "mama" and "papa" gag, but commandeered the bicycle at once.

I walked on north following the same road and two kilometers further ran into a group of Germans just as I was walking out of a wooded area into fields. They grabbed me and made me get into their trenches. I was not searched or questioned. Allied patrols were on the other side of the fields. Each time I made a move to leave they stopped me with an emphatic "Nichts."

I sat in the trench two hours with British shells passing over us into the woods. Finally one of the German soldiers was wounded in the stomach by a piece of shell. He was put in a wheelbarrow and I was ordered to take him back to the dressing station. I had noticed this field station when I passed it and they drew crosses in the sand in addition to motioning what I was to do. The German was still conscious and made me stop occasionally so that he could rest. Finally I dumped him with the medical people and was given chocolate and cigarettes. Then they motioned for me to go back toward Fontenay.

At Fontenay I followed a road leading west to Tilly and St. Pierre. On the outskirts of Tilly I went up to a farmer who was milking a cow and asked him how I could get to the British or American lines. I could tell about where they were from the gunfire and from the Allied aircraft that occasionally flew in low over the lines to draw fire and then popped back again. The Frenchman told me to follow a small dirt road north out of St. Pierre.

After following this road for 15 or so minutes, I began to see British helmets over the tops of hedges. I walked towards them and soon heard someone yell for somebody to get that French civilian out of the way. A British sergeant grabbed me from behind a hedge and when I told him I was an American flyer he radioed for permission to take me back to the forward HQ. After that I was interrogated at British HQ and brought back to my base in UK.

Comment to E&E 759: A cool and skillful job all the way through. The lesson it teaches is that in the confusion of a general engagement, when troops and transport are moving, there is an excellent chance to dodge controls and to bluff one's way in the tight spots. Enemy troops have their minds full of more pressing concerns than the examination of every ragged civilian on the off chance that he may be an evader.

The E&E report of Captain Ilfrey illustrates the use of hides in avoiding the Germans and the importance of assistance provided by local civilians. Ilfrey combined these two factors to return to the United Kingdom after only four days of evading.

Few downed American airmen had the wherewithal or opportunity to get themselves to friendly territory by themselves. Their fate often depended on local civilians—French, Belgium, Dutch—to provide them with food, hiding places, transportation, and disguise.

Helpers, though, had to be suspicious of Germans posing as evaders and they demanded that the Americans prove their identity. Some evaders went into detail in their E&E reports on how they proved they were American, but Technical Sergeant Kenneth P. C. Christian, a B-17 radio operator from Kansas City, Missouri, succinctly described his experience of his landing in France after being shot down on February 8, 1944. In his write-up he reported, "I was severely questioned by them (helpers) to establish my identity as an American."

Potential helpers had good reason to verify evader identity, as Staff Sergeant Emil W. Taddeo, a B-17 top turret gunner from Richmond Hill, New York, who was shot down on January 5, 1944, verified. In his report, he told of a Frenchmen who took him to a house where other villagers were gathered. He wrote, "He gave me food and asked for my name and identification. I showed them my dog tags. One of these men spoke some English and told me the Germans sometimes sent out men dressed in US uniforms to catch Frenchmen who were in the organizations."

Another French helper explained to Sergeant Richard A. Nyberg, a B-17 waist gunner from St. Paul, Minnesota, shot down in France by flak on June 14, 1944, that helpers had previously "trapped a German agent posing as an American evader." The helper said the German gave himself away by using German spellings of English words.

Repeated stories about the effort by helpers to verify the identity of American pilots merited a comment from the MIS-X staff to the E&E report of Second Lieutenant Bernard W. Rawlings, copilot of a B-17 from Kansas City, Missouri, that went down in France on January 29, 1944, after a bombing run on Frankfurt. The staffer emphasized the report, writing, "Note the extreme care the French must use to make sure that the evader is genuine."

Helpers verified the identity of Americans by the things they carried and by careful questioning. Second Lieutenant Daniel H. Goetsch, a B-17 bombardier from Hustisford, Wisconsin, landed in France on December 31, 1943. After a week of walking, he came to a farmhouse. In his report, he described what happened there, writing, "They became convinced I was a German because they said it was impossible to walk the distance that I had in the time I claimed. My German name and trousers were finishing touches. I was nonchalantly asked a simple question about America and I answered it correctly. Everyone relaxed. I was asked two more equally easy. Everyone became excited and I was accepted."

A farmer and his son challenged Second Lieutenant Jack R. Zeman, a B-17 pilot from Toledo, Ohio, when he came down on their farm in France on January 5, 1944. He wrote in his report, "I showed them my wings, uniform, and passport pictures. Also the QM tags on my clothes and the US stamp on my shoes. They then made me draw a rough diagram of my home town, Toledo, which they checked in a book of maps."

Fighter pilot First Lieutenant Harry E. Bisher from Arlington, California, crash-landed his P-38 in Belgium on March 4, 1944. In his debrief he wrote, "At the first place I was taken (by helpers) I was questioned very carefully to make certain that I was an American aviator. They did not seem to be convinced until I showed the three escape compasses which they asked to see. They seemed to know that we were issued an extra compass besides the one in the purse and aids box."

Sometimes common items served to verify an evader was an American. Staff Sergeant William C. Howell, a B-17 tail gunner from Goldsboro, North Carolina, went down over France on July 4, 1943. He wrote in his report, "I think I really proved myself (to French farmers) by showing the people an American penny."

Sergeant Norman P. Therrien, a B-17 waist gunner from Haverhill, Massachusetts, landed in France on December 12, 1942. He used his GI-issued comb, stamped U.S. Army, as proof to Frenchmen that he was an American.

Helpers also wanted to know how evaders would react if confronted by the Germans. Enemy fighters shot down B-17 pilot Second Lieutenant Homer E. McDanal over France on December 31, 1943. Farmers took the Denver, Colorado, native to a nearby house. McDanal described his test in his report when he wrote, "I was hidden in the next room and I could hear a lot of talking. Suddenly the door to my hiding place was flung open and there, with a gun, stood a man in uniform. He said a lot, but I played 'deaf and dumb.' Then he flung his arms around me, and I found out it was all a plot to test my reliability if we got caught."

Evaders' actions before meeting with helpers could cast doubts on their being Americans. After being shot down over France on January 7, 1944, First Lieutenant Neil H. Lathrop, B-17 pilot from Los Angeles, California, sneaked aboard a German truck trailer. A helper observed Lathrop's move and assumed he was an enemy soldier on the run. Later, after joining his helpers, Lathrop learned about the incident, as he wrote in his report, explaining, "I was suspected of being a German stool-pigeon and my life was temporarily in danger."

At times evaders were unable to convince their potential helpers that they were American airmen. First Lieutenant Norman C. Schroeder, a B-17 copilot from Harbor City, New Jersey, went down in France on September 16, 1943. In his debrief report he wrote,

On the 21st I stopped at a farm house at sundown. It so happens that I never took French in school, but did have two years of German. This evening the farmer tried speaking German to me, when he found that French would not work. He asked for my identity papers; I had none, not even my dog tags. I never had worn them, and I had reason to regret it now. The farmer decided that I was a German deserter. He distrusted me and I distrusted him. I showed him my maps, watch and compasses. In an effort to make him believe me, I even took off my shoes so that he could see where they had been made. He was still unconvinced . . . I put on my shoes, and said I was going to Spain and left.

Assistance came to downed airmen from men, women, and children of all ages and backgrounds. Some helped for only a few minutes while others hid evaders for as long as a year or accompanied them on their months-long journey to Spain or other refuge. MIS-X recognized the many helpers and the risks they took. In a comment to a March 5, 1944, report they wrote, "In this fine record of eight men back from one crew the credit goes mostly to the courageous and intelligent men and women who worked so well to get them out of sight. It is well to remind ourselves that few men would get back without such help, and that many helpers pay the last price. Twelve Belgians were shot in one group in April for aiding airmen to evade."

Another comment by MIS-X staff the following June 19 noted, "It is a rare French or Belgian workman who will refuse to help."

Both individuals and groups of civilians lent aid to evaders. Second Lieutenant Harry A. Hawes, a B-17 bombardier from Kansas City, Missouri, bailed out over France on September 3, 1943. After landing and hiding his chute, he joined a group of French farmers picking apples. He described how he handled his situation on the ground when he wrote in his report,

I made my fellow apple pickers understand that I was a bombardier. Down toward the village someone was firing rifles, and I understood it was the Germans. People passed on the lane, but they paid no attention to me while I picked apples. A lady came with a basket, said good morning, and passed me. After she had gone back and forth a couple of times, she came over, pulled a tape measure out of the basket, and took some measurements. For a moment I wondered whether she had a coffin or suit in mind. Another old woman came with a dog, looked me over, talked excitedly with the others, and went on. A boy brought a pair of black shoes, and a pair of felt and canvas slippers. Although the shoes were too large, I put them on. I went on picking apples and filled eleven bushels while I was being inconspicuous.

Another group effort assisted Flight Officer Ernest O. Grubb, a B-26 Martin copilot from Onalaska, Washington, after being downed by fighters over France on March 2, 1944. Shortly after landing, a helper gave him old clothes and a bicycle and then led him on back roads to a small village. Grubb wrote in his debrief report, "I knew I was getting good help because there was a Frenchman at every crossroads warning my helper if the way was not safe. I was told that the Germans were searching over a large area and stopping all young Frenchmen against the possibility of evaders having already obtained civilian clothing."

It was not just farmers who helped. B-17 copilot Second Lieutenant Philip B. Warner from Wayne, Pennsylvania, began his evasion on his own after landing in France on January 29, 1944. In his debrief report Warner wrote, "A gendarme stopped me and asked for my papers. Since I had no identity card, told him I was an American parachutist. There upon he at once explained to me the best way of getting through the town and over the frontier. He also told me that though most gendarmes might be eager to help me they could hardly risk doing so if other people were nearby." A day later another gendarme stopped Warner and asked for identification. Warner again admitted to being an American. The French policeman, according to Warner's report, directed him to a farmhouse where he was given food and permission to sleep in the hayloft.

Helpers also went beyond just providing clothing, hiding places, and guides. Staff Sergeant William S. Wood from Santa Rita, New Mexico, was a photographer aboard a B-17 shot down near a river in France on August 27, 1943. A Frenchman gave him a small boat, a glass of brandy, and told him to get away quickly. Wood related what happened afterward, writing,

I had no sooner made a good start than I saw a couple of bullets hit the water in front of me and I started to hear the crack of rifle shots. I did not think I had any chance of getting away, so I threw up my hands. When a couple of more shots were fired, I grabbed the paddle and started away as fast as I could go. I heard from the French afterwards that they killed the two Germans who fired at me, stamping their bodies down into the mud of the canal that night. Frenchmen told me that my pilot had been badly wounded and died in the hospital the morning after he landed. They said that another man broke his neck with his chest type parachute and they reported that two other men were shot by the Germans and that one had been bayoneted.

Helpers seemed to be much better at spotting evaders than the Germans. Staff Sergeant Stanley G. Langcaskey, a B-24 ball turret gunner from Trenton, New Jersey, went down in France on December 30, 1943. In his debrief report he wrote, "I took a southerly course by compass, stopping at two cafes for wine and coffee. At a third café, two or three miles to the south, a man was singing in French as he stood at the bar. When he saw me he switched to sing 'It's a Long, Long Way to Tipperary.' I waited until there were only three men seated and two others at the bar before going up to this man and declaring myself. He took me at once into a back room. From there my journey was arranged."

Another Frenchman also used the song to assure evaders that he was a helper. First Lieutenant Frank L. Lee of Dallas, Texas, and First Lieutenant Richard J. Gordon of Pelham Manor, New York, were both blown off course and ran out of gas in their P-38s above France on June 17, 1944. Their joint story includes the following narrative:

We landed in a field within 200 yards of each other, hid our chutes and Mae Wests, and joined forces at once. Several farmers came up and indicated that Germans were everywhere in the vicinity. We therefore took off and ran about two kilometers to a thicket where we were remained hidden until 2200 hours. Then we approached a woman working in a farmyard. She appeared to be suspicious of us, but she finally pointed out our position on our escape map. We then returned to the thicket and waited for nightfall.

It was our plan to walk to Normandy and get through to our lines. At dark we started southwards and after a half hour turned eastwards. We walked through fields until we came to a well-hidden farm and crawled into a hay loft, where we slept all day. At 2300 we resumed our way eastward. The terrain became rougher that night and we were continuously falling into holes and bogs. At about 0400 hours when the sky was just growing light we came to a farmhouse. Here we lay behind a haystack for an hour and a half until we saw that people were up and stirring in the house. We then knocked on the door and told the man who answered that we were Americans and hungry. The man called his wife, who gave us each three eggs and told us that there were Germans everywhere about. We left at once.

There was a town a little further to the east. We circled it first but then reconsidered our action and walked straight into it with the intention of entering the church. The church was locked, however, and we got out of town. We crawled into a hayloft; but we were too hungry to sleep, and at 0730 hours we heard people moving about so we went down and knocked at the farm house door. Two boys came into the yard at this moment. We declared ourselves to them, and asked the woman of the house to cook our eggs. She took us in and gave us breakfast, and the boys explained that there were swarms of Germans along the course that we had planned to take and that the only possible way to Normandy was by a long detour to the south. In view of this and since they assured us that the priest was in the town we had just left, we made our way back to the church.

Just as we approached the priest's house a woman came out to feed the chickens. She looked at us and then turned and ran back into the house. Fearing that she meant to call the Germans, we hurried out of town and hid in a hayloft of a deserted farm until the next morning, when hunger drove us out. We found a farm-house where the people gave us food; and then we walked along the highway, going into the ditch whenever a vehicle approached.

We approached another deserted farm. All the buildings were locked, but we got into a tool shed. Hardly had we settled ourselves when we heard someone whistling "Tipperary," and then a voice calling softly "comrade." We looked out and saw a man who waved a French-English dictionary at us. He told us to remain where we were and said he would return in an hour. Before the hour had passed he was back with a girl who could speak some English. At noon they brought us food, wine, and clothing, and at dusk returned again and led us across the fields to a shop in the town where we twice sought the priest. In this shop a dozen men and women greeted us enthusiastically, and from there our journey was arranged.

Another fighter pilot, Second Lieutenant William C. Hawkins from Langdale, Alabama, had a similar story after his P-51 went down in France on March 21, 1944. In his debrief report he wrote,

When I ran out of gas I bailed out at about 1,000 feet. There was an overcast at 400 feet, so the Germans could not see me parachuting. I landed in a tree, getting a gash in the leg. While I was trying to pull the chute down some Frenchmen ran up. They told me where I was. The Germans came to my plane almost immediately. They were driving down a road in a staff car when I crossed the road, but they paid no attention to me.

I stopped at about ten farms asking for help by means of my phrase card. First I asked for a place to hide and then I asked if Germans were near. They were only too glad to give me food, but they indicated that the Boches were all around and would kill them if they hid me, so I kept going. Finally in a field I found a young Frenchman and his brother who gave me blankets and arranged for me sleep in a field.

I had a certain amount of embarrassment because I did not have my dog tags with me. My French friends questioned me very carefully to satisfy themselves about my identity, and kept me under guard until they were convinced that I was all right.

They had had trouble from men pretending to be Allied aviators and they could take no chances. The next morning I was taken to a place from which the rest of my journey was arranged.

The French seemed to easily recognize evaders even after they had secured civilian clothes. Staff Sergeant Gary L. Hinote, a B-17 waist gunner from Chicago, Illinois, began his evasion on October 4, 1943, after being shot down by flak over France. Late in his evasion he walked into a barber shop. The barber, in English, said, "What do you want, a shave or a haircut?"

Civilians had good reason to fear retaliation from the Germans for helping evaders. Technical Sergeant Kenneth H. Nice, a B-17 radio operator from Souderton, Pennsylvania, went down in France on October 14, 1943. After evading for two months a collaborator tipped off the Gestapo about where he was being hidden by a farm couple. Nice escaped but the Gestapo questioned and beat the couple and took them away when they could not find the American. Nice learned later from the couple's daughter that the Germans had shot her parents.

Children who assisted evaders were not exempt from mistreatment by the Germans. Second Lieutenant Charles L. Moore Jr., a P-51 pilot from Rocky Mount, North Carolina, went down in France on April 30, 1944. A boy who first helped the airman after his landing later, according to Moore's debrief report, "fell into the hands of the Gestapo who tortured him to tell the names of people who helped me."

Second Lieutenant Michael L. Smith from Jacksonville, Florida, had to crash-land his P-47 in France after engine problems on March 17, 1944. In his report Smith wrote, "On my first day my helper took my passport pictures, and on the last day (10 days later) he gave me a complete identity card. He wrote me a note in English begging me not to disclose who it was who had helped me. He warned me of how grave the consequences would be for him and his family, and told me he had lost an uncle this way earlier in the war."

In addition to torture and execution of helpers, the Germans also used bribery as a means of locating evaders. P-47 pilot Major Paul E. Gardiner from Cherokee, Oklahoma, was hidden by a French couple after he landed on June 18, 1944. The Germans offered a bounty of 6,000 francs for information of his whereabouts, but the couple maintained their silence.

By early 1944, German efforts to curtail civilian assistance to evaders had made sufficient impact to be noted by the debriefers at MIS-X. B-17 navigator First Lieutenant Ivan E. Glaze from Indianapolis, Indiana, started his way south after being shot down in Holland on January 11, 1944. A comment made by his debriefer in his E&E report noted, "This is one of a number of recent cases in which evaders have been held up because organizations have been broken up by the Gestapo. Evader's course in such circumstances is pretty well defined by experience. After waiting until he is reasonably sure that his helpers can't move him further, he should move on, but only after a friendly understanding with them. They will usually try to dissuade him, being afraid that he will get picked up and betray them."

Civilian helpers rarely wanted anything in return for their assistance to evaders. They did keep parachutes and often stripped aviator's uniforms of badges and patches to help conceal their identity—and to keep as souvenirs. They asked for information about how the war was progressing and anxiously inquired as to when the invasion and liberation were planned. Some questioned why the United States was allied with the Soviet Union and expressed fear that the communists would take over their country after the war. Many said that they feared the Russians more than the Germans. It also was not unusual for a helper to ask an evader to carry a message back to relatives in the United States or United Kingdom.

One French helper had a different reason for assisting B-17 copilot Second Lieutenant John W. Bieger from Buffalo, New York, who went down on July 14, 1943. The farmer simply wanted him to stay and help with the harvest.

Evaders also had to be careful of the intentions of their alleged helpers. Staff Sergeant William P. Truesdell, a B-17 ball turret gunner from Evanston, Illinois, landed in France on August 15, 1944. On the ground he met a Frenchman who grabbed him and tried to make him follow. In his report Truesdell wrote, "I broke loose from him. He wanted to grab me again, but we had quite a fight as I understood he wanted to turn me in to the Germans. I was armed (personal weapon) with a .25 caliber automatic. I had no alternative, so I shot and killed him. Then I took his clothes."

At times it was difficult for the evader to determine the exact motives of helpers. A young man assisted Second Lieutenant William K. McNatt, a B-17 navigator from Lyons, Georgia, after he went down in France on August 17, 1943. About his experience McNatt reported, "The boy cut off my collar and sleeve insignia and we slashed my pockets so that I would not look military. When I rolled up my sleeves he saw my watch and held out his hand. In my position I had to give it to him. Someone in the crowd gave me an old cap."

Evaders were, of course, anxious for their units in the United Kingdom as well as their parents and spouses, to be informed that they had survived their plane being shot down and that they were at least temporarily safe. Helpers on the escape lines and members of the underground had two-way communications with England and radioed information about evaders when possible. Early in the war some helpers employed passenger pigeons to deliver messages.

A French couple who had a carrier pigeon service with the United Kingdom assisted P-38 pilot Captain Raymond R. Ray of Santa Rosa, California, after he bailed out on July 26, 1944. They could not get a message about his safety to England because they had "run out of pigeons."

Helpers were always interested in the ultimate success of evaders reaching England. Many made agreements for code words to be broadcast on the BBC at certain set times to communicate successful evasions. Often based on hometowns or first names and, at times, just whimsical conjecture, code words included such things as, "There were six beautiful days in Chicago," "Tex Bien arrived in Angletown," "Ashville has arrived," "Bon Jour Chicago," "Madam X your friend Pierre Amont is safe," "Charlie is safe," "Dorothy, the grass hangs high," "James and comrade are all well in England," "I'm drinka beir," "Schnapps is good," "The little dogs are safe," "The moon is full," "Two cases are safe," "The cheese is strong for three," and "Little robbed to Spanish cow."

All airmen expressed their admiration and appreciation for their helpers. B-17 pilot Second Lieutenant William G. Sheahan from Chicago,

Illinois, who landed in Belgium on March 2, 1944, expressed the feelings of all evaders when he wrote in his debrief, "A man named Jules Hassen, who lives at a mill in Vodelee, Belgium, kept four of us for four months. It was harder to leave there than it was to leave home. Too much cannot be done for this man."

Evaders, either on their own or with assistance from their helpers, made use of all kinds of resources to hide from the Germans. Most evaders spent at least one day or night hidden in a haystack or loft. B-17 waist gunner Staff Sergeant Kenneth N. Hougard from Portland, Oregon, who landed in France on May 8, 1944, took extra measures to ensure his hide in the hay went undetected. After hiding in a barn loft, he then pulled the ladder up.

Hiding in hay was not always that comfortable. Sergeant Norman Elkin, a B-17 waist gunner from Baltimore, Maryland, found help as soon as he landed in Holland on January 11, 1944. A Dutchman took him to his farmhouse. In his report Elkin wrote, "I was fed and given civilian clothes. Most of them were given me by a man who took them off his own back. I was taken to a barn full of pigs and cows, where I was hidden under the straw for the night. During the night the cows ate the straw right off of me."

Germans frequently searched haystacks. Staff Sergeant Charles H. Lambert, a B-17 waist gunner from East Boston, Massachusetts, was shot down by flak in Belgium on March 2, 1944. Lambert reported his experience with having hay as a hiding place, writing, "I hid in a haystack. The Germans bayoneted the stack, but I was in the middle."

Not all farmers were willing to share their barns and stacks of hay. Technical Sergeant Robert C. Giles, the top turret gunner on a B-17 from Detroit, Michigan, crash-landed in France on October 4, 1943. In his debrief report Giles wrote, "Before dark we found a shed in the fields and had just crawled into it when a farmer came up to the shed with a cow. He was not particularly unfriendly but said that we could not stay there because that was where the cow had to sleep."

In their initial efforts to hide from the Germans, many evaders had to use hides that were the most readily available. Staff Sergeant Lloyd G. Wilson, a B-17 tail gunner from Belleville, Illinois, went down in France on October 14, 1943. He wrote in his report, "I hid in some brush and covered myself with leaves."

B-17 navigator Second Lieutenant Allan G. Johnston from Bovina, New York, went a bit further in using the forest while evading in France after his plane ran out of gas because of severe head winds on September 6, 1943. While Germans on motorcycles searched for him on the ground, he climbed to the top of large tree, hiding sixty feet above ground. He commented on his choice, writing, "I thought that it was a good place to hide because of the German helmet—it would be difficult for the soldier to lower his head back far enough to look straight up."

Captain Denver M. Porter from Oklahoma City, Oklahoma, could barely move after being hit by flak and crash-landing his P-47 in France on July 23, 1944. He managed to crawl into a hedgerow only sixty to seventy yards from his plane. The Germans searched the area, and when they could not find him remained for thirty-six hours guarding the plane. Unable to walk, Porter remained in the hedgerow for two days before the arrival of the advancing Americans of the 90th Infantry Division.

Another fighter pilot, Second Lieutenant Michael L. Smith from Jacksonville, Florida, belly-landed his P-47 in France after being hit by German aircraft on March 17, 1944. For the next ten days he hid in hollow trees with a French boy bringing him food and moving him to other trees on occasion.

Staff Sergeant Robert E. Fruth, a B-24 waist gunner from Napoleon, Ohio, followed his evasion briefing instructions to the letter by not seeking assistance at wealthy homes. Instead, when he bailed out over Holland on January 7, 1944, he concealed himself in the vines and overhanging trees on a high brick wall next to a large house. In his report Fruth wrote, "I hid under the vines on top of the wall and stayed there until dark" while several German searchers passed by.

At times evaders had to share their hiding spaces with the unexpected. Flight Officer David G. Prosser, a B-17 navigator from Scarsdale, New York, went down in France on September 3, 1943, and hid in a crevice between two buildings. According to Prosser in his report, "I spent the day there. I tried to sleep, but I was pretty badly shaken up and did not seem sleepy. Some mice and snakes also kept me from making myself comfortable."

Some evaders refused to give up even after being spotted by the Germans. Technical Sergeant Nicholas Mandell, a B-24 radio operator from Phillipsburg, Pennsylvania, was shot down over France on November 13, 1943, on his first mission. He detailed his evasion techniques, writing, "My friend thought it useless to hide, as he knew we had been seen. I thought it worth the effort and ran over to the stream. I hid in the grass along the banks and wiggled my way upstream a good distance. Then I sat in the water pulling grass and weeds around my head and shoulders. At that point a thunder storm broke and I saw the Germans hurrying back to their bicycles."

Civilians often hid downed aviators in their homes as well as their barns. In at least one instance, it was not totally voluntary. B-17 waist gunner Staff Sergeant Edward M. Daly from Newark, New Jersey, parachuted into France on December 23, 1943:

Just before target (Paris) we were hit by flak. We dropped our bombs with the formation and were hit again. Fighters came in to attack and the alarm rang a few minutes later. By that time we all had our chutes on and had changed into GI shoes. I jumped at 10,000 feet, pulling the rip cord as soon as I was clear of the ship. An enemy fighter circled me all the way down.

I landed in an open field with no one around. I got out of my harness and ran over to a tree to which I clung until the fighter finally left. Then I threw my chute and Mae West under some hay and set off across the fields. It was already getting dark. I walked for almost eight hours. Once I fell flat between two rows of vegetables and a man stood beside me for some time but he gave no indication of having seen me. When I came to a brook I filled my water bottle and took some Benzedrine, which helped me feel better almost immediately.

Finally I came to a group of houses and hid in the shrubbery until it started to rain. Then I noticed a loft in one of the houses. I climbed into it and spent the night and the whole of the next day. Toward 1900 hours I let myself down through a trap door and found myself in a hallway.

I knock on a door which started a great deal of confusion as no one was found at the outside door. Finally I pushed the door open. A woman was cooking and was considerably startled. We stood staring at one another for some time. I showed her my cigarettes and dog tags, but she continued to look dazed, although she motioned me into the kitchen and fed me. When she turned on the radio, her husband came in and looked me over. Suddenly, he shook my hand and went to get civilian clothing. When he came back he told me not to worry that everything would be all right. The next day someone came for me and the rest of my journey was arranged.

Civilians hid Corporal Russell M. Smith, a C-47 crewman from Nashville, Tennessee, in a house a day after he landed in Belgium during Operation Market Garden on September 18, 1944. His helpers put a sign on the house door that said "Diphtheria" to keep the Germans away.

Waist gunner Sergeant Charles F. Payne from Lake Placid, Florida, was the only survivor of two B-24s that collided over France on March 18, 1944. After Payne landed, Frenchmen had him crawl down a ladder into a forty-to fifty-foot-high water cistern to hide.

Sergeant Ivan L. Schraeder, a B-17 tail gunner from Peoria, Illinois, landed in France on September 9, 1943. During his debriefing he wrote, "Four men arrived with civilian clothes. They took me in a boat along the river to a factory. A crane scooped us up into the factory. I smeared grease all over myself and walked into the shower room as I was directed. There I was given civilian clothes and the rest of my remaining uniform was disposed of."

Flak brought down B-17 navigator Second Lieutenant Rupert L. Phipps from Norfolk, Virginia, over Haarlem, Holland, on September 26, 1944. Phipps landed in the middle of the town, attracting the attention of most of the residents. Several Dutchmen hurried him away and rowed him across a canal to hide him in a greenhouse. When Germans arrived, the town mayor told them the pilot had drowned in a nearby lake. They accepted the story and left.

Evaders found other hiding places, either on their own or with the assistance of civilians. E&E reports note "hidden in cave," "hidden in church," "hidden in cemetery," "hid in a coffin in a hospital," and "hidden under a roof where tiles had to be removed to get in." Although effective, perhaps the worst hiding place was that of B-17 radio operator Staff Sergeant Harry D. Kratz from Collegeville, Pennsylvania, who went down in Holland on January 11, 1944. His civilian helpers, according to his debrief report, took him to a barn and "covered me in manure to hide me."

In some circumstances, the best place to hide was in plain sight. After receiving civilian clothing from the locals a day after he went down in Belgium on February 20, 1944, B-17 copilot Second Lieutenant Julius D. Miller from Hampton, Virginia, posed as a naturalist looking at trees in a forest.

Second Lieutenant John T. Boyle, a B-17 bombardier from Elmwood Park, Illinois, parachuted into France on August 16, 1943. He landed near a river where boys gave him a swimsuit, had him join them in the water, and then picnicked with him while the Germans searched.

B-17 bottom turret gunner Staff Sergeant Harold E. Tilbury from Canby, Minnesota, also arrived near a river in France by parachute on May 17, 1943. Tilbury reported, "A French boy came for me and we went to the river, got a boat, and pretended to fish."

Flak brought down Second Lieutenant John A. McGlynn from Cazenovia, Wisconsin, pilot of a photo reconnaissance P-47, in France on February 14, 1944. He found what was perhaps the best hiding space. As soon as he landed, he ran into a nearby town and ducked into a wine cellar. In his report he wrote, "There were only two bottles left. I took one and climbed up onto the top rack. It was very dark. The wine steadied my nerves. I lay there holding the bottle like it was a club. I filled my water bottle with the rest of the wine, and put 200 francs into the bottle before returning it to the rack. There were no signs of a search and I left."

McGlynn used more evasion skills in his search for help when he spotted an antique store. Aware that prewar American tourist had likely been customers, he approached the shop, learned that the proprietor did indeed speak English, and found help in his escape.

Chapter 8

Appendix B: Intelligence

HEADQUARTERS
EUROPEAN THEATER OF OPERATIONS
P/W and X Detachment
Military Intelligence Service

E&E Report No. 293
Evasion in France

12 January 1944

Name:	*Walter Hargrove*
Rank:	*2LT*
Unit:	*358th Bomb Squadron, 303rd Bomb Group (B-17)*
Home address:	*Huntley, Montana*
Target:	*Romilly*
MIA:	*3 August 1943*
Arrived in UK:	*26 December 1943*

Other members of the crew:

Pilot	*1LT*	*William J. Monahan*	*MIA*
Co-Pilot	*1LT*	*Louis M. Benep*	*MIA*
Navigator	*2LT*	*William P. Maher*	*E&E #118*
Bombardier	*2LT*	*Walter Hargrove*	*Narrator*
Radio Operator	*SSGT*	*Frank Kimotek*	*E&E #134*

Top Turret Gunner	*SSGT*	*Walter Gasser*	*MIA*
Waist Gunner	*SGT*	*Vernon E. Olson*	*MIA*
Waist Gunner	*SSGT*	*James A. Comer, Jr.*	*MIA*
Tail Gunner	*SSGT*	*David Miller*	*MIA*
Ball Turret Gunner	*SSGT*	*Alfred R. Buinicky*	*MIA*
Photographer	*SGT*	*Verdis B. Pryor*	*MIA*

The element leader aborted while we were still over England. We could never get into position to take over the element, because we were overloaded for the altitude, and therefore did not have enough power. We kept with the group, and were near Paris when we were recalled. We had gotten back to the coast, when it was decided to bomb the Amiens airfield. We all had to turn and go back in. As our aircraft made the turn, it started to drop behind the group. The oil pressure on number four engine dropped to below 60 pounds. The engine and propeller ran away, as they could not be feathered.

We went over the target, but after that the rest of the group pulled away, seven FW's jumped us, and we were hit in the left wing and nose. Number four engine was ablaze. The pilot told us to prepare to bail out. There was a two minute interval, during which the ball turret gunner, and the radio operator, who was at a waist gun, each got an FW. The bail out order was given.

After jumping at 22,000 feet, I delayed my jump until I saw two chutes open above me. I believe I was then at 18,000 feet. There was a slight jerk on my left leg, where the harness was loose, when the chute opened. I had had my harness adjusted at base, and wore it really tight over my thin flying jacket. There was a strong wind blowing from England and I was sent steadily inland. I could see the aircraft in a long steady glide. Smoke was pouring from it and the enemy fighters were still attacking.

At 6,000 feet I entered a solid cloud bank, in which I remained as I fell the next 4,000 feet. When I came out I was nearly over a town, but I was traveling towards woods at good ground speed. I looked the country over in order to decide in which direction to run. I decided to run to a large woods northeast of a small woods, in which I thought I would land. I did not want to go toward Paris or the coast for several days, and northeast seemed the least likely direction for them to look for me. On looking up, I could see a parachute just coming through the cloud bank: then all my attention turned to landing.

I was going to land in a tree. I pulled on the left hand shroud lines and swung my body so that the chute caught the top of the tree, while my body cleared it. The landing was as easy as falling out of bed. I pulled myself in toward the tree. When

I reached it, I sat on the limb, and unbuckled my chute and harness. Then I took off my Mae West and flying boots, and hung them in the tree with my chute. As I climbed down, I realized that my mouth was dry, and that I was very thirsty. I had a package of gum in my pocket, and chewed a piece. This made me feel much better.

I saw that I was going to have to cross an open field; so I took off my leather jacket and coveralls, and, rolling them tight, tucked them under my arm. I did not want to hide them, because I was sure I would need their warmth that night. I strolled nonchalantly across the field, trying to look like a Frenchman. As soon as I reached the large woods, I started to run, just as I had planned while still in the air. As I started to run I heard a car drive up and stop near the wood I had just left. When I reached the far side of the woods I put my jacket, coveralls, and gloves on again. Then I crawled into the middle of a large blackberry patch where I lay until dark.

Once, people talking passed nearby. I think they were Germans, but I did not investigate. One time they sounded as though they were running. At dark I came out and started walking northeast by the stars. I was lucky that it was a beautiful clear night, for I had no compass, as I had left my aids box in the plane. The box annoyed me when I was working a gun, because I kept it in my knee pocket, therefore I had put it down beside my chute, and not remembered it again until I was suspended in mid-air. Before I was finally picked up, I had plenty of occasions to regret forgetting my "aids."

There were several highways on my route, but I crossed them without trouble. At 2300 hours I paused to watch the RAF which was being shot at from Abbeville with red and green tracers. Most of the night was spent traveling across open country. At 0400 hours I came to a wood in which there was a piece of B-17, 4 × 10 feet in size. I looked it over, but the Alcoa stamp was the only mark I could find on it. At daybreak I came to an apple orchard and filled my pockets. The apples were green but that didn't matter. There was a grain stack nearby and I twisted and turned until I got myself into the center of it. I hid there until sundown.

At sundown I crawled out and headed back to the apple orchard. Once my pockets were filled again, I started off to cross the valley. When I came to the railroad tracks, however, I found them guarded. It was too dark to see if the man was French or German, but I could see his gun, and I did not have one. I went further down the track and crossed safely. I went through a cow pasture and crossed a little bridge over a stream that went through it. At 0200 hours on 2 September I lay down by a grain stack and tried to sleep.

Towards daybreak I got up and crossed a valley to a woods that I had seen ahead of me. I hid here all day, drying my dew drenched shoes and socks, in the sun on the southern side. I watched the French farmers working in the fields, and saw some Germans on motorcycles pass down the valley road. I heard what sounded like two groups of Forts going over, and I could see their vapor trails; almost immediately five or six FW's came over at not more than 100 feet.

That night I went down to an isolated garden about one kilometer from a village. Carrots and turnips were growing there. I ate all I could and then stuffed my pockets. I crossed a highway, and again traveled through open fields until midnight. I slept beside a haystack until daybreak. On walking I circled a village and stole into what looked like a tool shed or barn. I pulled myself up on to some boards laid across the rafters and watched what went on. I was next to a grain mill and there were a great many people about, including Germans. I decided that there were too many Germans present to find help in such a small town.

After sleeping until 1600 hours I left the building unobserved and crossed the mill stream into a garden, where I hoped to find more apples and carrots. After filling my pockets I walked down stream and hid in the bushes until dark. At dark I set off again and crossed a railroad track, this time without meeting a guard. At midnight I picked out another haystack and slept until dawn.

On 4 September, soon after setting out, I came to a road sign. I now knew exactly where I was and where I was going. I set out for a village shown on the sign. On reaching my destination I crept into a barn and waited for someone to come out of the main house. It was a poor farm, but I had been told that they were usually safest. I was badly in need of help; I had had no water for four days, because I had no halazone with which to purify it, and the streams I had crossed were not clean. My arm was beginning to hurt, because it was spattered with 20 mm fragments. All in all I was thoroughly dejected.

A boy 15 years old came out of the house and into the barn. I walked up to him and he asked if I was English. I said no: "American." He told me to stay where I was, and went into the house for his father. On returning they asked me, in sign language, about something to eat. They then took me into the house and fed me. I was given some hot water to wash my arm, and a cloth with which to bandage it. I went to sleep. At 1000 hours a doctor came and removed the shell that was irritating my arm. A young woman then questioned me, with the aid of a dictionary, to find out what I wanted and where I intended to go.

My first need, as I told her, was civilian clothing. Then I wanted food and a map. I asked if she knew of any way of getting to Spain. She thought it would be too difficult to get to Spain, and wanted to find me a place to stay until "the invasion." When she left, however, she promised to do all she could. I learned that her brother was in prison at the time, waiting to be shot for resistance work he had done. This did not seem to have frightened the sister.

That night I received the civilian clothing. The boy moved me to another house in which I was told to stay. Food was brought to me regularly, and I stayed here for two days. On the 6th of September someone came for me, and the rest of my journey was arranged.

Appendix "B" to E&E Report No. 293

a. *Ten batteries, of three 88 mm anti-aircraft guns each, were moved to Abbeville on 13 September. (hearsay)*

b. *Twenty-three Tiger tanks were at Le Phonchel and eight more were east of Auxi-le-Chateau on 15 September. They were orange and originally intended for Rommel, but were being camouflaged black and green for continental use. (hearsay)*

c. *An ammunition train came into Auxi-le-Chateau on 10 September and remained there for unloading until 14 September. The freight was unloaded into trucks: it appeared to be ammunition for small arms. (observation and hearsay)*

d. *There is a radio location station on the road (east side, on the left when heading for Amiens) between Auxi-le-Chateau and Amiens. The spot is 15 to 20 kilometers from Auxi-le-Chateau. There are two big screens here. (observation 25 September)*

e. *There are four rocket gun emplacements in a semi-circle around Auxi-le-Chateau. They are embedded in the hills in heavy concrete (hearsay 20 Sept)*

f. *There are 600 White Russians stationed at Quimper. They do guard duty and go on maneuvers. They are more feared and hated than the Germans ever were for they plunder, kill, and take anything they want. (observation and hearsay 20 Oct)*

g. *Two destroyers entered the Brest harbor at 1600 hours on or about 10 December. They came in at full steam, apparently undamaged. A seaplane tender was towed into the dry dock on 15 December. During the period of 10-15 December, a lone submarine came in beyond the break water. Four small freighters came into the harbor on 16 December. (observation)*

h. *The Germans at Brest go on nightly drinking sprees. They run around shooting out lights with their revolvers. One night a Frenchman was bayonetted. (hearsay and observation during the first two weeks of December)*

i. *The Italians stationed at Brest and Quimper wear a yellow band on their right arm. They are poorly treated by the Germans. In a group of twelve only one will have a gun. (observation 29 October Quimper—hearsay of Brest)*

j. *French morale is high. Most of the people are armed. Sabotage of railroads and power plants is a daily occupation. (observation October–December)*

k. *German fighter pilot morale is low. They have great respect for the B-17. (hearsay)*

l. *Twenty twin-engine aircraft, originally on the Russian front, were sent to Poulmic (airport for Lanveoc) on the Brest peninsula. Ten of these aircraft have been shot down. (hearsay)*

m. *There were eighteen locomotives in Auray on 15 October 1943. They were all in the immediate vicinity of the station. Most of the locomotives were on sidings and did not even have steam up. (observation)*

n. *The Le Bourget airfield was completely destroyed during the raid of 16 August 1943. 150 German aircraft were caught on the ground. (hearsay)*

o. *The area around Crozon is heavily garrisoned. The barracks are on the western side of the town. The Germans there wear green uniforms. They seemed to be seasoned troops, and were very professional in their appearance. There were always maneuvers of some kind. (observation October)*

p. *Twice a day a JE 52 patrol flies over the bay at Vannes. There does not, however, seem to be a set schedule. Anti-mine devices are attached to the aircraft. (observation 1-10 October)*

q. *American airmen parachuting in the area of Auxi-le-Chateau in August and September were shot at from the ground. In one case this only injured the airmen who were finished off by bayonets and rifle butts. (hearsay)*

r. *A poster is displayed, in German barracks in the north of France, which shows an allied airman with his "hands up." An automatic is stuck under his right armpit and in his right palm he holds a microflex with which to pull the trigger. The caption reads: "This is an allied airman who is apparently unarmed and surrendering. He is armed, and he will kill you, kill him before he kills you." (hearsay–October)*

s. *Nine airmen captured near a small town in northern France were shot by young troops while their officer stood with his back turned. Men are safe if they fall into the hands of older troops, but the young boys are maniacs. (hearsay)*

t. *The recent bombing of Toulon from Natousa was very accurate. Few Frenchmen were killed. (hearsay)*

u. *The bombing of Nantes created a great deal of bad feeling for Americans. The wrecking of Lorient, on the contrary, was cheered by the French although 300 of them were killed. (observation and hearsay)*

v. *There are observation towers on most of the high hills in northern France. During day light an armed look-out, with excellent field glasses, is posted in every tower. (hearsay)*

w. *Curfew in Auxi-le-Chateau is at 2300 hours. The first patrol is at 2315 hours. The patrol goes through the town on motorcycles every hour thereafter. (observation October 1943)*

x. *There are six batteries of 88 mm AA guns one block from the Porte-de-Versailles metro station. The guns are surrounded with brush in a vacant lot the size of a block. One turns left, leaving the station, and the guns are on the right-hand side of the street, probably between rue Delage and rue Hameau off the Boulevard Victor Lefebure. (observation 1 October)*

y. *There was a meeting of many high ranking German officers at the Army-Navy base at Poulmic near Laneveoc on or about 12 December. (hearsay)*

z. *The Germans have mined all the Brest docks. (hearsay)*

aa. *The flame throwers on the Brest Peninsula face inland. (hearsay)*

bb. *The Germans are posting Frenchmen to guard power lines and railroads. If there is sabotage, the Frenchman on guard is executed. (hearsay from guard)*

cc. *German officers and non-coms were observed entering apartment houses in Quimnper in uniform, and leaving in civilian clothing. French with Germans quartered in their home said it was quite common for the Germans to have civilian clothing on hand. (hearsay and observation)*

dd. *Several of the units stationed at Brest, Quimper, and Crozon have served on the Russian front. Four to five men in every squad wear a red ribbon two inches long and one inch wide on their tunic button. This represents service in Russia. (observation November–December)*

ee. *When German units left Vannes (in the winter of 1943) for service in Russia, many deserted or committed suicide. (hearsay)*

ff. *In September 1943, 400 Frenchmen were called up in Vannes for service in Germany. (observation and hearsay)*

gg. *The Germans have dug air raid trenches in the center of Auxi-le-Chateau next to the canal. The trenches are for Germans only, the French are not allowed in. (observation)*

hh. *A Lieutenant Colonel in the Gestapo told an informant that he knew of the whereabouts in Auxi-le-Chateau of six American airmen whom he could ar-*

rest. He knew, however, that the Americans were not engaged in espionage work, and therefore, he felt he could leave them unmolested; he knew that the war was lost and felt that he might just as well stay in the best graces of the allies that were possible. (hearsay)

ii. *The airfield at Pluguffan is said to be good. There are only a few transports and old training planes stationed there now. (hearsay)*

Hargrove's appendix B is lengthier than those of his fellow evaders. However, it contains information similar to those found in all of their accounts.

Each E&E report included a section on what the evaders had observed or heard that might be of intelligence value. A preprinted form labeled "Appendix B" directed: "List all military information which you observed or were told while evading. (Airfields, troop encampments, coastal and interior defenses, AA batteries, radar installations, troop movements, results of Allied bombing, locations of enemy factories and ammunition dumps, enemy and civilian morale, etc., etc.)."

Other than aerial photo reconnaissance, evaders were the primary source of information on enemy locations and activities. Upon their return, their observations were immediately analyzed and included in future bomb mission planning. Their direct observations were also an important source of evaluating the morale of the enemy and of the civilians whose lands they occupied.

Length and details included in appendix B reports depended upon the evader's time evading, the area of evasion, and the observation skills of the individual. Some of the reports are only a few paragraphs in length while others list thirty or more observations. Explanations of whether or not information was from direct observation or hearsay was also included. Most reports were as written by the evader while some were taken down by a recorder.

The amount and importance of evader intelligence information did not diminish until after D-Day on June 6, 1944. After that time, many reports in the appendix B section merely stated that the evader's experiences occurred in areas that had already been retaken by the Allies.

Location of airfields and troop concentrations often led appendix B reports. Some of these were brief while others went into great detail with accompanying diagrams and maps. Sergeant Raymond F. Chevraux, a B-17 waist gunner from Louisville, Ohio, went down in France on January 5, 1944. In his appendix B Chevraux reported, "An airfield between Muret and Toulouse was observed January 23, 1944. There were five large hangers. Bombers were taking off, landing, and flying above the field. From observation would state 80 aircraft here, later, from hearsay, 100. The runways appeared to be made of concrete. The field was in good condition." He attached a map.

B-17 waist gunner Staff Sergeant Leonard J. Kelly from Everett, Washington, landed in France on September 23, 1943, after being shot down by German fighters. He reported in his E&E, "Evader learned that there was a large concentration of heavy caliber anti-aircraft batteries in Rennes, particularly at the railroad station."

Another B-17 waist gunner, Staff Sergeant Jacob J. Dalinsky from Hazleton, Pennsylvania, went down in Belgium on August 17, 1943. Attached to his appendix B a staffer noted, "In traveling from Brussels to Ghent by train evader passed a dummy airfield about eight miles outside Ghent. There was some netting camouflage on the field but no aircraft, either dummy or real."

Staff Sergeant Charles K. Bailey, a B-17 waist gunner from Wynnewood, Oklahoma, was shot down after bombing Regensburg on August 17, 1943. He included one of his observations, writing, "In every railroad station in Belgium and France a great number of flak guns were observed on flak cars. Sometimes there would be one gun with a little ammunition, sometimes two smaller guns and even four small guns on one car."

As one of only five crewmen to bail out of their B-17 before it exploded in midair after being attacked by fighters on June 26, 1943, radio operator Staff Sergeant Lester Brown Jr. from Austin, Texas, made his way to Paris. He included his observation, writing, "One end of the building housing Napoleon's tomb was being used as an ammunition dump and was heavily guarded by armed guards."

P-38 pilot First Lieutenant Harry E. Bisher from Arlington, California, crash-landed in Belgium on March 4, 1944. He reported, "[W]as told that deep under the post office at Courtrai the Germans have one of their largest telephone exchanges in occupied territory."

E&E reports also included recommendations for methods of attacking enemy targets. B-17 navigator Second Lieutenant Homer Contopidis from the Bronx, New York, landed in France on May 17, 1943. He wrote in his appendix B, "French suggested that bombing runs on Brest submarine pens be made paralleling the coast because the targets of opportunity on either side of the pens. Also the city would be missed while bombing from this approach."

Many of the evaders heard rumors from their helpers about new fighting techniques as well as secret weapons, including various rockets, jet propelled airplanes, and gas warfare. B-17 copilot Flight Officer Billy James Hooker from Collinsville, Texas, went down on July 30, 1943. An interrogator added information to Hooker's appendix, writing,

> Evader heard that there was a small airfield on the Helpe River at which was based one German pursuit ship. The German flyer of this aircraft was supposed to have perfected a technique in which he patrolled the Helpe River area at night and got above raiding aircraft so that he could silhouette them against the river before attacking. The Belgians stated they had heard a great deal about this pilot and that he was credited with shooting down over twenty RAF bombers. The Germans claim that he shot down over 200 aircraft."

Technical Sergeant Gaetano A. Friuli, a B-17 top turret gunner from Catskill, New York, landed in France on January 21, 1944. According to Friuli's appendix B notes added by a staff member,

> Informant was told in February that the Germans are trying to invent some mechanism to stop aircraft motors. He was told that there is a large square building in the woods somewhere to the north of Auxi-le-Chateau in which the Germans have installed some sort of light or magnetic device. This thing had been tried

on two Marauders, so informant's source declared, and they had crashed, source claiming to have seen the crash.

Paratrooper Technical Sergeant John D. Kersh from Autaugaville, Alabama, was captured shortly after jumping into France on D-Day. He escaped six days later and made his way to Allied lines on June 17, 1944. In his appendix B, Kersh provided the following details: "German SS troops of the Totenkopf Division moved into the Muneville-le-Bingard area on way to front." His interviewer added details, writing,

Informant had opportunity to observe various officers and men. Equipment was in good state. Sixty tanks were with this unit. French who talked with attached medical personnel reported that all complained of food. They drank a good deal, and told the French that flying bombs would soon be used on a large scale in Normandy, as they had been so successful in England, and had killed a million persons in London alone. One man maintained Germany could not win the war without secret weapons but still hoped to destroy US army after it got to France. Said Hitler still had three million "hidden reserves" in Germany and occupied Europe, and was saving his best troops for a final battle.

One evader brought back information on what was likely a German prototype for a jet fighter. P-38 pilot Second Lieutenant Leroy V. Hukinson from East Moline, Illinois, was shot down by a ME-109 over Holland on January 31, 1944. He delivered details of the information he had gleaned, writing in his appendix B, "On February 15, 1944 I saw plans for a twin engine rocket plane, as large as a B-26, in hands of a Dutch draftsman who had escaped from a plant near Berlin. Single fin, streamlined, rounded tapered wings, engines far behind, not much in front. Pilot's place in front. Reported one plane in production."

Gathering information about the status of development of German rockets that could reach England was also an important part of evader debriefings. Technical Sergeant Trafford L. Curry from Hollis,

Oklahoma, was the top turret gunner aboard a B-17 before he bailed out after a collision with another Fortress near Paris on September 3, 1943. His appendix B included potential intelligence: "Informant was told that a concrete emplacement near St. Omer, in the bombing of which he had participated, was a place where the Germans were experimenting with a rocket 'torpedo.' He was told that five or six hundred Germans had been killed in the bombing of this site, and that the position had been completely destroyed."

Evaders heard many rumors that the Germans had plans to use poisonous gas. One rumor reaching England came from B-17 bombardier Second Lieutenant Thomas B. Applewhite from Memphis, Tennessee, who bailed out over Holland on November 11, 1943. The only member of his crew to successfully evade, Applewhite observed that most of the Belgians seemed to think the Germans would use gas as their secret weapon. The word was that English gas masks would do no good against the deadly gas called "nickel carbonyl" made from nickel ore the Germans had procured from the Dutch East Indies in prewar imports.

Information on the morale of the occupying Germans and the local civilians was highly sought from returning evaders. Included in Curry's report quoted above was a note from his interviewer who added, "Informant noticed that the occupation troops which he saw in France were very inferior. Some seemed no more than 15 years old. He saw some cripples, some hunchbacks, and many with thick lensed glasses."

Second Lieutenant Carl W. Smith from Mineral County, West Virginia, was the copilot of a B-17 that went down in Belgium on August 17, 1943. A staffer added to the intelligence he provided, writing in Smith's appendix B,

Belgian helpers told informant that morale of many German soldiers seemed very low. A German soldier by himself would admit that the Germans have lost the war, that he is tired of it all, and wants to go home. A few Germans were supposed to have deserted. It was rumored that pilots over 30 refused to bomb England and that only young pilots would make the missions.

About the only people giving the Hitler salute in Belgium were the black-shirted Belgian traitors. German soldiers give a sloppy version of our own salute.

B-17 top turret gunner Technical Sergeant Bertil E. Erickson from Grassbelt, Pennsylvania, went down in France on August 27, 1943. "In October was told by a Frenchman that in the vicinity of Douai and Valenciennes there is a water supply for mines and factories in the area which, if destroyed would shut down all the factories and mines. Was told that a single German will admit that Germany has lost the war." About the locals Erickson said, "[M]orale is good, but the French are impatiently awaiting the invasion of the continent."

After enemy fighters killed his pilot and copilot, B-17 waist gunner Technical Sergeant Erwin D. Wissenback from Klamath Falls, Oregon, parachuted into France on October 9, 1943. For his contribution to his appendix B, Wissenback wrote, "In N. France Germans shabby and not as good as in S. France. Italians in S. France very poor. I heard Italians were ready to fight with us."

The French were eager for an Allied invasion that would liberate them. As evaders revealed, these Frenchmen had harsh plans for collaborators as well as the Germans themselves. Second Lieutenant Lawrence E. Grauerholz, a B-17 navigator from Kensington, Kansas, evaded capture in France after going down on January 5, 1944. In his appendix B he wrote, "The first question the French asked was when the invasion was coming. We told them either that we didn't know or that probably in the spring. They gave us the impression that many a jerry will die at the hands of the French on the day."

German fighters shot down B-17 navigator Second Lieutenant Jennings B. Beck from Sharon, Pennsylvania, over Belgium on January 29, 1944. He wrote his observations, reporting,

Gestapo creating bulk of trouble in Belgium; German soldiers rather decent to inhabitants. In France both the Gestapo and army are actively engaged in annoying the populace. Also in France there is great hatred against all those who have collaborated with the Germans; almost every man has a list of those he is going to liquidate when the invasion starts. Great admiration for Russia throughout France, and some disgust with the Anglo-American procrastination. There is no political unity in France. The majority of the population is engaged in some sort of anti-German activity.

B-24 pilot Second Lieutenant Murray L. Simon from New York City began his evasion on May 6, 1944. A staff member of the debriefing team included in Simon's appendix B the soldier's oral assessments, writing, "All Frenchmen in this area who worked for the Germans had been sent a card on which a noose was printed. This card came from the resistance people. In St. Etienne evader overheard two German soldiers discussing the raids on Germany. They were depressed about it and expected to find only ruins when they returned."

Second Lieutenant Conrad M. Blalock from Winston Salem, North Carolina, was the navigator of a B-17 that went down in France on February 6, 1944. Based on his observations he wrote, "French civilians in Paris have been storing quantities of food (potatoes, flour, tinned goods) to tide them over the initial stage of the invasion." He noted that at the same time Parisians were hoarding food, they were angry about black market prices, believing farmers were getting wealthy. Blalock added his own assessment, writing, "Peasants in the country have more and better food than the wealthy people in Paris."

Evaders also brought back information on German propaganda. On January 23, 1943, a combination of flak and Nazi fighters brought down the B-17 on which Staff Sergeant Frank W. Greene from Maywood, Illinois, served as the ball turret gunner. In July he observed in his appendix B, "The newest propaganda poster in Paris, especially in the Metro, seems to be directed at the Americans alone. The new poster shows a young girl with a dead child hanging limp in her arms. A cross figures prominently behind her and in the background are ruined and burned buildings. In the upper right corner looking down on the scene with a very smug and approving look is President Roosevelt. This replaces the poster showing Roosevelt and Churchill tearing Africa to pieces."

Second Lieutenant John A. McGlynn from Cazenovia, Wisconsin, was flying a P-38 on a photo reconnaissance mission to Paris when he was shot down by flak on February 14, 1944. He reported, "The principal theme in German propaganda today is communism. It is having a definite effect on timid or conservative Frenchmen. Many Frenchmen feel that an army of occupation should be left in France for a period after the war to prevent bloody revolution."

Shot down on a mission to Frankfurt on February 8, 1944, Sergeant Francis F. Higgins, a B-17 tail gunner from Bangor, Maine, made his way to Paris. His appendix B reports a unique evaluation: "Went to movies a number of times in Paris and noted that the news reels concentrated on Anglo-American bombing of French civilians. Audiences in Paris cinema stamp on floor or make catcalls when President Petain appears on the screen."

Second Lieutenant Robert O. Lorenzi, a B-17 pilot from Spokane, Washington, was quickly aided by helpers after being shot down on February 8, 1944. He summarized his view by writing, "From time of parachuting in France, nothing of military importance was observed by myself. All traveling was done in a closed panel truck and nothing was observed while in route from place to place. Morale of the French people was very high with blood hatred for the Germans and hope for their annihilation."

MIS-X was always interested in learning the fate of airmen who did not evade or were captured. Staffers queried returned evaders for any and all information they had about what happened to fellow crewmen. They recorded reports of deaths as well as some locations of burial. B-17 radio operator Staff Sergeant Robert H. Johnson from Selma, Alabama, was shot down by flak over France on June 22, 1944. He was the only survivor of his plane that exploded in midair. He reported on his appendix B, "I saw the graves of all these men and have their identification tags."

Some of the evader E&E appendix B reports contained a bit of irony or humor. Second Lieutenant Roy E. Waller, a B-24 bombardier from Washington, DC, went down in France on June 25, 1944. He offered insight into local thinking when he wrote, "The average French peasant thinks that everyone in the plane is a pilot therefore their report on our 'pilot' being captured may pertain to any member of the crew."

Second Lieutenant John J. Maiorca, the bombardier from Manchester, Connecticut, sited earlier, made his way to Paris upon parachuting into France on November 5, 1943. In his E&E report a staffer added a note from his interview, "Informant visited the Louvre in middle November and wondered where all the statues were for which there were marble pedestals. His guide indicated that the Germans had rifled the works of art."

At least one evader provided intelligence on hidden art. B-17 pilot Second Lieutenant Myrle J. Stinnett from Benld, Illinois, was shot down in Holland on April 8, 1944. In his appendix B entry he wrote,

> We were taken by a Dutch Underground man to an old barn where we hid for eight days. Then we were taken by train to Maastricht where we remained for ten days. On May 4 we were guided across the Holland-Belgium border by an Underground worker. He took us through an old mine which has an entrance in Maastricht and which extends almost all the way to Liege, Belgium. We were told that the mine was 18 kilometers long. All the Dutch art treasures were stored in the mine, along with enough food to feed 70,000 people. A huge store of weapons and ammunition was kept in the mine. I noticed that huge ovens had been installed in the mine to feed persons who were hiding from the Germans. Some paintings on the walls were marked with the year 1497. We were told this was an old cement mine. There were thousands of passages in the place, and one could not pass through it without a guide for fear of becoming lost.

Nazi fighters brought down the B-17 piloted by Second Lieutenant Earl B. Duarte from Livermore, California, on December 31, 1943, in France. He reported, "Hearsay that most of the Allied leaflets dropped over Toulouse in early February (1944) were collected by the Germans. Very few copies were circulated. This was because the pamphlets were dropped in bundles and not scattered. This is the pamphlet that showed a picture of Frankfurt with an overlay showing coverage by 600 B-17s."

Belleville, Illinois, native Staff Sergeant Lloyd G. Wilson, tail gunner aboard a B-17, went down in France on October 14, 1943. Attached to his appendix B was information added by a staff member reading, "The day after the informant's plane crashed the Germans had removed the tires from the wreckage. Within three days they had removed the whole wreck."

Information in other appendix Bs do not particularly fit into any single category.

Staff Sergeant William C. Howell, a B-17 tail gunner from Goldsboro, North Carolina, was shot down over France on July 4, 1943. His interviewer added to his appendix B, "Informant was told that gasoline for the Germans is carried out of Spain in tanks underneath truckloads of oranges. In Paris in September informant saw movies showing multi-barreled rocket gun in use on the Russian front. The movies also showed an American plane toggling out its bombs, apparently on non-military targets, while it fell out of formation."

Hit by debris from another damaged Fortress, pilot Second Lieutenant Charles B. Winkelman from Plains, Illinois, crashed in France on September 8, 1943. He reported that copper telephone lines in Paris and other large cities were being dug up and replaced with alloys. Also, coastal defense concrete bunkers were poorly constructed with cement mixed incorrectly and were eroding or were without proper foundations.

Second Lieutenant Glen S. Call from San Francisco, California, was copilot of a B-17 that crashed in France on May 27, 1944. The intel he reported in his debriefing forms included, "The Germans leave white Ukrainian Russian Cossacks (forced into German army) in certain sections to restrict movement of parachutists and Maquis. They will surrender to Americans in order to enjoy status POW, but will fight Maquis."

Flak and enemy fighters shot down B-17 bombardier Second Lieutenant John C. Vollmuth from Richmond Hill, New York, in France on February 25, 1944. He reported, "In Toulouse a large number of Japanese soldiers were seen entertaining. They wore a field-gray uniform much like that of the regular German army, but the officer wore red piping."

Evaders also provided confirmation of the reports of the Nazi persecution of Jews across Europe. Staff Sergeant George W. Jones from Tipp City, Ohio, the top turret gunner on an A-20, heard broadcasts from Germany while hiding with his helpers after landing in France on May 27, 1944. He reported an example of the propaganda he heard, "Do you realize that all your sacrifices are made for Jewish power and profits directed from Washington and Moscow?"

Direct reports of the extermination of the Jews came from two additional evaders. Second Lieutenant William R. Hartigan, B-17 pilot from Unionville, Connecticut, went down in Belgium on October 20, 1943. He reported on what he had heard, writing, "According to an escaped French prisoner, a million Jews have died in a gas chamber, over a six-month period, at Rawa-ruska, a small town on the Russo-Polish frontier. Seven thousand Russian prisoners, who could not be fed, were also put to death here. The Red Cross at Geneva was to investigate but the Germans quashed the investigation. The Belgians believe this story and want another investigation."

Second Lieutenant Clayton C. David from Topeka, Kansas, parachuted from his B-17 over Holland on January 11, 1944. His appendix B report included, "Hearsay that the Jews in Poland were often used for experiments. They were in houses on which explosives were to be used, burned alive in locked houses, and killed by gas. Many were machine gunned."

CHAPTER 9

Appendix D: Escape Aids Kits and Purses

HEADQUARTERS
EUROPEAN THEATER OF OPERATIONS
P/W and X Detachment
Military Intelligence Service

E&E Report No. 326
Evasion in France
                                    24 January 1944

Name:	William L. Utley
Rank:	TSGT
Unit:	368th Bomb Squadron, 306th Bomb Group (B-17)
Home address:	Gary, Indiana
Target:	Stuttgart
MIA:	September 6, 1943
Arrived in UK:	January 17, 1944

Other members of the crew:

Pilot	2LT	Wesley D. Peterson	MIA
Co-Pilot	2LT	Edward L. Maslanka	E&E #222
Navigator	2LT	Donald E. Phillips	MIA
Bombardier	1LT	August Winters	E&E #179
Radio Operator	TSGT	William L. Utley	Narrator
Top Turret Gunner	TSGT	William B. Plasket, Jr	MIA

Ball Turret Gunner	SGT	Frederick E. Huntsinger	MIA
Waist Gunner	SSGT	George S. Monser	E&E #169
Waist Gunner	SGT	William E. Scott, Jr	E&E #173
Tail Gunner	SSGT	Douglas G. Wright	E&E #262

We were on the way back from target when the pilot called me on the inter-phone and told me to start transferring gas. We held formation as long as we could, then we pealed off, and the pilot gave the bail-out order. I opened the bomb-bay with the emergency release, and stood there a second. I stepped off at 17,000 feet.

Before leaving the plane, I had decided to make a delayed jump. I wanted to get to the ground as quickly as possible, and not let a crowd watch me float down. I tumbled for a while and then went into a spin; I could not get out of it. I had been told that one could control a spin by pulling ones knees onto ones chest and grasping them in ones arms. I did not want to let go of the ripcord and only used one arm, this may have been why I kept spinning. I started to have difficulty breathing, and pulled the ripcord at 10,000 feet.

The chute opened immediately, but the spinning had twisted the shrouds. I had to unwind myself before the chute would open fully. Now, when I looked up, I could see eight chutes far above me. I decided that the missing one must belong to Lt Peterson, as he was still at the controls when I jumped, and I could not see the plane. I had my aids box in my pants pocket and this caused the harness straps to bruise me badly in the crotch. Over two months later this hampered me when I was crossing the Pyrenees, for I could not lift my legs to stride along properly.

I reached a cloud, but just missed the corner. I seemed to be drifting into a small town, so I worked the shrouds in an effort to avoid doing this.

I landed on a high piece of ground a half mile from the village. Six or eight people arrived immediately, and I knew that they had been watching me. I asked, in English, if there were Germans in the neighborhood. I thought that "German" was the same in every language, but soon realized my mistake, when no one knew what I was talking about. They did, however, understand that I wanted to hide and they left me free to do so. The sides of the hill, on which I had landed, were heavily covered with brush; I started down one side. As I started to walk through the brush, I realized for the first time that, while jumping, I had lost my left flying boot, heated boot, shoe and stocking. I had not been wearing the shoe, my shoes were tied around my left hand, and the laces of one shoe, the left, broke.

When I reached the bottom of the hill, I started to look for a place to bury my chute, I still had my chute, harness, and Mae West with me. I was half way through hiding them, after searching for a good place for what seemed to be 15

minutes, when I heard someone coming. I hurried off to a spot I had seen while trying to hide my equipment. I thought this a particularly good location, because trees
growing low over the brush here, blended well with my green flying suit. I walked
into this cover backwards, trying to pull the tall grass back again over my trail.

When I was safely settled, I started to watch the searching party. There were
no Germans in it, and I recognized one of the Frenchmen. I called him over to
me. About five people trooped over. I told them I wanted civilian clothes and they
went off the get some. While they were gone, I finished hiding my chute, then I
settled down again and opened my aids box. The first thing I did was to get out
the language card, so that it would be handy. Then I separated my money from the
other objects as I did not know how far I could trust these people.

In an hour my friends returned. The shoes they brought were a little too small,
but they had to do. I put on a baggy pair of trousers, and a grey coat that had gone
white with age. I looked like a real tramp. Then I moved to a tree covered swamp
that was thick with brush. Food was brought to me here, and I learned that one of
my helpers was himself anxious to leave the country. He said he would take me to
Paris, and maybe the whole way to Spain. Then I was left alone.

Toward the end of the day they came back and asked me to work in the fields
with them because I would be so obvious there that I would be sure to be safe. We
went through a turnip field, and my companions poked about, looking, I later
learned, for .50 caliber ammunition. One of the boys had been almost hit on the
head by a 100 rounds, which had fallen from a plane that day. They drew me,
in explanation, a picture of a cartridge, I then thought we were looking for bugs.
We went on to another field and worked for two hours handling brush. I believe
it must have been soy beans. Then we worked for another three hours, loading the
bundles onto the wagon. We stopped once to watch a formation of P-47s.

After supper I was given a bed in an empty house, I spent the night here. The
next morning, clean, pressed clothes were brought to me. They also brought me a
better pair of shoes, but these were even smaller than those I had, and could not
be worn. After breakfast we walked to the bus line. The bus was jammed, but we
crowded in and rode to the nearest city.

We went to the railroad station, and my friend bought us third class tickets.
There were lots of Germans about, but they paid no attention to me. The people
in the carriage talked all the time, and a German stood in the doorway chatting
endlessly with a woman. I passed unnoticed.

In Paris, we got on the metro and went to an apartment in which I was hidden during my stay in the city. I was never free to see the sights, and the whole
stay passed off without anything interesting having happened. My friend decided

to take me on beyond Paris, and we went to the railroad station on the morning of 11 September.

We again traveled third class; I still had no identity papers. I was traveling as deaf and dumb. The story seemed to be well accepted, for my traveling companion explained that this happened as a result of shell-shock during the recent Paris raids. When we reached our destination in central France, we went to a café for something to drink. My friend left me there while he went to check bus schedules. I tried to be nonchalant and look like one of those Frenchmen who is always sitting in a café with a drink.

Taking another bus, we got off near a river. There was a bridge over the river, and guards on the bridge. My friend took both suitcases, and walked across the bridge on one side, while I crossed on the other about 10 feet behind him. Neither of us was stopped by the guards, although this is where we crossed the Line of Demarcation. At the moment I was angry with my companion, because he took both the suitcases, leaving me, so I felt at the time, to look very obvious. I later learned that carrying packages and baggage, in France attracts the Germans' attention. They will stop a man to investigate black market activities, whom they did not suspect of being an evader.

We went to a home in which I stayed for a month. During the entire month, I never left the vicinity of the house. When I arrived I was told that I would be leaving in from ten days to two weeks. As I now knew that the French always underestimate time, I guessed I would be there almost a month. My Intelligence Officer had also told me to obey my helpers, so the only get-away plans I made were for use if the Germans found me.

At the end of the month, my friend wanted to complete the journey south by train. This would not have taken much time, but I reminded him that I was still without papers. I thought it would be too dangerous for me to risk a control on a train in the coastal area. I knew from my I.O.'s talks that this area is more heavily guarded. We took a long taxi ride to the nearest big town south of us. We had tried for two days, but we could not get places in the bus. This ride made quite a dent in our funds. It should have cost 400 francs, but the driver, who knew something was wrong, charged 1,000 francs. We were in no position to complain.

Two Germans stopped and commented as we left the taxi, and I thought it was all over, but they went on again without questioning us. Something had gone wrong with the train schedule, and we found that we had six hours to wait. I suggested going to the movies, but there were too many Germans around the ticket window. We spent time walking around the town. By now I knew some French and my friend had learned some English. We were thoroughly familiar with one another's gestures and with the aid of a dictionary could talk about anything, except, of course in public.

We caught the train and rode all night and next morning. This time there was a goose over my head. It would honk at odd intervals all through the night; everyone else would jump and look up, as I was supposed to be deaf and dumb, I was in a bad position. No jumping, when there was sudden honk, was one of the hardest things I had to do during the whole evasion.

While traveling on the trains I noticed that many of the French cannot understand the Germans, even when they speak French. The Germans therefore are not surprised when people do not understand, and turn away. This would not work of course, with Vichy police or soldiers. They wear a green uniform and do not, however, seem to bother people much. French people are as conversational as Americans on trains, and an evader should have a good reason for not talking; boarding a train and going to sleep for twelve hours is suspicious in itself.

We walked 7 ½ kilometers after we got off the train, and went to place from which the final stages of my journey was ultimately arranged. I was, however, here thirty-seven days before negotiations were completed. During this time I was kept in one room. I had nothing to do except read seven Penguin books. Once a week I was allowed to come down stairs and listen to the radio, but all they would ever tune in were French programs.

When I finally started across the Pyrenees, I was startled to learn that we were going at night. I had never considered it as anything but a daytime journey. We were soaked to the skin, and it was mud and water all the way. We spent the last hour that night in the snow, and when we reached the barn, at which we stopped, I thought I was going to pass out. There were some stairs, but I couldn't get up them alone. We buried ourselves in the hay and fell asleep. We stayed here two days and a night. Our food was bread, wine, and fat. I now started to use my aids box, and was very glad that I had kept it. Just eating, when I was dead tired, kept me going for the rest of the journey. I thought it gave me energy, but it may have only diverted my mind. Whatever the process, it worked.

The guides had not been over the trail in seven years. We only walked three hours, but were lost throughout one of these hours. We stopped and rested another two days and a night in a smoke filled barn, where we ate out of pails. When we left here we could hear the barking of the dogs in the German patrol. We had to make a detour at a quick trot. This detour forced us to cross a small village. The guide checked it first, and then we went through "silently" running in cleated boots.

During this night we also had to pass a patrol station. Our hearts were in our mouths, this time one could really have heard a pin drop. The snow started to fall, *and as it grew colder, there seemed to be rivers to wade across. We started up one mountain, and kept on going up for six hours. By the time we reached the top, the snow was up to our knees. We slid down the far side, and were at the bottom in fifteen minutes.*

We kept on walking and walking. Sixteen hours later we reached the Spanish frontier. I was arrested a day later, and spent the next month in jail.

Appendix D to E&E Report No. 326

1. *AIDS BOX*

    a. *Did you use your aids box? Yes—but the kit was pretty beat up and old. I was going to dispose of it, as I had no place to carry it, but my French helper realized this would be a mistake, so the box was kept for the Pyrenees.*

    b. *Which of the following items did you use?*

        Horlicks tablets. Inside wrapper had to be eaten too, but we sucked them and it help keep my mouth moist. In the mountains one can never get enough to drink.

        Chocolate. It was all broken up but I ate it just the same. Chocolate helped but sugar helped more. The paper around it was covered with English print.

        Milk (tube), Tasted good (like honey) on top of buttered bread. Thought it might be milk.

        Benzedrine tablets (fatigue). Used them in the mountains, but they were no good. I had been given a bag of sugar and this gave me more pick-up than anything when I was completely exhausted.

        Matches. For cigarettes—when matches were finished I kept box to carry French matches.

        Adhesive tape. For cuts and blisters—tape was no good, wouldn't stick.

        Chewing gum. None in box.

        Water bottle. No good—loops broke. Used bag for waterproof cover for bottle in my pocket.

        Compass. Phosphorescent compass came through laundry okay

    c. *Did any of the items prove unsatisfactory? Water bottle—rubber was rotten so could not draw string.*

    d. *How did you dispose of the box? Broke it up last place before crossing mountains and transferred contents to rubber bottle.*

2. *PURSE*

    a. *Did you carry a purse? Yes*

State color: Red. Mark II, Purse came in handy for papers, as I turned it inside out, and used it that way. Later gave it to a Dutchman in Spain as a tobacco pouch.

b.   *Did you use the purse? Yes*

c.   *Which of the following items did you use?*
Maps. Which ones? Lower France
Compass: Used it in the mountains.
Foreign Currency: 2,000 French Francs
How did you spend the money? 1,000 Francs for get-away taxi and train-fares

d.   *How did you dispose of—*
Maps. Gave upper France to a helper—lost lower France in mountains
Compass.
File (hacksaw)
Surplus currency. Gave to helper

3. <u>AIDS TO ESCAPE – (GADGETS*)</u>
*(Issued separately from aids boxes and purses)   Not Issued

4. <u>PASSPORT SIZE PHOTOGRAPHS</u>

a.   *Did you carry passport-size photographs? Dressed in a hurry before raid, put on clean khakis leaving pictures in old set. Believe this delayed me for two weeks in France. French took some (with difficulty) for French papers.*

5. <u>LECTURES</u>

a.   *Were you lectured on evasion and escape? Yes*
State WHERE, WHEN and by WHOM.
306 Bomb Group, April to September

b.   *Did you find the lectures of value? Yes, I knew just what to do when I hit the ground*

6. <u>GI SHOES</u>
I carried cadet shoes with laces tied around my hand, laces snapped in jump, lost one shoe. From the time I landed I wished for GI shoes, for the French shoes were all too small, and the soles of the English army boots I was given wore out, although the tops looked like new. The ideal set up would be GI shoes and oxfords. GI's for walking and mountains. Oxfords for trains and towns, where police check airmen by their feet and look at shoes when any doubt on identity papers.

Appendix D of Technical Sergeant Utley's report provides a fair representation of similar information found in those of other evaders. Once safely on the ground USAAF airmen had several tools to aid their escape from the Germans and to help gain assistance from civilians. These items changed over the months in accordance with the recommendations of successful evaders.

Escape kits contained sufficient food to sustain an evader for a day or two. Included were malted milk Horlicks tablets, condensed milk, chocolate, chewing gum, and a water bottle with halazone purification tablets. Benzedrine pills for fatigue, matches to light fires, and adhesive tape for wounds and blisters were included. Some aid packets contained fishing hooks and others had a razor and soap, and a file or saw.

Policies on the carrying of individual weapons aboard aircraft varied from squadron to squadron. Those who did arm themselves carried M1911A1 .45 caliber semiautomatic pistols, though a few carried Smith & Wesson .38 caliber revolvers. Most crews did not carry side arms for two reasons: First, their harnesses already had too much attached, making it difficult to move around in or to exit the aircraft. Second, and most important, they realized that a single airman with a pistol was not going to do very well against the entire German army. Some of those who did carry pistols threw them away with their parachute upon landing or handed them over to their civilian helpers as a reward for their assistance.

One of the few to actually use his pistol was Flight Officer Earl W. Green, a P-47 pilot from Klamath Falls, Oregon. His flight leader reported that on June 6, 1944, Green attacked a German road convoy and "released his bombs at too low an altitude for safety. His ship was apparently seriously damaged by the blast . . . he was last heard on the radio saying, 'I ran too low. Hit my own blast.' I heard this and then observed him parachute from the smoking plane."

Safely on the ground, Green discarded his holster and carried his .45 caliber pistol inside his flight jacket. Soon, he heard shots fired nearby. He next "met three enemy soldiers, shot all three by walking up to them first with one hand in the air."

Completion of the two-page appendix D form varied with individual evaders. Some, like Technical Sergeant Utley, answered each question in detail. Many skipped a portion of the questions while still others included a paragraph or two on escape aids and purses without using the form.

The adhesive tape in the escape kit received the most specific mentions for its help in treating blisters. Airmen, unlike infantrymen, were not accustomed to walking. Except for moving from their barracks to mess hall, briefing room, and their aircraft, they were mostly a sedentary lot. The word "blister" is so pervasive in the reports that it eventually lent its name to all evaders as the Blister Club.

Although not specifically requested in the two-page appendix D, the opinions of the returned evaders often appeared in reports, like that of Utley's, and included advice about GI shoes. In fact, shoes are the single most items mentioned it all the E&E reports. Aboard their aircraft, crew members wore insulated boots that were good for keeping their feet warm but fairly useless for hiking. The boots were also readily recognizable by the Germans as American issue. Some airmen cut the tops off the boots to make them blend in better. Even so, because the flying boots were not designed for walking, they were the source of many blisters for the evaders.

Airmen learned early in the war to take their brown lace-up shoes with them. Some tied them to their parachute harness while others reported jumping from a plane with one hand on their rip cord and the other grasping their GI shoes.

From their briefings, airmen knew the importance of footwear. When ordered to bail out of his B-17 on September 6, 1943, ball turret gunner Staff Sergeant William W. Rice from Liberty, Mississippi, made his way to the escape hatch only to go "back to the turret for my GI shoes."

If time permitted, crewmen changed from their flying boots into their GI shoes before bailing out or crash-landing. On December 31, 1943, German flak and fighters crippled Sergeant George Jasman's B-17 over France. The ball turret gunner from Brooklyn, New York, and his fellow crew members prepared to crash-land. In his appendix D Jasman wrote, "All equipment was dumped overboard. We got rid of our flying clothing, changed into GI shoes, and everyone except the navigator got into the radio room before we made a wheels-down landing."

Shoes, like aids kits, did not always make it to the ground with the airmen. Technical Sergeant Walter L. House, a B-17 radio operator from

Bowling Green, Kentucky, went down in France on September 6, 1943. He noted in his report, "I always kept GI shoes with me, intending to hook them to my parachute if I had to jump. But on the occasion I had no chance to grab the shoes. I think every evader should wear GI shoes, but it would be well to cut off the heel so that the maker's name does not show in the footprint."

Bombardier Second Lieutenant Lloyd A. Stanford's B-17 went down in France on October 10, 1943. Stanford, an Augusta, Georgia, native carried his shoes when he jumped but lost them on his way down.

Even though most of the appendix Ds included comments on how the aids package could be improved, the unanimous opinion was that they proved helpful in the evasion of those who got to the ground with them. Second Lieutenant Clayton C. David, copilot of a B-26, from Topeka, Kansas, was shot down over Holland on January 11, 1944. David explained his experience with the aids provided to him when he wrote,

> I used the Benzedrine in the mountains and it was very helpful. I wish I had had more so that I could have given it to others who had been forced to abandon theirs. The box was an American one, stamped all over with the manufacture's name, and was considered incriminating. I carried a red purse. I shared my money with another man in the party whose money had been confiscated. I carried three side view photographs and three full face. In Holland they used the side view, but my print had too glossy a finish. The Dutch made a reprint of my picture on a matt surface.

First Lieutenant Dale R. Sandvik, a P-47 pilot from Palmer, Alaska, declared his escape kit to be a great help after being shot down on March 18, 1945. Referring to his compass he said, "It saved me from capture."

On April 7, 1945, Staff Sergeant Carman Francis, a B-17 bombardier from Costa Mesa, California, was shot down west of Ludwigslust, Germany, and became one of the final airmen to evade before the end of the war. Over the first three days, he used his escape kit compass to walk west and met Allies nineteen miles east of Hannover. A comment by his interrogator in his E&E report stated,

The evasion of SSGT Francis demonstrated again that it is possible to evade capture in Germany if airman are bailing out are not captured immediately upon hitting the ground. Avoiding all people, civilians and soldiers, can be accomplished if the evader will take advantage of wooded areas and travel by night. It takes determined walking and the will to get back. SSGT Francis is enthusiastic about the usefulness of the escape kit. He believes he could not have reached allied lines without the compass and the rations.

Money from the purse helped Second Lieutenant Edward J. Carey, a B-17 navigator from Baltimore, Maryland, evade after going down in France on February 8, 1944. He used the cash to purchase clothing and shoes at a secondhand store near where he landed.

Food in the aids packet could sustain the evader for several days. First Lieutenant Meyles A. Sheppard, a B-17, navigator from Kalamazoo, Michigan, shot down on January 29, 1944, said that he lived for five days on contents of his escape kit before he "began to get hungry."

Food in the kit could also be used for other purposes. First Lieutenant William H. Banks, a P-38 pilot from Rochelle, New Jersey, used the aids box milk tube to treat his burns after being shot down in France on July 27, 1944.

Aids kits materials also played direct roles in escapes. Sergeant Herve A. Leroux, a B-17 ball turret gunner from Hebronville, Massachusetts, landed in France on January 5, 1944. His fluency in French aided his evasion as did the file in his escape kit that he used to cut a boat lock so he could cross a river.

Phrase cards proved invaluable as well. Staff Sergeant Lloyd G. Wilson, a B-17 tail gunner from Belleville, Illinois, had advice for fellow airman about his successful evasion from France after going down on October 14, 1943. In his E&E report he wrote,

From my journey I found that it would be a very good idea for aircrews really to study the phrase lists which they are given. You never think that it is you who is going to be shot down, but if you are, it is extremely useful to know the phrases on the phrase list. Furthermore, if a man is around France very long, it is an excellent idea for him to pick up all the French he can. He may find that it comes extremely handy when he is riding on trains, not so much so that he will be able to speak, but so that he can understand what questions the inspector is asking.

The E&E reports reveal that nearly all airmen were briefed on evasion techniques prior to their being shot down during training in the United States, at their units in England, or both. Major Walker M. Mahurin, a P-47 pilot from Fort Wayne, Indiana, was the USAAF's first "double ace" with ten kills and had a total of 19.75 victories when shot down on March 27, 1944. He wrote,

> I had been lectured at my unit on escape and evasion. I had heard from many evaders from fighter and bomber groups. These lectures were most worthwhile. Their emphasis that the first 24 hours are the hardest was most valuable. I thought that I would fall right into a bunch of Germans but I did not see any Germans until four days after I landed. Remember the average German soldier is dumb as hell and that all the Germans are not looking for you—as I was convinced they were for me.

MIS-X recognized the importance of evasion briefings. Eight of the ten-man crew aboard a B-17 with waist gunner Technical Sergeant William J. Miller from Pittsburgh, Pennsylvania, evaded after being shot down on September 16, 1943. His debriefer added a comment to his E&E report, stating, "It has become such a commonplace to get back six to eight men from one crew that it no longer excites comment. Whatever is responsible for this remarkable record, it would not be possible without the efficient work of our intelligence officers in briefing crews."

False identity documents played an important role in many evasions. Passport-size photos of airmen in civilian clothes were a part of each escape kit. Due to changes made by the occupying Germans, these photographs did not always meet minimum standards. Evaders often commented in their reports about the photos and made recommendations for their improvement.

First Lieutenant Harry E. Bisher, a P-38 pilot from Arlington, California, was shot down over Belgium on March 4, 1944. In his debrief Bisher wrote, "I carried seven passport size photographs and used them on identity papers. It was most helpful that I had been told to do exactly as my helpers instructed, for a number of things they directed I thought dangerous, but I did what they said and it turned out all right."

It took a while for the USAAF to correctly make the photographs. An earlier evader, Captain Elmer E. McTaggart, a P-47 pilot from Redmond, California, found his photos to be useless after being shot down in Belgium on May 14, 1943. He critiqued the efforts, writing, "Photographs were of the wrong size—background and color wrong."

More recommendations on photos came from Second Lieutenant Arthur J. Horning, B-17 navigator from Cleveland, Ohio, shot down in Holland on October 10, 1943. Horning had six photographs but said he could not use them because he had a moustache in them, and Dutch do not have facial hair in document photos. He also recommended rings and jewelry be removed and that a cap be placed over a military haircut.

Sergeant Carlyle A. Van Selus, a B-17 ball turret gunner from Huntington, West Virginia, shot down in France on February 8, 1944, also found fault with the photographs. He wrote, "Photos now being used are no good. They are a 'give away' to the Germans." Van Selus accompanied his remarks with diagrams and descriptions showing that the "full face" photos needed to show more torso.

When evader photographs were not available or acceptable, the airmen and their helpers had other sources of pictures. Second Lieutenant Grady W. Roper, a B-17 navigator from Albany, Georgia, parachuted into Belgium October 9, 1942. His plane had lost three engines and its tail before it disintegrated, killing six crewmen. Germans captured three of the survivors, leaving Roper as the only evader from his aircraft. He wrote of his efforts to get identity papers, explaining, "On December 20 an identity card was brought me. The picture used was the one taken at St. Amand (Belgium). Also, I was given a paper which stated I received a pension from a workers' union because of a disability."

German fighters shot down Staff Sergeant Richard A. Mayhew's B-24 in France on January 21, 1944. The tail gunner from Reno, Nevada, made his way with two other evaders to Paris. Mayhew told his story, writing, "We had pictures taken of all three of us in a small store booth, and waited next door until they were developed. My photograph was then put on the identity card and the names and signatures filled in."

The best, or perhaps the worst, excuse for not having usable photographs came from B-17 ball turret gunner Sergeant Walter R. Snyder from San Diego, California, who went down in Holland on January 11, 1944. He simply wrote, "I left my photographs at base because I was sure I would never be shot down."

The largest problem with the aids kits and purse lay not in their contents but in the actions of the airmen themselves. Second Lieutenant Eugene V. Mulholland, copilot of a B-17 from Hammond, Indiana, landed in France on September 3, 1943. He reported, "I used the North Star to get my bearings as I had lost my escape aids in the jump."

Losing escape aids while parachuting or leaving them behind on the plane were common occurrences. Fully one-quarter of the evaders admitted to not having the kits when they reached the ground. Captain Robert H. Copley, a B-17 pilot from Davenport, Iowa, landed in France on April 27, 1944. In his report he wrote, "I lost my aids box, purse, photos, and other items when parachuting because I had forgotten to fasten my coveralls knee pocket."

Both Second Lieutenant Clyde S. Manion, a B-17 bombardier from Minneapolis, Minnesota, downed in France on December 20, 1943, and First Lieutenant James P. Cater, a B-17 pilot from Maribeth, New York, downed on April 28, 1944, also reported they lost their aids packets and purses while parachuting from their planes.

CHAPTER 10

Pyrenees

SECRET—AMERICAN
MOST SECRET—BRITISH

HEADQUARTERS
EUROPEAN THEATER OF OPERATIONS
P/W and X Detachment
Military Intelligence Service

E&E Report No. 367
Evasion in France

February 14, 1944

Name:	*Richard Arthur Stakes*
Rank:	*2LT*
Unit:	*337th Bomb Squadron, 96th Bomb Group (B-17)*
Home address:	*Glen Head, New York*
Target:	*Bordeaux*
MIA:	*January 5, 1944*
Arrived in UK:	*January 30, 1944*

Other Members of the crew:

Pilot	*2LT*	*Richard Arthur Stakes*	*Narrator*
Co-Pilot	*2LT*	*William Mack Foley*	*In neutral country*
Navigator	*2LT*	*Lawrence Emil Graurerhole*	*In neutral country*
Bombardier	*2LT*	*J. B. Tennyson*	*MIA*
Radio Operator	*SGT*	*Elton Royce Aldridge*	*In neutral country*

Top Turret Gunner	SGT	Herbert Gilman Ruud	In neutral country
Ball Turret Gunner	SGT	Paul James Farmer	MIA
Waist Gunner	SGT	Charles Joseph Robinson	MIA
Waist Gunner	SGT	Humerto Rocha	In neutral country
Tail Gunner	PVT	Richard Monroe Cox	MIA

I was flying an old plane, the engines were good, but it had thirty-three missions behind it, and I had to use full manifold pressure and 2,300 RPM all the way to target in order to keep formation. This naturally weakened the engine. Over the target, flak knocked out number four engine. We dropped our bombs with the formation, but even with the loss of their weight, could no longer keep formation on three engines. Fighters attacked and hit number two engine, which caught fire and poured oil. I tried diving to the low squadron, but the fighters followed me; I could not keep up with this formation either. Then the nose gun jammed.

The wind was off land so I did not want to give a bail-out order. There was a wounded man (Sgt Robinson) on board, and therefore I did not wish to ditch in the sea. I saw a lake and headed for it, after ordering the crew into the radio room. I ditched in the lake and beached the aircraft in one operation. The only one hurt was the ball turret gunner, he was hit by the dinghy radio and somehow sprained his ankle. Everyone cleared the aircraft. The crew dispersed and set off as soon as we settled Sgt Robinson well away from the plane.

I took the dinghy out of the ship and stuck part of my chute into a gas tank to act as a fuse. I stood off about 100 feet and fired flares into the dinghy. I couldn't hit it, and had to get to within 10 free before I succeeded and it started to smolder. I moved off then, and soon heard the ammunition begin to explode (it continued to explode for over an hour). I moved across the marshy ground, and there seemed to be no place to hide. A German flying boat came over and I ducked into the reeds. There was an explosion from the plane and a great black cloud billowed into the air.

I caught up with my navigator, ball turret gunner, and top turret gunner and we started to push our way through the thickly overgrown swampland. We pushed and stamped, and fell on our faces in the ice cold water for a good two hours. Finally we reached dry ground. We walked up to some men cutting fir bows and they immediately warned us of German patrols. They left their work and led us well into the dense woods. Here we joined the radio operator and left waist gunner who had already been concealed there. Sgt Rocha is a Mexican and speaks fluent Spanish. One of the woodsmen had already gotten them food and clothing and the Sgt now made the same arrangement for us. The co-pilot, now in civilian clothes, joined us in a meal of bread, meat and wine. We were led deeper into the woods to a very secluded cabin. As we were wet and cold we built a fire. After dark the bombardier walked in, and we all spent the night together.

Before dawn the next morning, a friend pointed the way down the railroad track to the nearest city. We split up into twos and threes and started off. I set out with two other crew members. We followed the tracks a while and then started to skirt a town. My companions were so much more cautious than I, that I had to stop every 30 yards and wait for them to catch up. When this happened several times, I stopped no longer. From then on I was traveling by myself.

It was daylight when I finally got around the town. I cut back to the railroad tracks and walked until 1400 hours. I did not think it would be safe to approach anyone until I was well away from the area in which we had landed. Then I started to cut across the fields, and crossed two main highways. By now I was very hungry, and when I saw a farmhouse, I went up to the back door and knocked. A man came to the door and I said: "Bon soir Monsieur." Then pulling out my map, "Espagne." He gave me a map of the sector, and showed me which route to follow. He tried making conversation, but I was no good at this, so he offered me meat, wine, bread, and marmalade. I ate heartily, and was very thankful that I had sat in the cabin the night before studying the language card. I had learned my few words of French and how to count to ten while drying by the fire.

I started walking again. It grew dark, but I kept walking and passed through a small village. It was very cold. At a crossroads I saw a German sentry and realized that it was too late for a Frenchman to be out. I retraced my steps to the village and stopped at the first house. The people were Spaniards, and I could not make myself understood. They took me next door. The man in this house had learned some German, while serving as a conscripted laborer in Germany. I know a little German and we were able to understand one another. I was fed and put to bed.

On the 7th I started off again after having said: "Bon jour" and "merci, merci." I walked all day without stopping and reached a town at dusk. Here I again tried to find shelter, but the person I approached advised me to catch a train. I went to the railroad station. There were no Germans about.

I stood and watched a Frenchman buy a ticket. He just put down the money, gave the name of the town, and picked up his change and ticket. I put down 100 francs and gave the name of my town. The ticket agent could not understand me, I repeated, he said "ah" and gave me the ticket and some change but he wanted some more change from me, as cashiers often do, so as to make it come out evenly. This left me absolutely stumped, I just stood and stared in silence. Finally he fixed the change up by himself and wrote the train time on a piece of paper.

A train came in at that time and I got on. Fortunately it was going in my direction. There was only one woman in the compartment. I had my G.I. flashlight with me. I flashed it on my map and gave the name of the town I wanted. I was shabbily dressed and she was wrapped in furs, and I realized I was in a first class carriage. I had stayed in the station because I knew there were no Germans there, when the train pulled in I had gotten into the carriage opposite the door, without checking the class. The train came into a station; she told me the name of the station and started to push at me. I realized that I had to change trains here.

I walked to the station buffet and gave the name of the city I wanted. The woman at the counter gave me the time in French. I handed her a pencil and paper, then pointed to my watch saying "Train . . ." and the name of the town.

I remained in the buffet, and I was hungry. I pointed to some sandwiches and pulled out some francs. The woman said: "Non-ticket." There were too many people about for it to be safe to explain who I was. I saw a man getting some wine, so I got some. Then I sat there smoking my last cigarette. A German walked in. The French all stared at him, so I stared at him too. He walked up to the buffet counter and said "Bouillon" and it was given to him. I waited until he had left, and then I went up and got some. It did not help me much, however, for I was very cold, and the bouillon was cold too.

The proprietor started to close up and I realized that he wanted me to leave, but my train was not due until 0130 hours. I had another glass of wine which warmed me a bit, and then walked down the road and sat in the woods. I saw a light in a brick building and moved over there in search of warmth. I was practically inside the door when a German walked out. I realized that the building was a barracks. He stared at me. I turned around and left. He followed me a short distance and left. At 0030 hours I went back to the station masters room. There was a good fire here and no Germans. Whenever I was spoken to, I would say: "Non Monsieur" until I was finally left alone. At 0120 hours I heard a train stop and looking up said the name of my station. The answer was "Non." Another man, who was waiting for my train, took me to it when it came in. I traveled until 0800 hours on 8 January and was much too cold to get any sleep.

I took out my compass, and started walking south, noticing, as I did so, which way the rivers ran. The second river I came to, the largest in this area, ran north. I knew therefore that if I crossed to its southern side on the town bridge, I would not have to cross it again. I crossed over and followed the ox-cart road along the river to a town. Here a whole lot of little tributaries came into the river, so I retraced my steps to some peasant bridges. There was not enough detail on my map, so I took the first road south and followed it for the rest of the day, eating Horlicks tablets as I went.

At dusk I reached a small village and went into a bakery. The woman here said: "Ticket" to which I replied: "Americain." She then said: "Americain!" and I continued "Espagne." She went into a back room and, after a conference, I was taken in and fed bread and coffee.

As I left the shop, she handed me two loaves saying: "Espagne—Montagne." I followed an ox-cart trail across the fields, and a person from the bakery rode up on a bicycle to point the way and say 10 kilometers. I figured the 10 kilometers would take me two hours. At the end of two hours I saw a town and thought I had reached Spain. Seeing a bus, I went up to it and: "Madrid." The driver pointed to the ground and said: "France" and added "Espagne" after pointing south.

I went to a hotel in search of a room, but was unsuccessful. One of the men, at the hotel desk spoke English, and I asked for advice on where to stay, but he just said, "very dangerous."

I went to a café and took out my bread and bought some wine. There was a fire here, and I told them I was an American. This did not help at all. They were very scared and kept repeating "Allemand, Allemand." A man in the café had been drinking quite a bit, and he took me out to the field and pointing said: "Espagne."

It was so cold that I went back to the town and tried the house doors, until I found one that was open. I went inside and slept on the hall steps. Two hours later I woke up shivering and disgusted. I decided to walk. I followed a muddy ox-cart trail south, and was thankful that I was wearing G.I. boots.

I started over the mountains on a winding trail. I was heading south southeast, for I saw on my escape map that I could not go wrong if I did this. After two hours of walking, I rounded a corner and saw the lights of Spain shining in the moonlight. It was another three hours before I cleared the intervening hills and actually reached a town. I went to a store in search of food and heat. I told them I was an American, and met a New Yorker married to a Spaniard. I was given coffee, bread, and cake. Before I went to sleep we had a little party over a bottle of anisette. Someone wanted to take me to San Sebastien, and I wish I had let them, but the American told me to turn myself into the police, and I did.

The police confiscated everything I had, and the next day, 10 January, they photographed and fingerprinted me. I had a nasty scare when they took me back to the border patrol house, to register me properly. I thought I was being sent back to France. When that was over I joined several other American flyers in a hotel, and returned to UK on 30 January 1944.

Lieutenant Stakes had an easier journey over the Pyrenees than most of his fellow evaders. His story, however, contains many of the dangers and hardships experienced by his fellow airmen in their trek across the mountains.

Of all the natural difficulties encountered by the evaders seeking to escape to Spain, none surpassed the obstacles of the Pyrenees Mountains, the rugged chain across southwestern Europe that separates Spain from France. The nearly three hundred-mile range from the Bay of Biscay on the Atlantic Ocean coast on the west to the Mediterranean Sea on the east scales to a height of 11,169 feet in the central area, known as the Maladeta (Spanish for accursed)—where it reaches eighty miles in width. At its eastern end where the mountains narrow to only six miles wide, the lowest passages are at 6,500 feet. Evaders approaching these formidable peaks from France could see the Pyrenees from a great distance. As they drew closer, they faced what appeared to be shear walls descending abruptly with few or no foothills.

By the time an evader reached the mountains, he was likely exhausted from his long trek across Nazi-occupied Europe, his feet were blistered, and he was hungry. Those assisted by helpers from the Pat O'Leary and Comet Lines had their guides arranged for them. Evaders who arrived at the frontier with no assistance had to seek help on their own to cross the barrier.

P-47 pilot Flight Officer Robert E. Sheehan from Seattle, Washington, went down in Holland on November 7, 1943, when his plane experienced mechanical problems. When he finally reached the Pyrenees two months later, he had close encounters with German sentries. He related his experience, writing,

> We had a rough Pyrenees crossing. When we were just one hill from Spain, we heard a loud cry, "Halt! Halt!" The guides exclaimed "Allemands!" and started running. I was not inclined to be left behind, so I ran with them as fast as I could. The Germans opened fire. I ducked as best I could and saw the flashes of rifle fire. Within 30 yards of a creek at the bottom of the hill I lost my beret. When I was about to stoop to pick it up on the run, I

noticed a German police dog coming up behind me at top speed. I forgot all about the beret and gave myself the biggest push I could. The dog just by-passed me and ran on to the creek. While the dog was busy with his own personal affairs, I crossed the creek about five feet from him and started up the opposite hill as fast as I could run. Actually it was probably not much more than a crawl. The dog started after me and came up close behind. I gave him a resounding whack with my walking stick, and he did not even bark. He just turned and went back to the French side after one of the other fellows in our party. He backed him against the rocks. I could hear the Germans below me, shooting and whistling for their dog. The dog answered the Germans' whistles, and this fellow got away as soon as the dog moved. One of the guides had been grazed on the hand and on the head by bullets. We waited for the rest of the guides to catch up with us. One of the guides told me that my two comrades had been taken by the Germans. We felt pretty miserable about losing these fellows. Several days later, however, we met them again and found that they had managed to get over all right.

Sergeant Ivan L. Schraeder, a B-17 tail gunner from Peoria, Illinois, crashed-landed off the French coast on September 9, 1943. Helpers, likely from the Pat O'Leary Line, assisted his movement toward Spain. In his E&E report Schraeder had some advice for future evaders, writing, "I think aircrews should be told that they should not be discouraged or disillusioned by rumors that they will be returned to England in 10 days, flying back or coming some other way. Whatever version of this story you are given, you just walk over the Pyrenees anyway."

B-17 pilot First Lieutenant Olof M. Ballinger from Newton Falls, Ohio, went down over France on July 4, 1943. Four months later he finally reached the mountains. He later recalled what other evaders had discovered: "Crossing the Pyrenees alone is a pretty desperate journey."

Ballinger continued,

I walked over the Pyrenees by myself. Because I was in poor shape and would have been unable to keep up with them on the climb, I separated from the party with whom I had traveled. I waited around the foothills for some days expecting to meet a guide but he never came. After some miserable days waiting around in woods in the rain during the day and trying to sleep in the hay in a cold barn at night, I set out by myself. I did not have a compass, so I directed myself by the sun. From an old Frenchman I learned that I was walking in the right direction. I followed a trail over the mountains, apparently crossing the highest peak for some distance. I was in snow for about two hours going up the peak and for a little longer going down. Just when I came below the snow line, it got dark, and I could follow the trail no longer. I had to sit under a tree all night, trying to keep from freezing while I waited for morning. The next morning I found I was over the Spanish border, but I still had long hours of walking before I came to inhabited sections of Spain.

Staff Sergeant Robert G. Neil, a B-17 ball turret gunner from Providence, Rhode Island, went down in France on May 17, 1943. In his description of his evasion he wrote, "The hike to Spain was pretty rough going, but it was much easier for us crossing the mountains than for most Americans. We had been walking 30 kilometers or so a day for some time, whereas the others had been cooped up for weeks. None the less, it was far from an easy walk."

P-47 pilot First Lieutenant John Balcunes from Riverside, California, landed in France on May 21, 1944. By foot and train, he quickly made his way to St. Jean de Luz on the far southeastern border. On May 27, he began walking across the mountains on a route that was considered one of the most dangerous because of the number of German patrols. Balcunes recounted his crossing, writing,

I walked until the moon set. At that time I had reached the crest of a mountain. There I remained until 2200 hours when I took up my hike once more. About midnight I came upon a group of

Spanish cattle rustlers. When I told them who I was they said that they had stolen the cattle from the Germans and that I could come with them. I was given a stick with witch [*sic*] to drive the cow at the end of the column, but after a while I became so exhausted that I clutched the cow's tail with both of my hands and let her drag me up the mountains, down valleys, and over the border into Spain. Without the aid of that cow I would have never made it over. When we had got some distance into Spain the party split up. I followed the chief of the rustlers, who had four cows as his share. Presently he pointed out to me the lights of a village in the valley and told me to go there. When I reached the village I found the bakery open. The baker allowed me to sleep in his shop for the rest of the night and in the morning on his advice I went to the police station. The police put me up at an inn and the next day, May 29, took me to the military commandant in Irun. I spent the night of May 29 in jail and on May 30 was taken to a hotel in Irun where I met a representative of the American embassy.

Flak brought down the B-17 on which Staff Sergeant Nick Asvestos from Astoria, New York, served as a waist gunner on February 28, 1944. He made his way to the mountains and crossed to Spain on one of the more direct routes. Despite his success, the MIS-X debriefers included the comment, "The escaper had apparently not been briefed to avoid the easiest ways across the Pyrenees, which are the most closely guarded."

Most of evaders who reached the mountains did so with the aid of helpers from the O'Leary or Comet Lines who had prearranged guides waiting for them. Although some of the guides worked for the lines for no wages, many were not members and basically performed as subcontractors. Basque sheep herders and others who lived on both sides of the border had earned or supplemented their income for years, if not centuries, by smuggling wine, food, and other products across the mountains. Following narrow pathways that had existed for generations, the guides, for a price, were able to lead evaders and other European refugees across the heights. Since it was more practical, as well as profitable, groups rather than individuals were the norm for the cross-mountain trek.

Second Lieutenant Fred W. Glover from Ashville, North Carolina, was a veteran of the Royal Canadian Air Force before transferring to the USAAF. His P-51 went down over France on April 30, 1944, and helpers led him to the border where he joined a guide and a group of civilians. In his E&E report he recounted,

When we started over the Pyrenees, I had no idea of what was coming as there was no other English speaking person in the crowd. We set off one morning at 0600 hours, stopping briefly at 1000 hours and 1400 hours to eat. Each of these times I ate no more than a quarter of a bar of chocolate. I was in good shape and knew that over-eating could affect my wind and heart. At 1600 hours two men got very sick from over-eating. Because of them we now had to stop frequently. At 2000 hours the guide motioned me to take over the lead. From then to midnight I spelled the guides at leading the party. As I had no pack of my own, I was carrying the 40 pounds of meat for the party. Our sick got better and were able to walk. We had two hours of steady hiking, and then we were working our way through the clouds across a peak, a thunderstorm broke. The older men in the party began to have trouble with their hearts. I carried one of them until we stopped at 0400 hours to build a fire and drink some wine. The guides were nervous, and one of them went on ahead to scout while I led the party, and the second guide rounded up the stragglers. When we had to cross a torrent I stood in the water and got one heart case safely across. The men next to me had just started the second old man across when he slipped and fell and was washed away and drowned. One of the sick men collapsed completely and I had to take turns carrying him and leading the group. We were near a German camp and had to be extremely careful. At daylight we were five kilometers short of our destination and had to spend the rest of the day hidden in the woods. We had traveled 83 kilometers in 24 hours. That night we finished the trip without further incident. When it was over the guides gave everyone a glass of wine and when they got to me they grinned and produced a whole bottle.

Not all, or even the majority, of the E&E reports contain information about crossing the mountains to Spain. MIS-X commander Lieutenant Colonel Holt included in Glover's report, "Comment on 656: Once in a while a story about crossing the Pyrenees will be included in an E&E report. This one gives an accurate picture of an average passage. Note the commonplaces of mountain climbing: Heavy exertion stops digestion and causes food to ferment, the gases from which oppress the heart and cause 'heart failure' in the mountains. Lt. Glover's fine help to his party was made possible by his good physical condition."

First Lieutenant C. R. Clonts Jr., from Oviedo, Florida, also crossed the mountains with a group of civilians. German fighters had shot down Clonts' P-47 on his first mission over France on May 8, 1944. In his E&E report he wrote,

When we started over the mountains we were joined by a band of Jewish refugees. Our mountain guide had made a financial arrangement to take them across unknown to the patriots who had been helping the Allied airmen in the party. There was a girl of eighteen, two women over forty, and two old men in their group. It was suggested that we carry the luggage of these five people, as we were traveling light. We did, which was a mistake, for we had little food, and the guide only gave us one meal during the three-day trip through the clouds. The luggage added to the strain, and while the refugees had an ample supply of food, they would not share it. The guide had to spend most of his time keeping order in this mob and had particular difficulty in making them be quiet when we passed through danger zones. We finally reached Spain and were glad to be arrested. It was another thirteen hours, however, before the police treated us to a meal of boiled potatoes.

Some of the evaders reached the mountains in poor physical condition from their long journey or from injuries from bailing out of their damaged planes. Even those who reached the Pyrenees in good physical condition suffered injuries, mostly frostbite, during their crossing.

B-17 top turret gunner Staff Sergeant Joseph L. Kirkner from Radnor, Pennsylvania, went down over France on December 31, 1943. About his crossing he wrote,

I was expected to start over the Pyrenees on 9 January, but it was 14 January before my feet were in condition for me to do so. I was the only American in the group. My knapsack was filled with cheese, two tins of sardines, bread, and a bottle of cognac. We walked the whole night and were still only in the foothills. After spending the day of 15 January in a barn we walked for ten hours over much steeper hills, before stopping at a farm. The night of 16 January we were really in the mountains. We came to a road patrolled by the Germans and watched their bicycle lights as they traveled up and down the road. We hid in the bushes, and each time the patrol passed, one of us would slip across to the bushes on the far side. After much more climbing the guide pointed to a stake on top of a mountain and told us it marked the border. We climbed up through heavy snow and at 0230 hours on 17 January the guide said, "Espagne" and left. We followed the road down between the mountains and were arrested five kilometers from the nearest town. We were registered and searched. All compasses, knives, and files were confiscated, as were my 2,000 francs. When I reached a hotel at Pamplona, I rejoined my pilot. We had both lost so much weight that we had difficulty recognizing each other. I was taken to the internment camp at Lecumberri on 18 January. The consul sent us clothes and cigarettes. He also saw to it that the Americans had an extra ration of food. On 5 February I left the camp and started on the final phase of my journey, arriving in UK on 2 March.

Frostbite was a problem for B-17 bombardier Second Lieutenant John S. Trost from Detroit, Michigan. Shot down over France on December 20, 1942, he survived while seven of his fellow crewmen were killed and two were taken prisoner. Trost was one of the earliest evaders to make it over the mountains. He described his journey, writing,

On February 9, 1943 at 0100 hours I started across the Pyrenees in company of people. At the top of the first mountain we stopped in a small cabin to spend an hour around a fire. At 0400 hours we started walking again and continued until 2300 hours. We spent time this night in another cabin. It was there that my feet started suffering. They were wet and my socks and shoes were soon frozen to my feet. The next day they were badly swollen. We had to walk all day but reached a settlement that night. Arrangements were made for us to stay there. We were there two days and nights. Arrangements had to be made for transportation because I had a severe case of frostbite. I spent a month in a hotel under doctor's care. One of my toes was amputated. Later the Military Attaché took me to Madrid. I spent six weeks in a British-American hospital. Arrived at Gibraltar on April 21 and UK April 24.

Some evaders had to attempt to cross the mountains several times before successfully reaching Spain. Second Lieutenant John Betolatti, a B-17 bombardier from Danbury, Connecticut, was shot down by fighters over France on April 13, 1944. Several weeks later he reached the Pyrenees. He wrote in his E&E report,

At dawn I set out on the road south. As I neared the mountains the road petered out into a thin trail. I still had some sugar, and I ate it now along with the candy from my escape kit. It took me a whole day to climb the first peak. There was no trail now and the snow was up to my chest. When I got to the valley I thought I was in Spain, but the shepherds all pointed south. I spent one night with a Frenchman and another in a deserted cabin. I wanted a

Benzedrine badly, but it had all disintegrated in my pocket. I got over another peak, but I was exhausted. Every few steps now I would collapse. I finally saw a road and decided to follow it east to the international highway, for I was so weak that I was afraid of dying of exposure if I continued through the snow.

I reached the road, and there on a wall sat three German officers. There was only one way to go, and besides I had passed many of them in north France, so I went on. I had forgotten that I was soaking wet now, as no peasant would be. I got past but then it dawned on them that I must be a refugee and they called me back and asked for my papers. I tried a trick I had heard of in an evader's lecture at base. I reached in my pocket, looked blank and then set off again. It did not work, and I had to come back. I had a loaf of bread under my shirt. They evidently thought it gun, and I had to stand at attention while they investigated. They asked if I was Polish, French or Italian, and as they questioned me they went through my pockets. I started to laugh, and could not stop, which irritated them. One asked if I was Russian. This had a strange effect on another; his expression grew hard and he came over and started to kick my legs apart. This made me mad and I told them I was an American officer and expected to be treated according to the Geneva Convention. They asked for proof and I showed them my dog tags. They knew what these were immediately, and we moved off pleasantly enough to the village hotel at St. de Salau. Then I realized how near I was to my goal when I was captured.

After three days of confinement, Betolatti escaped. He recorded his plight, writing, "My first thought was to clear town. South meant the Pyrenees, but I was too weak to try them again, so I headed north hoping to find a farm at which I could rest until I was fit again."

French peasants provided the American airman food and shelter until he sufficiently recovered to approach the mountains once again. Describing his journey he wrote,

During my second Pyrenees crossing we were badly delayed due by the poor condition of one of the party. Then we were caught in a snow storm and the guides got lost. By the time we got back on the trail we could not make the final pass before the arrival of the German patrol. At the top of a mountain, the guides told us to follow a river in the valley below and then deserted us. We reached the river and followed it to a highway. Here the party split, some of the men following the highway. I thought this much too dangerous, and got off with two Englishmen along the mountains paralleling the road. It was hard going, as the mountain kept forcing us down to the road and it was torturous getting up again. It was with a great deal of relief that we finally stumbled past France into Spain.

Staff Sergeant John L. Swenson, a B-17 radio operator from Somerville, Massachusetts, came down in France on December 30, 1943. Frostbite also forced him to retreat on his first attempt to cross the mountains. He wrote, "I traveled with other members of my crew, but it took me two Pyrenees crossings finally to get into Spain. I had shoes which were too small for me the first time, and when my feet were frozen, I was unable to complete the journey."

A MIS-X note to Swenson's report detailed the difficulties encountered in his first trip and recommended him for a Bronze Star:

For courage and determination in evading from France under the most difficult conditions. Made one unsuccessful Pyrenees crossing before the second successful one. In this first crossing he helped Sgt. Stumpfig (Conrad P. Jr.) (E&E 568), practically carrying him for more than eight hours. Lt. Compton (Charles W. Jr.) (E&E 566) reported this effort as one of the most amazing feats of human endurance which he had witnessed. Because of his efforts, Sgt. Swenson froze his feet so badly the he was unable to continue the journey and had to be left behind in France.

Technical Sergeant Archie R. Barlow, a B-24 top turret gunner from Hattiesburg, Mississippi, went down over France on January 21, 1944. On his first attempt to traverse the mountains, he got separated from his guides and found himself alone. He recorded his story, writing, "I was too exhausted to continue. I had not taken care to keep myself in good physical condition, and I was wearing shoes which were too small for me." Barlow went down the mountains and took a train back to Paris where his original helpers arranged a second trip. On April 22, he finally made his way to Spain. A comment to his report states, "Napoleon's soldiers may have marched on their stomachs, but evaders cross the Pyrenees on their feet."

B-17 top turret gunner Sergeant Herman F. Hermanson from Austin, Texas, was shot down over France on his third mission on March 27, 1944. He took a train to the nearest border. He wrote, "I set out at once on foot southwards to the mountains. That night I slept on a hillside and early the next day I came within sight of the snow-covered peaks. I had exhausted my stock of food, my feet were very sore, and when I saw the height of the mountains and the snow I knew that I could not get to Spain alone in my present condition." Hermanson turned back, found helpers, and successfully made it across on his second attempt.

B-17 bombardier Technical Sergeant Bertil E. Erickson from Grassbelt, Pennsylvania, came down in France on August 27, 1943. He reported,

Our Pyrenees crossing was an especially rough one. Four Europeans with us had to drop out completely. I had some wooden sole shoes, and my feet were pretty sore, but I manage to carry on. It was a tough trail; for a long distance we walked in deep snow. When a man fell down in the snow, we were all so exhausted there was little we could do for him. A couple of men had a bottle of what seemed to be pure alcohol. I was awfully thirsty and drank too much of it. It almost knocked me out, and I was pretty sick and miserable. Some sugar was the only thing I had to eat and I was getting more and more thirsty and started eating snow; once I started, I could not stop myself. I took a Benzedrine tablet and we finally made it across.

Captain Eugene A. Wink Jr., a P-47 pilot from Tampa, Florida, was only a year out of West Point when he bailed out over France because of engine failure on March 2, 1944. He reported,

> We started over the Pyrenees on March 16 after having had nothing but potatoes to eat for several days. The next day we stopped at a place where I was able to buy enough lump sugar for the whole party. This later proved very helpful as it gave us quick energy without making us thirsty. On March 19 our guide left us. We were still three hours from the border, but the guide said that we were out of danger. The snow was hard and slippery, and once as we walked along the side of a mountain a Frenchman fell and slid to a stop just short of cliff. We walked for five hours before reaching Spain.

B-17 waist gunner Sergeant Edward F. Chonskie from Shenandoah, Pennsylvania, began his evasion on July 4, 1943, after his plane was shot down by fighters. When he and two fellow crew members reached the Pyrenees, they paid guides to take them over the mountains. When the airmen refused to pay additional money, the helpers slipped away leaving the airmen on their own. It took six days of staying off trails and only approaching shepherds for help for them to reach Spain and return to the United Kingdom on October 18.

Second Lieutenant Paul A. Marriott from Fort Worth, Texas, was acting as the tail gunner aboard a B-17 that Nazi fighters brought down in France on January 7, 1944. About his trip over the Pyrenees he wrote,

> During the actual crossing we walked for 60 hours in five days and had to leave one member of our party behind. We were all exhausted by the long pull in deep snow and made without proper equipment or food. The guides deceived us about the distance ahead of us and continually kept telling us everything would be all right the next day. They demanded money for all food we ate on the way. Some of us had the remains of our escape kits with us, and the Benzedrine and Horlick's tablets helped us to get

through the ordeal. We reached Barcelona on March 22 and then went through to Gibraltar after spending a week in Madrid at the British Embassy.

Evaders used the money from their escape kits and funds provided by helpers to pay their guides and to buy food. Sometimes this was not sufficient. Technical Sergeant Donald C. Stairs, a B-17 radio operator from Mt. Pleasant, Pennsylvania, went down in France on March 20, 1944. "Most of the money that I had gotten from the French Resistance had been used up during the trip down, especially for liquor." Before crossing mountains, Stairs and others stopped and worked for a farmer for wages. He reported, "We sawed lumber for the rest of the day."

Difficulties came from more than just unreliable guides, lack of food, and the weather. B-17 copilot Second Lieutenant Carl N. Smith was shot down over the North Sea on July 26, 1943, rescued, and returned to his unit. Three weeks later, on August 17, 1943, he was again shot down on a mission over Belgium. He broke his leg upon landing but helpers, likely from the Comet Line, picked him up on a motorcycle. In his E&E report he wrote, "I had to ride on it and put my legs on a couple of steel rails and look just like another Belgian out on a motorcycle jaunt."

The helpers took Smith to a doctor who set his leg. By December he had recovered sufficiently to head south and cross the mountains. He continued, writing,

Because of my leg the hike over the Pyrenees was worse than the annual rough climb. We seemed to be going up and down continually, and my leg was bothering me badly. Part of the time I had to go on hands and knees and was pretty miserable. The others would get ahead of me, and by the time I caught up with them they were resting some place. Then they would start out immediately with the result that I got no rest at all. We slept, or tried to sleep, in barely adequate shelters and nearly froze in them. The barns were the closest we came to real comfort. The guides were continually saying "just ten kilometers more," and then we walked for a couple of more days. We seemed to go over the highest peaks you could find in the mountains. For some reason we kept walking deep into Spain. Afterwards I wondered how I had actually made the hike.

B-17 pilot Second Lieutenant James A. Grumbles from Sumter, South Carolina, went down in France on December 31, 1943, and quickly made his way south. He reported,

> We started over the Pyrenees at 2000 hour on 3 January and walked until we reached the frontier at 0100. Here the guide left me. The frozen ground was snow covered. I started down the mountain alone, without any clear idea of the way. At 0800 hours on 4 January I reached a village and started on the main road to Barcelona. The police caught me at 1000 hours. The police kept me comfortable for a night and then after a day of being checked into the local jail, I went to prison. I was in prison for four days when the American consul arranged my release.

Sergeant Francis F. Higgins a B-17 tail gunner from Bangor, Maine, bailed out over France on February 8, 1944. He joined a group of other evaders and civilian refugees when he reached the Pyrenees. The most remarkable part of his report is that he "carried a baby the entire way."

CHAPTER 11

Spain

2LT Jack E. Williams
B-17 Copilot
Highland Park, Michigan
Crash landed in France on December 12, 1942
Arrived in UK on January 29, 1943

STATEMENT BY LT WILLIAMS
"WHAT HAPPENED TO ME AT MADRID AND GIBRALTER
and SUGGESTIONS FOR IMPROVING CONDITIONS
AND HELPING US PERSONNEL"

When we arrived in Madrid we were taken to the British Embassy. We were quartered in a small building in the rear of the Embassy which had several cots for sleeping. There was also a small building where two Spanish women cooked our meals. The British Red Cross gave us clean clothes, soap, tooth brushes, tooth paste and shaving articles. We were also paid 35 pesetas a week for buying things we wanted such as wine and coffee. We were interviewed by the Embassy officials who wanted our names, rank, squadron and the names of the personnel in our plane for future identification. We stayed at the Embassy several days until it was arranged for us to leave by train for Gibraltar.

The night we left we were taken to a hotel in Madrid where we had our supper. We then proceeded to the railway station. There were about 76 men leaving with us who had been released from Miranda prison camp. We had compartments on the train and after a very long journey we arrived at a small Spanish town just north of the border with Gibraltar. We were put in buses and taken to a town on the border of Gibraltar. At the British Vice-Consulate we filled in forms giving false names, birthplace and fathers name, mothers name and rank. I was given the name of Sgt. Jack Roger of the Canadian Army at Madrid by Major Haslan and told to make up false answers for everything else they asked me. After an hours wait we were driven across the border to Gibraltar. We were taken down to the docks and interviewed by British officers after which we were taken out to the S.S. Ormonde, which was lying in the harbor. After being on board the boat a day and night we realized we weren't being treated as thought we should be. The British authorities would not let us go ashore to communicate with the American authorities, and we did not have clean clothes or money. After doing a lot of complaining to the C.O. of the boat, they sent out an American Finance Officer who gave us $100.00 uniform allowance and took back word to Col. Holcomb, the military observer at Gibraltar to do everything he could to get us off the boat, which he did, and they took us off the boat about 1800 hrs that same day. When we arrived in the town we were issued British battle dress and taken to an officers camp called the Laretto Camp. The next day I went to the military hospital in Gibraltar with acute tonsillitis. I stayed in the hospital nine days. When I was released I got in touch with the American Operations Officer, Capt. Gable, who told me there was an American B-24 bomber leaving for Porthreat that night. I then made arrangements with the pilot of the B-24. Late in the afternoon Mrs. Carole Landis Wallace arrived by plane from Algiers. She also received permission to go on the B-24 to England if the weather permitted. At 2 a.m. on 29 Jan we took off and after an uneventful trip landed at Porthreat at 8.30 a.m. We had breakfast and we were then told we were to go on to London on a small De Haviland plane. After testing the plane it was found unfit to fly, so being very anxious to get to London, Mrs. Landis and I motored over to another field, 20 miles from Portreath where a government C-47 cargo plane was waiting to take off for London. We took off at 1400 hrs and were in Hendon airport at 1530 hrs. I then took a bus to London and reported immediately to H.Q. ETOUSA, where I was identified.

SUGGESTIONS
In Madrid the American Embassy should take care of all US personnel escaping from France. Instead of paying us 35 pesetas for buying coffee and wine they should have it there. The British authorities in Gibraltar should have let us get in touch with the Americans instead of shipping us on a boat in the harbor without clean clothes or money.

Lieutenant Williams experienced many difficulties not encountered by subsequent evaders. However, his statement, included with his E&E Report No. 9, offers insights into problems aviators faced in Spain after successfully crossing the Pyrenees.

Evaders were not necessarily safe even after they crossed over the mountains into Spain because that country's tumultuous history had left its populous divided in its loyalties. Officially neutral, the government of dictator Francisco Franco nevertheless played both the Allies and the Axis powers to its advantages, leaving the people in the countryside to choose their own responses to evaders. In many cases, civilians welcomed arriving airmen and assisted them in their reaching British or American consuls. In other cases, civilians turned evaders over to German border guards. Treatment for the evaders was likewise unpredictable from the Spanish police. Some arrested evaders for entering their country illegally; other policemen detained them in order to deliver them to the Allied consuls. Still others turned them back over the mountains or directly to the Nazi border guards. Even after reaching the safety of the consuls, evaders frequently faced questioning by German agents at local inns and restaurants regarding their units, escape routes, and identification of helpers.

Kings had ruled Spain for centuries until Alfonso XIII was replaced by a democratically elected government in 1931. In 1936, Spanish monarchists, fascists, and nationalists, supported by much of the Catholic Church, rose up in rebellion. Nationalists, as they were known, led by Francisco Franco, quickly took over much of the country. Communists and anarchists, known as Republicans, opposed the Nationalists in what became a bloody civil war with both sides massacring prisoners and civilians alike. By war's end, with a Nationalist victory in 1939, an estimated half million Spaniards had died.

The Spanish Civil War served as a proving ground for much of the tactics and weapons of World War II. Germany and Italy aided the Nationalists while the Soviet Union provided support for the Republicans. The British and Americans officially remained out of the conflict other than to provide volunteers for the Republican International Brigade. About 2,800 Americans, 900 whom were killed in action, fought in the Brigade's Lincoln Battalion.

Franco met with both German and Italian leaders after the outbreak of World War II and offered to join the Axis. In return he demanded island territories in the Atlantic and colonies in Africa. The Axis thought the demands too much for too little and turned down the offer. For much of the war, however, Spain provided raw materials to Germany, particularly tungsten, to pay off their debt for support during their Civil War. The Spanish also provided a volunteer unit, the "Blue Division" to assist the Germans against Russia on the Eastern Front.

Franco attempted to maintain good relations with the United States as American imports were his primary source of petroleum and other products. The United States continued to maintain an embassy in Madrid and Consulates General in Barcelona, Bilbao, and San Sebastian.

Great Britain, which honored Spain's neutrality, had offices in the country as well as occupying the fortress of Gibraltar, a narrow peninsula on Spain's southern Mediterranean coast. The three-mile square "rock" was heavily fortified, and its air and naval base guarded the Strait of Gibraltar. Hitler sought, but did not receive, permission from Franco to cross Spanish territory to attack the British stronghold. Franco positioned much of his army along the Pyrenees to prevent such an incursion by the Nazis. Ultimately, these soldiers impeded the crossing of the mountains by evaders while Gibraltar served as their final exit back to the United Kingdom.

American airmen were wholly unprepared to deal with the intrigue of the fractured political situation in Spain once they arrived on the other side of the Pyrenees. Americans experienced difficulties in not having been briefed on what to do on arrival in Spain. Second Lieutenant John W. Herrick, a P-47 pilot from Metuchen, Pennsylvania, was shot down by fighters over France on November 26, 1943. He recounted his experience, writing,

After I reached Spain, I jumped a freight train in an effort to get to the consul in Barcelona. The train made a stop and I got off and stood beside it. When it started up again, I was unable to get aboard. I went to the station and tried to persuade a priest to buy me a ticket, but he would not, even when I offered him my ring. Two policemen stopped me for papers, and I was arrested. In jail

I rejoined many of the Americans with whom I had crossed the mountains. The next day three of us were taken for interrogation in the office of a man in civilian clothes. He asked if we were aviators, the type of aircraft we flew, and how we had gotten over the border; he wanted to see the precise spot on the map. We did not tell him. He knew we had come over the southern end, and what he did not know and wanted to know, I believe, was the name of the town we had started from. The next day the consul told us that this man was undoubtedly a German agent or a Spaniard working for Germany. I knew what to do when interrogated in enemy country, but what to do in neutral countries had never been made clear to me. All that I had ever been told was to get in touch with the American consul.

The Spanish police were the final barrier to successful evasions. Once an airman reached, or were reached by, American or British officials their evacuation to the United Kingdom was ensured. Difficulties with the police did not ease until the passage of time and the recognition of the Spanish government of the likelihood of an Allied victory.

P-38 pilot First Lieutenant Wendel S. McMurray from Philadelphia, Pennsylvania, was shot down over France by flak on May 7, 1944. He wrote,

I crossed the Spanish border on June 11 and two hours later came upon a border patrol of Spanish police to whom I gave myself up. The patrol consisted of four privates and a corporal. I told them that I had been taken prisoner by the Germans and had escaped, and apparently satisfied with this story they took me to a mountain hotel for the night. The next morning they awaken me and walked along a road with the intention I presumed of taking me to the nearest Spanish town. Presently, however, I suspected that we were going in the direction of the French border; and when I asked the corporal directly whether this was the case he admitted it, saying that they had orders several days before to allow no one to enter Spain who had not a proper passport. I protested that

I was an escaped prisoner of war and that my right of asylum in neutral territory was guaranteed by the Geneva Convention. He stubbornly insisted that his orders were to put me back into France. Then I told him that the American consul knew that I had escaped and was on my way to Spain, that he was expecting me, and that there would be serious trouble if I was not allowed to communicate with him. Finally, after two hours of arguing the corporal agreed to return to the hotel and from there telephone his superior about my case. He left me under guard and after an hour or two returned saying that he had after much difficulty received permission to let me remain in Spain.

MIS-X added a comment to McMurray's story noting, "This is the first instance of Spanish admission of direct collaboration with the enemy—the patrol's action was entirely illegal and the evader did a fine piece of work in insisting upon his rights under the Geneva Convention. Crews should be briefed to regard Spanish officials as allies of the German in everything but belligerency; to insist upon their treatment as escaped prisoners of war, to have the nearest American consul notified of their presence, and to give no information other than name, rank, and serial number."

Staff Sergeant Irwin Gassaway, tail gunner on a B-17 from Norwood, Ohio, was shot down in France on December 31, 1943. Smugglers helped him over the mountains, and he arrived in Spain on January 27. His guides then turned back toward France. Gassaway reported his plight, writing, "I followed the road into Vera and reported to the Spanish police, who searched me and took my remaining French money. I had already destroyed my identity card. I said I was an American officer and that I had escaped from the Germans. They let me stay in the police barracks, but did not restrict my movements at all." Gassaway passed through several police stations before being turned over to Allied officials. He landed back in the United Kingdom on March 24.

Second Lieutenant Henry M. Heldman, a B-17 copilot from Hartford, Connecticut, went down over France on February 11, 1944, and reached the mountains six weeks later. He crossed into the microstate of

Andorra on the French-Spanish border where he stayed for five days. A representative of the British consul arrived and walked him into Spain where, after clearance through the police, he was fed and taken by car to Barcelona. Heldman was then provided clothes, given money, and placed in a private home. Then he was taken to the British embassy in Madrid, bussed to Gibraltar, delivered to the American attaché, and then flown to Casablanca and on to the United Kingdom where he arrived on April 4.

Evasion reports of those who made it to Spain are consistent in noting harassment and worse by the Spanish police and then fairly good treatment once in the hands of Allied representatives. Their primary concerns mentioned in their reports were efforts by German agents to discover how they had escaped and who helped them on their journey.

MIS-X interrogators, after review of the report of B-17 pilot First Lieutenant Royston T. Covington Jr. from Baltimore, Maryland, who went down in France on March 8, 1944, warned of new evidence of German agent activity in Spain. In a comment on Covington's June 15 report they wrote, "Note evader's suggestion on necessity of silence in Spain. New evidence has come in that border hotels are hangouts for German spies. For example, there is an American named William F. (Bill) O'Brian at the Hotel Norte in Irun who buys drinks for evaders at the hotel bar and pumps them about helpers and military matters."

More information on O'Brian came in through a memo to Lieutenant Colonel Holt from First Lieutenant Theodore M. Purdy Jr., a member of the MIS-X staff. On April 5, 1944, with the subject "Possible Informer in Irun," Purdy referenced the report of Staff Sergeant Emil W. Taddeo, a B-17 top turret gunner from Richmond Hill, New York, who went down in France on January 5, 1944, and made his way to Spain at the end of January.

According to Purdy's memo,

SSGT Emil W. Taddeo (E&E #516) reports that there was an American named Bill O'Brien living at the Hotel Norte in Irun whose actions appeared suspicious to the group of which Sgt Taddeo was a member. They were at this hotel from 30 January to 4 March and had full opportunity to observe him. He claims to have escaped from a concentration camp in Germany. He was a student in Munich at the beginning of the war, stayed on, got in trouble with the Gestapo, and spent 18 months as an internee in 1942–1943. He was later used by the Germans to interpret for captured American and British fliers and in this capacity visited several prison camps. Finally he claims to have escaped through France and made his way to Irun. He says that his family (mother and sister) are in Madrid, which explains why he does not return to the US, but he makes no attempt to explain why he stays in a border town and does not return to Madrid. He became friendly with Sgt Taddeo and the other members of their party, loaned them money, and bought them drinks. He appeared to be anxious to get information concerning their experiences as evaders, and asked whether they had gotten any military information on the way out, and whether they had made underground contacts. Mrs. Stevens, wife of the US Military Attaché, who came over from San Sebastian to see this party, and later invited them to San Sebastian, said she had no information about this man. During their stay at Irun, the rooms of Sgt Taddeo and the group were searched several times, presumably by the Spanish police. They think O'Brien may have tipped off the police that most of this group were not officers, though they claimed to be, and that they had information about underground activities. A German officer is stationed in police headquarters in Irun, according to Sgt Taddeo, and information about escapers and evaders is undoubtedly passed on to him by the Spanish police.

Staff Sergeant Nick Asvestos, a B-17 waist gunner from Astoria, New York, was shot down by flak on February 28, 1944. He was quickly captured by the Germans but escaped and found helpers who guided him to the mountains and into Spain on March 14. Spanish police imprisoned him for six days before turning him over to the American consul. He detailed his experience, writing,

While I was being kept in the prison in Figueras a young man who said that he was a Spanish playwright came into my cell. He spoke English perfectly and told me that he was writing a play about American bomber raids in Germany. He then talked to me about Hollywood and motion pictures but now and then would put questions to me about American bombers and bombing tactics. When after a half hour he had failed to get me to talk to him he left the cell; but a little while later I was called out and this same young man told me the Spanish police wanted me to answer a few questions. I told him that I wouldn't answer anything until I had seen the American consul. After that I was returned to my cell and did not see this young man again, but two old men in the same cell told me that he was a Gestapo agent.

B-17 tail gunner Sergeant Francis F. Higgins from Bangor, Maine, had a similar experience after bailing out over France on February 8, 1944. In Spain he mistakenly gave a civilian occupation to authorities rather than maintaining he was an escaped prisoner of war. As a consequence he was interred for several weeks in the civilian concentration camp at Miranda de Ebro. Besides the great discomfort of the camp, he was questioned by a man said to be a colonel in the German secret service.

P-47 pilot Second Lieutenant Bert I. Smith Jr. from Long Beach, California, had an even worse experience after being shot down by a FW-190 on August 28, 1944, over France. With the assistance of French helpers, he made his way to Spain only to have the Spanish policemen arrest him, return him to the border, and turn him over to the Germans. Smith remained in a German POW camp until it was liberated by Allies near the end of the war.

Switzerland

E&E REPORT NO. IS9 (WEA)/6/661/2522
SECRET IS9 (WEA)
(Applies to all British, Canadian, US & Allied Personnel)
Escaped from Switzerland

November 30, 1944

Name:	Elmer P. Israelson
Rank:	2LT
Were you wounded?	Small flak wound on right cheek
Unit:	358th Bomb Squadron, 303rd Bomb Group (B-17)
Job:	Bombardier
Private Address:	Milaca, Minnesota

Other members of the crew:

Pilot	2LT	Raymond Hofmann	Interred in Switzerland
Co–Pilot	1LT	Robert Snyder	Interred in Switzerland
Navigator	1LT	Samuel Minkowitz	Interred in Switzerland
Bombardier	2LT	Elmer P. Israelson	Narrator
Radio Operator	TSGT	Seymour Berman	Interred in Switzerland
Top Turret Gunner	TSGT	William Blakeney	Interred in Switzerland
Ball Turret Gunner	SGT	John Barr	Interred in Switzerland
Waist Gunner	SSGT	Tracy Lawson	Interred in Switzerland
Waist Gunner	SGT	Ollie Crenshaw	Interred in Switzerland
Tail Gunner	SSGT	Thomas Hickey	Interred in Switzerland

We were on a mission to bomb a German airfield near Munich. When we got over Wurttemberg, German fighters swarmed into us. From that time until we hit the I.P., the fighters made at least eight sweeps through our group; but I don't think we were even hit.

Over the I.P. flak got our No. 4 engine and my interphone was shot out. We had to drop out of the formation with the prop on No. 4 windmilling. The pilot and co-pilot decided we would never be able to make it back through the fighter screen; so we headed for Switzerland.

We brought our ship down on a small field at Dubendorf and immediately found ourselves surrounded by Swiss military police. I wanted to go up to inspect the No. 4 engine, but the guards quickly hustled us into a truck waiting near the plane.

We were driven to a barracks on the field, and there ordered to lay out all of our equipment for inspection. Our escape maps were taken from us, along with our compasses. Then we were given Red Cross cards to fill out. These asked for our units, but we just put down 8th AAF and nothing more. We were asked a few questions, none of a military nature, except that our interrogators wanted to know what our target was and where we had come from. We refused to give our target and said merely that we had come from England.

The next day we were taken by train to Adelboden, where officers were separated from the EM's. We officers were put under quarantine for two weeks in the Kuln Hotel in Adelboden, where we remained for two weeks after which we moved to the Regina Hotel. At both hotels we received excellent treatment, our only complaint being that the food was not good. However, I believe we received the same fare as the general run of Swiss civilians.

On 27 June most of the officers were moved to the Palace Hotel in Davas-Platz. This was in one of the most pro-German sections of Switzerland. When we first came there some of the café owners in the village were openly hostile and told some of the officers that they wanted no Americans in their establishments. However, their attitude soon changed to one of real friendliness towards us. We heard rumors that the Swiss had deliberately sent us to that section to counter-act the pro-German attitude there.

I started thinking about escaping early in June, and several of us purchased civilian clothes for this purpose. However, the Swiss authorities searched our rooms and picked up the clothes.

In the latter part of October I heard that a druggist in Lucerne had arranged the escape of F/O Roger Buckholz, 2nd Lt. Parks and 2nd Lt. Clark. They had escaped from Greppen on about 6 Nov.

I got a pass and went to Lucerne to see the druggist. He arranged that I should escape on Nov 22, but the date was later changed to Nov 26, as he said he had not yet "fixed" the guards at the Swiss frontier. I was to pay him 750 Swiss francs for the help.

On 26 Nov I got a pass into Lucerne and met Rudolph Lutchen at Rothen's drugstore. Lutchen was working with Rothen and had come to see me at Greppen to arrange the escape.

Lutchen had a complete set of civilian clothing for me, a fishing rod and ruck-sack. He told me I was to act as if we were going on a fishing trip, as internees were often given passes for this purpose. We boarded a train at Lucerne and arrived in Basel that evening.

As this was almost on the German border, I began to have doubts about Lutchen, thinking that he might be working with the Germans and would turn me over to the enemy. My fears had been further aroused when the legation in Berne had told me before I left to avoid Lutchen because his activities had not been "checked." His plans, too, had sounded almost too good to me.

I slept in Basel that night in an artist's studio where Lutchen had taken me. He, himself, disappeared, which made me more suspicious.

The next morning, however, we took another train going South. We changed at Delemont, and took another train to a small village. There we changed to a bus which took us to within a few miles of the French border. We got off the bus along the Doubs river, and there found Rothen fishing the river and waiting for us.

Rothen and Lutchen then guided me to the Swiss customs house on the border and there left me. I walked across the border, actually going across the back porch of the customs house.

Rothen had told me previously that he bribed the customs house officials, and by bringing them something to drink now and then kept them quiet.

Neither Rothen nor Lutchen could have made any profit on my escape, for the fishing equipment and civilian clothes must have cost them as much as I had given them. All my railroad fare had been paid by Lutchen.

After crossing the border I contacted some French soldiers at the first small village. I caught a ride to Besancon, and there met two American officers who took me to Paris.

Although the E&E report format differed somewhat for evaders to Switzerland, Lieutenant Israelson's narrative closely resembles those of his fellow airman. Switzerland became a country for evaders to both escape to and escape from during the war. Surrounded by the Axis powers, the Swiss were nevertheless able to establish and maintain their neutrality throughout the entire conflict. Their large standing army and air force, supported by extremely defendable mountain terrain, deterred any invasion. The Axis also recognized the benefits of having a neutral country's vast banking system available. With more than 60 percent of its population of German descent and their first language, much of the Swiss population supported Adolph Hitler and his Nazis. The remaining citizens, mostly of French linage, favored the Allies. Most Swiss, both of German and French backgrounds, favored the peacefulness of neutrality and the profits from a raging war that cost them no blood and added to their treasure.

The proximity of Switzerland to France and Germany made it an obvious place of possible refuge. Whatever waited in a neutral country certainly appeared better to the crew of a damaged American bomber than sitting out the war in a German POW camp.

On August 13, 1943, pilot First Lieutenant Alva "Jack" Geron determined that his B-24 with two engines out and other battle damage could not make it back over the Alps to their North Africa base. He set course for Switzerland where he crash-landed, and it became the first American plane to reach the neutral state. Over the coming months, 166 USAAF aircraft with 1,517 crewmen landed in Swiss territory. Not until the Allied invasion of France secured airfields did the flow slow and then halt altogether. While Geron and his crew burned their aircraft on landing, most of the planes, nearly all B-17s and B-24s, despite damage were somewhat salvageable and were confiscated by Swiss authorities.

Swiss police arrested the crewmen on their arrival, placing them in loosely guarded and rundown hotels and labeling those who crash-landed into the country as "internees." Conditions in the camps were at best only adequate. Most internees, who found the food poor but not that different from that provided their Swiss guards, were forced to sign papers stating they would not attempt to escape. Hundreds did, however, quickly tired of confinement.

Sergeant John J. McCanna, a waist gunner on a B-24 from Aledo, Illinois, crash-landed in Switzerland on July 21, 1944. He remained an internee for only a little more than a month before he stole a bicycle, rode to a train station, and purchased a ticket to the border. There he rented a rowboat, crossed a river, and joined the French Resistance who delivered him to the advancing American army.

Those whom the Swiss apprehended in their attempts to escape were placed in pretrial confinement for their crime. They were moved to much more secure camps where harsh treatment rivaled that of the Nazi POW camps for airmen in Germany. Particularly bad was the Swiss internment camp at Wauwilermoos where the camp commander was a Nazi sympathizer. Conditions were so hostile in the camp that, after a lengthy lobbying effort by former internees, the United States posthumously awarded Prisoner of War Medals to 143 veterans held at Wauwilermoos and on April 30, 2014, presented the award to eight survivors of the camp.

While a few of the crashed-landed airmen escaped Swiss interment, most remained in the camps until near or at the end of the war. MIS-X did not consider internees to be evaders and only interviewed those who escaped from the internment camps.

Although briefed that there was a much better chance of returning to the United Kingdom if they made their way to Spain, some airmen shot down over France and Germany preferred to seek refuge in Switzerland if they were near the border and had a choice. For most, the reason was simple—they could evade from German-held territory in a matter of days rather than the months it took to reach Spain. A total of 224 evaders crossed the Swiss border.

Unlike internees who had crash-landed, evaders who walked across the borders were not confined to hotels or camps but rather were turned over to the military attaché at the US legation. After a twenty-one-day quarantine period, their only restriction was to sign a statement that they would not attempt to escape from the country. As evaders, they received their military salary, which meant they were required to pay their own way. The most common complaint was one made by Staff Sergeant Robert L. Williams, a B-17 gunner from Manistique, Michigan, who reported about a lice infestation and related, "[T]hey cut off all our hair which I think was very unnecessary."

Staff Sergeant Benjamin St. John, a B-24 gunner from Oneonta, New York, shot down over Belgium on January 29, 1944, took longer than most evaders to reach Switzerland. He lived with the Belgian resistance for a month before walking on his own to cross the Swiss border. St. John found that it "cost too much to live, enlisted men had to spend much of their pay for food and clothing." On May 9, he left Switzerland and successfully made his way to France and, after the D-Day invasion, joined advancing US troops.

Most of the stories by evaders who escaped to Switzerland are brief and to the point. Second Lieutenant Bill B. Banias, a B-24 crewman from Kerman, California, wrote, "Crash landed in Germany on July 11, 1944 approximately 45 minutes from target. Headed for France. Seven days without food, walked day and night. Received aid from French in France. Night of seventh day was guided across frontier into Switzerland." Banias became a double evader by crossing back into France on July 19 to join the advancing Allies.

First Lieutenant Marion E. Brown of Louisville, Kentucky, the pilot of a B-24 was shot down over Belgium on February 24, 1944. The Belgian resistance assisted his evasion to near the Swiss border, which he crossed "independently." Evaders who wanted to become escapees from Switzerland also had assistance. Brown wrote, "I escaped uneventfully by the aid of Werner Lier's organization in Geneva, on September 8 crossing the border at Geneva and joining the FFI who took me to Annecy where I came into American hands."

Some airmen remained in Switzerland for an extended time before making their escape. Staff Sergeant George Kemp from Milford, Connecticut, was the tail gunner on a B-17 shot down in France on September 6, 1943. While the other nine members of his crew were captured by the Germans, Milford evaded apprehension for almost a month before crossing into Switzerland. A year later he told his storywriting, "On September 2, 1944 I escaped from Switzerland as follows: Marius Pernet, taxi driver of Glion, who had helped many others get away, took me to the border near Geneva, where I met Maquis who took me across and sent me, two days later, to Grenoble, where I joined Allied forces."

Staff Sergeant Joseph D. Loss, a B-17 ball turret gunner from Wellsburg, West Virginia, evaded in France for a month after being shot down on May 29, 1943, before reaching Switzerland. He lived in a Swiss hotel for three months before going to work for the US military attaché in Zurich. On August 23, 1944, he went to Geneva where he climbed in a railroad box car, rode across the border back into France, and joined a US infantry unit.

According to Second Lieutenant Harold E. Bentz, copilot of a B-17 from Cleveland, Ohio, "I went across the border at St. Gingolph. We bribed the guards. The Maquis met us."

American paratroopers also made their way to Switzerland. Private First Class Richard Vatalaro of the 101st Airborne Division from Akron, Ohio, jumped into France on D-Day and was captured by the Germans on June 30, 1944. He escaped on June 30 and with assistance from the Maquis entered Switzerland on August 9. With aid of the American consul he left for England on September 13 where MIS-X debriefed him and compiled his E&E report.

Private John E. Tweer from New York City jumped into Holland with the 101st Airborne Division as a part of Operation Market Garden and was struck on the head and captured by the Germans on September 26, 1944. In route to Germany aboard a hospital train, he escaped. After walking for seven days, he was not aware he had crossed into Switzerland until two Swiss soldiers detained him. After treatment at a Swiss hospital Tweer was delivered to the French border on December 6 and turned over to Allied officials.

The repatriation of Vatalaro and other evaders was the result of ongoing negotiations between US and Swiss officials. As it was now evident that the days of the Third Reich were numbered, Switzerland began to make efforts to get along better with the Allies to include the return of evaders.

Sergeant William E. Wyatt, a B-17 gunner from Pittsburgh, Pennsylvania, who had been in Switzerland since shortly after being shot down in France on March 16, 1943, was released on the same day as Vatalaro. In his E&E report he stated, "I was released and taken by truck to Annecy."

While most of the evaders had returned to Allied control by the end of 1944, some internees were not released until the German surrender. Of the 166 US aircraft that landed in Switzerland, 120 were moved to an airfield outside Zurich. After the war, American mechanics repaired the planes, and they were flown back to England where they were scrapped.

Sweden

LEGATION OF THE UNITED STATES OF AMERICA
OFFICE OF MILITARY AIR ATTACHE
STOCKHOLM, SWEDEN

13 May 1944

SUBJECT: *Personal narration of escape from Denmark.*
TO: *AC of AS, Intelligence, Headquarters, AAF, Washington, DC*
THROUGH: *AC of S, G-2, War Department, Washington, DC*

This is the personal narrative of 2nd Lt Robert R Kerr, co-pilot, 303rd Bomb. Group, 427th Bomb Squadron, B17G, from Chicago, Illinois. Departed England 0700 hours, 29 April 1944, to bomb the target Berlin, Germany.

Heavy flak was encountered over the target area. A concentrated burst knocked out #4 engine, and caused a severe gas leak in #3 feeder tank. The pilot, 2nd Lt Howard J Bohle, feathered the engine, but the gas remaining was insufficient to return to England. He asked the navigator, 2nd Lt John K Brown, for a heading to Sweden.

    Flying over 9/10 undercast the ship crossed the Baltic Sea, through a hole in the clouds land was seen. At the same time a ME 210 attacked the plane, but was shot down by the tail gunner. However, the German pilot evidently had radioed the ship's position to the ground AA batteries, for a barrage of flak was shot up. It was very accurate, hitting the plane square, jammed the stick in a fixed position, knocked out #2 engine; the pilot could not recover control, so he ordered the crew to bail out. The approximate position area was 54 degrees 55' N, 11 degrees 15' E, 1300 hours, 29 April 1944.

Before I left the ship I noticed the altimeter read 15,000 feet, so I waited about 45 seconds before pulling the rip cord. I was directly over the water, but drifting towards land and was able to aid my direction of descent by manipulating the shroud lines. Landed in an open field, about fifty yards from a farm house, where a young boy was watching my actions. Immediately upon touching the ground I released the chute harness, which was a British type, gathered the equipment, placed my Mae West in the folds of the silk, and hid them in nearby bushes. I learned from the boy that I was in Denmark, that the Germans were close.

I started to walk towards the wooded area, but just before I reached it, a man on a bicycle approached, removed his hat and made signs of friendship. I told him that I was American flyer. Speaking broken English he said that he would help me. I followed him by a back road to his home where I was given a good meal and a bottle of beer. After the meal he told me to hide in the woods until dark, that he would return and do all possible to aid in my escape. His wife furnished me with candy, sandwiches and beer; I proceeded to the wooded area he indicated and hid. During the late afternoon I could hear the Germans searching, but they did not come near my hiding place. There were several German planes flying low in search also.

The man and his wife returned at dusk with food, civilian clothing, and a bicycle. He rode with me to a nearby town, where we were met by another man on a bicycle. They escorted me to the village of Eskilstrup, to the home of a school teacher, where I stayed until Monday night. There was the question as to the best way for me to reach Sweden. At first the plans were to put me aboard a boat at Stubbekjobing, bribing the fisherman 4,000 Crowns. The money was obtained, and all the arrangements made when word was received from Copenhagen to wait. Monday afternoon, 1 May 1944, a lady arrived from Copenhagen to accompany me there. I left all my flying clothing, escape kit, and equipment with the school teacher to be destroyed. We left that night and arrived at Copenhagen at 2300 hours, making the trip without incident. Two men met us at the station, and took us to one of their homes, where I stayed until the night of 9 May, receiving excellent treatment. I was in a position to observe many interesting things, and met influential people in the Danish underground.

Tuesday morning, 9 May 1944, a man called and escorted me to the home of a friend, where I stayed until 0200 hours, 10 May 1944, at which time we took a taxi to a rendezvous point at a harbor near the city. Here we were joined by nine Danes, six men and three women, who were escaping also. We boarded a small fishing boat, hid in various spots, then waited until daylight. At 0620 hours the engines were started, and we proceeded cautiously from the harbor, avoiding

German patrol boats and planes which were in the vicinity. At 1000 hours we were in international waters, within sight of Malmo. We waited for the arrival of a Swedish fishing boat, which drew alongside at 1100 hours. We transferred, arriving at Malmo 2200 hours, 10 May 1944.

We were taken to the police station, where I was separated from the Danes, interrogated, given a medical examination, and ration coupons. I was then taken to the American Consulate office.

I departed Malmo for Stockholm Wednesday night, arriving there 0758 hours, 11 May 1944. Lt Herman F. Allen, of the Military Air Attaché office, met me at the station.

Felix M Hardison
Lt Colonel, AC
Military Air Attaché

Evaders who reached Sweden were debriefed by US attaché officials. These reports, like that of Lieutenant Kerr, were added to their E&E reports.

Since the end of the Napoleonic Wars in 1815, Sweden maintained a neutral stance in all international relations and hostilities. When World War II began on September 30, 1939, it appeared that Sweden's neutrality would be challenged, but because of their location on the Scandinavian Peninsula, political maneuvering, and the buildup of their own military, they were able to discourage any outside aggression.

After occupying Denmark and Norway, the Nazis looked toward Sweden. In addition to having a formidable army, the Swedes had another powerful factor in their favor. Germany's primary source of iron ore was Sweden, and the Swedes agreed to continue to provide the important resource if allowed to remain neutral. They threatened to blow up the mines if the Germans invaded. Sweden permitted the Nazis to use their railways to move troops for the invasion of the Soviet Union and allowed their soldiers on leave from Norway to pass through on their way to Germany.

Sweden also provided refuge to Danes and Norwegians and helped train them for the liberation of their countries. Damaged Allied aircraft were permitted to land in Sweden, but their crews were interned for the duration of the war. On July 26, 1943, the "Georgia Rebel," a B-17 from the 535th Bomber Squadron crash-landed on Swedish soil as the first arrival after sustaining damages during an air raid on Norway. The ten-man crew all survived.

Over the next months and years, 129 American aircraft, mostly B-17s and B-24s, landed in Sweden. Their crews, totaling about 1,200, were housed in camps at Falun, Vasteras, and Granna as well as in local hotels and pensions. They were not confined and were free to visit local restaurants, cinemas, and other public facilities. A few were transferred to Stockholm to work in the American embassy.

Swedes, many of whom had relatives living in the United States, were friendly to the airmen. The Americans continued to receive their pay; an aircrew NCO (i.e., noncommissioned officer) was paid more money than a senior Swedish officer and spent it freely. This made them popular with local merchants as well as young Swedish women. A hotel in Karlstad even advertised a dance saying that Americans would participate.

None of the 1,200 airmen who landed in Sweden are considered evaders. MIS-X prepared E&E reports for only thirty-three American airmen who reached Sweden after their aircraft went down in German held territory—thirty-two from Denmark and one from Norway. These reports were primarily based on interrogation by US embassy officials.

As the war progressed, Sweden became more friendly toward the Allies. They continued to sell iron ore to Germany but at the same time designated five airfields for the landing of damaged Allied planes. This was not officially documented, nor were maps provided the Allies, but their locations were common knowledge.

In March 1944, the Allies established an office in Sweden separate from their embassies to assist airmen and others to be repatriated to the United Kingdom. Evaders, unlike crews from planes that landed in Sweden, were not considered internees. According to the Geneva Convention, evaders were considered to be escaped prisoners of war. As a result they were on the initial planes to England.

First Lieutenant Glyndon D. Bell from Richmond, California, was one of the first airmen to successfully evade from Denmark to Sweden. Bell's B-17 had mechanical problems on its way to bomb Danzig on October 9, 1943. Pilot Bell ordered his crew to bail out and then crashed-landed the plane on an island east of Varde, Denmark. "I obtained help from a farmer who loaned me a bicycle and went with me to Hojen. We traveled at night over the main road. A farmer and a doctor in Hogen helped me. They bought two tickets to Copenhagen, the doctor's wife used one; I used the other. One ticket covered the whole travel, ferry (to the mainland) included."

During the ferry ride, two German officers joined Bell at the ship's railing but did not question him. In Copenhagen the Danish underground, including a policeman, put Bell on a fishing boat for Sweden where he went ashore five days after crash-landing.

B-17 pilot Second Lieutenant Howard S. Pauling from Muncy, Pennsylvania, headed for Sweden on April 11, 1944, after his plane suffered severe damage from flak and fighters after their bombing mission over Settin, Germany. He crash-landed in a grassy field on an island that he thought belonged to Sweden. Local farmers informed him that he was on the German-occupied island of Bornholm in Denmark. All ten of the crew survived the crash, but four were captured by the Germans.

The six evaders made their way northwest using their escape kit compasses. Shortly before dark the evaders approached a woman working in her garden to ask for water. Their "phrase list which we carried had no Danish," and they could not communicate what they wanted. At the next farmhouse "the people understood what we wanted and took us in and gave us sandwiches and milk."

Pauling and his five men tried to sleep in a field in a pile of hay and sugar beets, but the cold forced them to return to the farm's barn hayloft. On April 14, the farmer and friends took the evaders to a fisherman and his boat. After the exchange of money and staging to make it look like theft, the fisherman handed the boat over to the Americans. Pauling wrote in his report,

The boat was about 16 foot long, painted green and equipped with four oars, an engine, and a gaff rig sail. We rowed north until daylight, all the time trying to start the engine, but it would not run, so we set sail. About 0600 hours we turned west and sailed in this direction until 1150 hours. At this time we were picked up by the Swedish ship *Borga* about five miles northeast of Hano Bay.

We were brought to Kalmar by them and turned over to the police there at about 0200, April 15, 1944. We remained in the custody of the Kalmar police, under the care of the British vice consul, until we came to Stockholm by train on the morning of April 21, where we were met at the station by Lt. H. F. Allen of the Military Air Attaché Office.

On April 27, 1944, the six evaders returned by air to the United Kingdom.

Pauling also included in his report an incident that followed their arrival in Sweden, writing, "[W]e had the bad luck to have a newspaper man, who falsely claimed to be from the Associated Press, hound us, and we made the mistake of talking to him and letting him take our picture." When the picture and story were printed, representatives of the Danish underground strongly protested to US authorities saying that they could not ensure the safety of future evaders if such information continued to be made public.

The B-17 on which Staff Sergeant Mansfield Hooper from Olympia, Washington, was the ball turret gunner crash-landed on the Danish island of Lolland after sustaining damage from flak on April 9, 1944. Although the plane was mostly destroyed on impact, the Germans later claimed to have recovered four hundred gallons of fuel from one undamaged wing tank. Hooper and another crew member evaded for two weeks, first walking and then hopping a freight train on their way north.

On April 22, the two airmen made contact with the Danish underground who hid them in a small shed covered by a haystack. Two days later they were taken by taxi to Copenhagen where they, according to Hooper's report, "strolled around town, went to a football game, and rested up in general." On April 26 the underground put the two evaders aboard a four-cylinder small boat and took them to Sweden.

After brief interrogation by Swedish police, Hooper and his fellow crewman were given a room in a hotel by the American attaché. Hooper concluded,

> Just before we left Denmark our helpers in the Danish underground gave us a note that is of particular importance because of all the recent newspaper publicity there has been about American airmen coming out of Denmark. The note complained about press announcements of the "great victories" in getting American airmen out of Denmark. It also complained about BBC broadcasts mentioning help for allied airmen. Because of such publicity the Germans were tightening their patrol activities. Unless such releases were stopped, the note said, the Danes would have to discontinue their "ferry command" for British and American airmen. The Danes begged that no mention at all should be made of successful evasion from Denmark.

Nazi fighters knocked out two engines of the B-24 being flown by Hamline, North Dakota, pilot Second Lieutenant Byron E. Logie. He reported,

> I bailed out of the plane at 1100 hours on April 9, 1944. I did my best to make sure that the rest of the crew had jumped, but was unable to be certain because of the interphone being out. I landed in a field near Venslev, where a farmer hid me in a haystack until 2200 hours. At that time a young Dane took me in his truck to a small town nearby where I changed clothes. We then drove to Slagelse where I stayed until the night of April 11 and then to Roskilde where I stayed the day and night of April 12. Thursday, April 13, I took a taxi to Copenhagen where I lived for four days.

On April 17, Danes put Logie on a boat for Sweden where police met him and took him to a courthouse before turning him over to the American vice consul.

Copilot Second Lieutenant Tony P. Gill of Shelburn, Indiana, and navigator Second Lieutenant Charles F. Markowicz from Wellboro, Pennsylvania, crashed-landed in their B-17 on Denmark's island of Lolland on April 9, 1944. They walked northeast for a week, hiding from German patrols in dense woods and barns until a farmer took them into his house and contacted the underground. A guide came, provided them civilian clothes and bicycles, and led them to Copenhagen where, in their E&E report, they said they "mingled with the people on the streets, joined a crowd of onlookers who were watching the Germans unload the remains of our plane from a flat car on a railroad siding, and watched a football game."

On April 24, a guide took Shelburn and Markowicz by taxi to the docks where they went aboard a ship and hid in a coal bunker. When the ship reached Sweden, they left the vessel with the Swedish pilot after he guided the ship into port. They were turned over to local military officials in Malmo and given rail tickets to Stockholm where they were met by the American military air attaché. In their report to the office of the military attaché, the two noted that 150 Danes had recently been sent to Germany as forced laborers for helping a German soldier desert and escape.

One of the quickest and most successful evasions to Sweden took place after pilot Second Lieutenant Kenneth E. Bethe from Abilene, Kansas, crash-landed his B-17 in the vicinity of Store Heddinge, Denmark, on April 11, 1944. A farmer hid the entire crew in the nearby woods and used his tractor to harrow the field to cover their tracks. Later in the afternoon another farmer guided them to his barn where they hid in the hay loft until a truck arrived.

The crew lay concealed beneath hay on the truck that transported them to Copenhagen. There they were hidden and fed by a series of Danes over the next few days. After a week they were placed on a small boat that took them to a larger vessel that delivered them to Sweden. The entire ten-man crew safely arrived back in the United Kingdom on April 26, just fifteen days after crash landing.

Second Lieutenant David C. Besbris, a B-17 navigator from Raynham, Massachusetts, was the only one not captured when his crew bailed out over Norway on November 16, 1943. Besbris, who had survived—as part of a ten-man crew—the ditching of his Fortress into the English Channel just two months before, walked rapidly southwest. After sleeping in a hayshed, he contacted friendly farmers on his second day who told him, according to his E&E report, "not to be afraid of the Quislings (collaborators), because out of 900 people in the district there was only one Quisling." While Brebris discovered walking toward Sweden in the snow difficult, he also found that the Norwegians continued to be helpful, one family serving him rainbow trout. Though not members of any organized effort, the very anti-German locals advised him, "to pretend I had a toothache and couldn't speak if anybody stopped me."

On his third day, Bresbris linked up with members of the Resistance who arranged the rest of his journey that included a ride on a horse-drawn sleigh. In addition, the downed navigator recorded, "I went to Pytten on skis—my first skiing lesson. I found it hard going." On February 8, after nearly three months of evading, he walked across a frozen lake and the border, becoming the only American to successfully evade from Norway to Sweden.

Another unusual route to Sweden was that of Staff Sergeant Norman C. Goodwin, a B-17 ball turret gunner from Bradford, Massachusetts. Goodwin's Fortress was shot down over the North Sea while returning from bombing Bremen on June 23, 1943. In his report he related, "A 20 mm shell exploded in my left leg." Goodwin parachuted and landed in water about fifty miles off the coast where a German rubber dingy picked him up. The Germans treated his wound and transferred him first to a medical sea plane and then to a hospital in Norderney in the Frisian Islands. He was later evacuated to Germany where his injured leg was amputated. On October 19, 1943, the Germans repatriated Goodwin to the United Kingdom via Sweden in an exchange of wounded prisoners. Goodwin is the only former prisoner in the group to have made an E&E report.

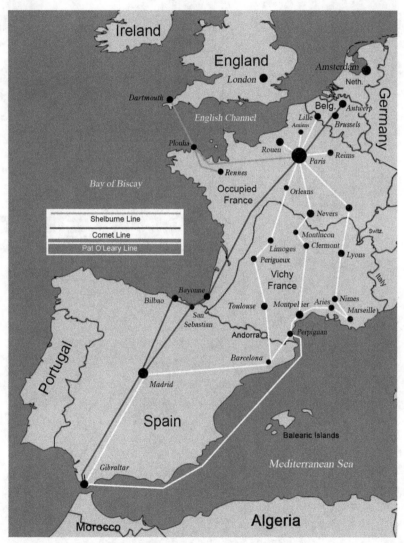

World War II Escape Lines. Map courtesy of Bob Rosenburgh.

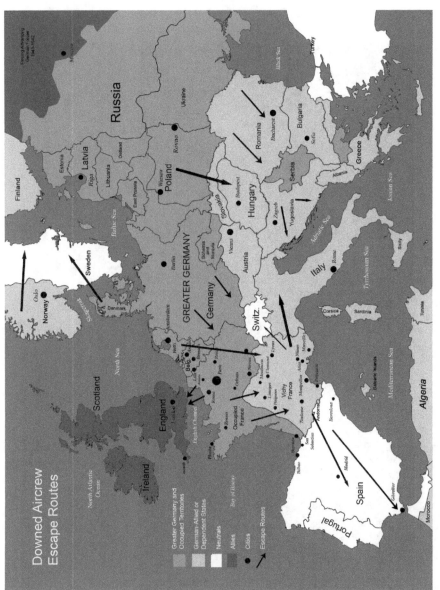

World War II Escape Routes. Map courtesy of Bob Rosenburgh.

B-17 Flying Fortress

C-47 at Gibraltrar

Paratroopers aboard C-47

B-17 Flying Fortress and B-24 Liberator

B-24 Liberator

B-25 Mitchell

A-20 Havoc

P-38 Lightning

P-47 Thunderbolt

P-51 Mustang

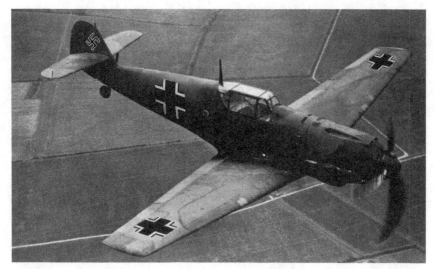

ME-109

FW-190

ME-292

German 88 anti-aircraft gun

LISTS OF PHRASES

FRENCH
ITALIAN
GERMAN
SPANISH

FRENCH

ENGLISH	FRENCH	ENGLISH	FRENCH
One	Un	Twenty	Vingt
Two	Deux	Thirty	Trente
Three	Trois	Forty	Quarante
Four	Quatre	Fifty	Cinquante
Five	Cinq	Sixty	Soixante
Six	Six	Seventy	Soixante-dix
Seven	Sept	Eighty	Quatre-vingts
Eight	Huit	Ninety	Quatre-vingt-dix
Nine	Neuf	Hundred	Cent
Ten	Dix	Five Hundred	Cinq cents
Eleven	Onze	Thousand	Mille
Twelve	Douze		
Thirteen	Treize	Monday	Lundi
Fourteen	Quatorze	Tuesday	Mardi
Fifteen	Quinze	Wednesday	Mercredi
Sixteen	Seize	Thursday	Jeudi
Seventeen	Dix-Sept	Friday	Vendredi
Eighteen	Dix-huit	Saturday	Samedi
Nineteen	Dix-neuf	Sunday	Dimanche
Minutes	Minutes	Week	Semaine
Hours	Heures	Fortnight	Quinzaine
Day	Jour	Month	Mois
Night	Nuit	O'clock	heures

ENGLISH	FRENCH
I am (we are)	Je suis (nous sommes)
British (American)	Anglais; (Américain)
Where am I?	Où est-ce que je suis?
I am hungry; thirsty	J'ai faim; J'ai soif
Can you hide me?	Pouvez-vous me cacher?
I need civilian clothes	J'ai besoin de vêtements civils
How much do I owe you?	Combien vous dois-je?
Are the enemy nearby?	L'ennemi est-il près?
Where is the frontier?	Où est la frontière
BELGIAN	Belge
SWISS; SPANISH;	Suisse, Espagnole
Where are the nearest British (American) troops?	Où sont les forces anglaises (américaines) les plus proches?
Where can I cross this river?	Où est-ce-que je peux traverser cette rivière?
Is this a safe way?	Est-ce-que ce chemin n'est pas dangereux?
Will you please get me a third class ticket to . . .	Voulez-vous me prendre un billet de troisième classe pour . . . s'il vous plaît.
Is this the train (bus) for . . ?	Est-ce-que c'est le train (autobus) pour . . .?
Do I change (i.e. trains)?	Dois-je changer de train?
At what time does the train (bus) leave for . . . ?	A quelle heure est-ce-que le train (autobus) part pour . . .?
Right; left; straight on	A droite; A gauche; tout droit
Turn back; stop	Revenez en arrière; arrêtez vous
Thank you; please	Merci; s'il vous plaît
Yes; No	Oui; Non
Good morning; afternoon	Bonjour
Good evening; Night	Bonsoir
Consulate	Consulat
Out of bounds;	Défense de pénétrer;
Forbidden	défendu

Phrase card

Winged Boot Badge

CHAPTER 14

Italy

SECRET—AMERICAN
MOST SECRET—BRITISH

HEADQUARTERS
EUROPEAN THEATER OF OPERATIONS
P/W and X Detachment
Military Intelligence Service

E&E Report No. 200
Evasion in Italy

November 28, 1943

Name:	Philip F. Teraberry
Rank:	SSGT
Unit:	67th Bomb Squadron, 44th Bomb Group (B-24)
Home Address:	Malcom, Iowa
Target:	Naples
MIA:	July 17, 1943
Arrived in UK:	November 17, 1943

Other members of the crew:

Pilot	1LT	Curtis S. Griffin	MIA
Co-Pilot	2LT	Joseph H. Potter	MIA
Navigator	2LT	Samuel E. Levinson	MIA
Bombardier	2LT	Charles E. Rouser	MIA
Radio Operator	TSGT	David Harrington	MIA

Engineer	TSGT	James C. Corcoran	E&E #199
Top Turret Gunner	SSGT	Ernest V. Swanson	E&E #198
Waist Gunner	SSGT	Robert W. Nicholls	E&E #145
Waist Gunner	SSGT	Gordon H. Greattinger	MIA
Tail Gunner	SSGT	Philip F. Teraberry	Narrator

I left Benghazi on 17 July 1943 as tail gunner in the same crew. We test-fired our guns twice. The first time was at 20,000 feet, and I thought that all the guns were firing except mine. The second time we test-fired was at 22,000 feet; then my gun was firing but the right waist gun was not. When the fighters attacked us, I thought Sgt Swanson shot down one of them and that I got one too. After we were hit by fighters, I saw part of the wing and a supercharger fly by. When we started losing altitude, I came forward in the ship, passing the radio operator, who was taking pictures. He soon followed me. I thought we were at 20,000 feet when I bailed out the rear hatch. I counted six parachutes on the way down. I saw one chute flutter as if it did not work. I thought afterward that it must have been Lt Potter's, for I was told in the hospital at Avellion that the Italians had found someone in the ground up to his knees, and from their description I gathered that it was Lt Potter.

On the way down German fighters circled me, but did not fire. When I neared the ground, I hear bullets zinging by me, and I figured that I was being shot at by civilians from the ground. I saw one man land before me, not far from the place where I landed. I thought it was about 1615 when I came down. In landing I hit a tree and the bank of a gully and broke my nose. I put some cloth from my first aid kit on my nose and then tried to pull my parachute from the tree, but it was too securely entangled. I walked toward the place where I thought the other man had landed and found Sgt Nicholls. We walked to a nearby house. Just as we reached it, a crowd of Italians came, armed with pitch forks and shot guns. Some of them led Sgt Nicholls away, and others took all of my flying kit, escape kit, and purse from me. Soon they walked me to a town, which I understood was Avellino, and put me in a room with Lt Rouser and Sgt Swanson. Sgt Nicholls and Lt Levinson were in another room, as I recall.

After a time some Italians brought in Sgt Harrington, who was unable to walk. They swabbed my nose a bit with alcohol and put some tape on it, but they did absolutely nothing for Sgt Harrington. About 1800 he and I were taken to the Avellino clinic. There we remained from 16 July to 9 August 1943. I did not see any of my crew members afterwards. I have never seen as filthy a hospital: it was uncomfortably full of bed bugs and lice. We were given execrable medical attention *by the Italians. They did not even bother to give us much to eat; we had a little bread and macaroni each day and almost nothing else. They never set my nose, and they did nothing for Sgt Harrington, though, I learned afterwards, he had a broken pelvis. When he could limp a bit, they sent us off to Bari.*

We arrived there 11 August and were put in a camp which I understood had been the headquarters for the 4th Italian Air Force Fighter Command. A number of American aviators were there as listed in E&E Reports 146–155. There was also a Lt. Wilson from the Twelfth Air Force. Again we had little to eat and we were ourselves almost devoured by the mosquitos and bed bugs.

The night I came in an Italian colonel interrogated me through an interpreter. The interpreter was an officer who spoke English like an American. The colonel asked me my home address and some other personal questions, but mostly about our planes. He asked how many bombs we carried, what size they were, how many guns we had on our plane, where we were flying from, what our range was, why we bombed Italian cities when Italians did not bomb the United States, and so on. I did not answer his questions. I was amazed at this interrogation, for I had expected them to use third degree methods on me. The Italian colonel did not press his questions very hard, and his heart did not seem to be in his work. He seemed to think Italy was ready to pull out of the war, and he did not seem to think it could do it too fast for him. He talked to me for only about twenty minutes altogether.

After I had been at Bari for about 18 days, Sgt Sigle came in, and we left the same day that he arrived.

We went to Sulmona with the party who reported in E&E Reports 146–155. Sanitary conditions in the camp were bad. Latrines were completely inadequate. Water spigots were turned on for half an hour twice a day. There was some yellow jaundice in the camp but little foot disease. The camp was a British camp and only some 20 Americans were there. Some of the British prisoners had been there for two years or more, but their morale was astonishingly good.

We understood that there had been a number of escaping Britishers, but it seemed that most of them had been caught again. We heard of one man who spoke Italian and who escaped, dressed himself in a monk's robe, found a bicycle, and cycled right into the Vatican City. There were some tunnels in the camp, but we were not there long enough to begin one of our own. If we had been there longer, we would certainly have begun tunneling simply to keep for being idle continually. One tunnel went under the wall and came up too near the surface of the road outside the camp, giving it away.

A sergeant major in the Italian army who was serving as an interpreter in Sulmona was born in Chicago. There was also an Australian serving in the Italian army.

While we were in the camp, American airplanes hit the munitions factory and railroad near Sulmona. They turned over the camp, apparently using it as a pinpoint.

While we were watching a football match between the English and Scots about 1630 on 11 September, 1943, we heard a crowd of Italians shouting, "La inite inite!" The Italian camp padre had heard the news over the BBC. We were not convinced of the report until we saw Italian papers in the camp the next day and then heard the news over the radio ourselves. Major Cochran of the South African army took charge of the same on 12 September, and we understood that he had information from Pescara about an allied landing and that we should sit tight in the camp. A bugle system of dispersal to the hills and recall was established. We hoped that the major would distribute the Red Cross parcels among the prisoners, in case we had to make a break, but he did not.

We had seen German convoys going through the town ever since 11 September. About 1800 the evening of 12 September we saw a German staff car coming up the road to the camp. We went out one of the holes in the camp wall along with a party which included Sgts Sparks, Winter, Strandberg and several British (among them Penn and Knocker, or something like that). Some of the group wanted to wait for the recall, but we figured that, once out, we had better go on to the Allied lines. It was a moonlight night; we walked on to Campo di Giove. We slept all day in a hay loft near there. An old man offered to keep us in his home for a month until the allied troops came to that area, but Strandberg, Penn, and the two of us thought it was too close to Sulmona, so we walked on.

The night of the 14th we walked up a river bed, heading southeast, and came to Mt. Secine; we slept out near there. From an English-speaking Italian we heard something about the boys in the camp defending it, but we could not straighten out what his story was. We heard that 1,700 prisoners had been taken. We ran into Lt Kinsey who had escaped from prison camp after the Germans had come in.

We were directed over the mountains to Castel di Sangro by an Italian. On the way we saw German patrols going along the roads in Volkswagens.

On the night of the 16th, we walked until 0300 and slept in the woods. The next morning we got food from some goat herders who warned us to avoid Campo Basso since the Germans were there. We slept in an old house the night of the 17th.

On the 18th we came to Agone, where the local police fed us. A Carabiniere warned us to keep to the right of Campo Basso and we started on about 1030, walking up another river bed. Near Belmonte we ran into two other escaped prisoners Sherburn and Langabeer; they did not join us, but we saw them frequently thereafter. We came to Carpinone and wanted to stay there, but a Carabiniere seemed anxious to get us out of town so we slept in some corn shocks outside. On 19th walked to Duronia and spent night in deserted pub. Then walked to near town of Molise and stayed there about two and a half weeks after being warned that our camp clothes were easy to spot by Germans. Finally, on October 22 we reached Canadian lines and were evacuated to Bari and then back to the UK.

Staff Sergeant Teraberry's E&E report is a good example of those of airmen who evaded to Allied lines after the Italian armistice. In 1922, Benito Mussolini and his Fascist Party had seized power in Italy. Although he did not have the support of the *contadini* (mountain people), the communists, or the Royalists, he controlled most of country by the outbreak of World War II. Although Mussolini and Adolph Hitler were friends, Italy did not join the Axis against the Allies until June 10, 1940. The Italians joined the Germans in opposing the British, and later the Americans, in North Africa.

By the summer of 1943, the International Red Cross in Italy had registered more than 84,000 Allied service members as POWs. Most of these had been captured in North Africa, but some, including several hundred American aviators, had been shot down over Italy itself.

On July 9, 1943, the Allies invaded Sicily and completed the takeover of the island on August 17. The Allies crossed into mainland Italy on September 3 causing the Italians to agree to an armistice. That did not, however, bring an end to the fighting in the country. German units still occupied the northern half of Italy where some of the war's most intense fighting took place over the following months. In fact, the Germans in far Northern Italy were some of the last to surrender after the fall of Berlin.

Most of the Italians operating their POW camps simply walked away once the news of the armistice reached them—some as late as September 8. Orders came from Allied command for the prisoners to remain in place until liberated by advancing units. The Germans had different ideas and dispatched units to gather POWs and transfer them to camps in Germany.

Unrest swept through the POW camps as none of the prisoners had any desire to be transferred to German work camps. An estimated 55,000 crawled or walked out of their wire prisons and took to the hills. A few walked north attempting to reach Switzerland, but most headed south toward Allied lines. The Allied advance slowed, and the Germans recaptured most of the escapees and only a few successfully evaded.

Evaders in Italy faced many of the same problems, but also the same assistance, of their fellow aviators who came down in Western Europe. Italians, especially the contadini, had little use for the Germans and had a strong sense of humanity in helping those in need. They shared their meager food and directed evaders to safe houses and provided guides for escape.

The Germans countered with patrols and English speaking plants to root out helpers. Bounties were offered to those handing over evaders or to those who revealed the identity of assistors. Italians who were caught assisting evaders paid with their lives and the destruction of their property. In the town of Anversa, the Germans posted the death sentence of one of the most prolific helpers. "The German Military Authority has condemned to death Michele del Greco, shepherd, of 47 years, for having sheltered 56 English, French, Russian, and American POWs escaped from concentration camps."

Most of the successful American evaders were shot down on bombing missions that originated from bases in North Africa. Waist gunner Sergeant Clarence H. Rothrock from Spokane, Washington, took off from Benghazi in his B-24 on August 16, 1943, to bomb the Foggia, Italy, airfield. Enemy fighters shot down his Liberator shortly after they made their bombing run. Captured by Italian soldiers after bailing out near Attela, he was taken to a hospital with a leg injury sustained in his parachute jump. Rothrock escaped from the hospital on September 10 but was quickly recaptured. When bombers flew over Attela causing a diversion, he escaped once more only to again be recaptured. He escaped a final time during still another bomber attack. He related his experience, writing,

We walked all that night and the next day until 1800 hours. We then slept in a farm house [*sic*]. The next day we rode mules to Brindisi where we stayed in a schoolhouse until the morning of the 17th. A British commando patrol arrived and took us to their headquarters outside Taranto. We were taken to Taranto the next day and stayed until October 1. We then flew to Salerno, then to Catania, and then to Algiers, and on to the UK where we arrived October 18, 1943.

Staff Sergeant Ernest V. Swanson, a B-24 top turret gunner from Smolan, Kansas, took off from Benghazi on July 17, 1943, to bomb Naples. After making the bomb run, enemy fighters and flak shot down his Liberator. Swanson bailed out and was immediately captured by Italian civilians who spit on him and beat him with sticks. Once in jail he was treated badly by officers but, he reported in his debriefing documents, "the guards, however, were very good." When he refused to give any information more than his name, rank, and serial number, his captors told him his parents would not be notified of his status. He maintained his silence.

His Italian captors moved Swanson through several camps to Servigliano where, he reported, the food was "abominable" and "it was the Red Cross parcels which really kept us alive." The only problem with the parcels was that canned goods had to be eaten quickly because the guards punctured containers to be sure they contained no contraband.

On the night of September 8 Swanson learned of the armistice and, afraid he would be taken north by Germans, escaped and headed south to Allied lines. At one time during his evasion, he pretended to be a shepherd herding three sheep when approached by a German patrol. He successfully reached British lines on October 12.

Technical Sergeant James C. Corcoran from Brockton, Massachusetts, was a radio operator on the same B-24 as Swanson. After landing, he evaded capture for a day by hiding in olive groves until Italian militiamen took him to a local jail where town people came to see what they thought was "a really curious object." He was then moved to and interrogated at several camps before the armistice was declared. He then left camp and headed south. Corcoran briefly joined an Italian partisan group and continued to walk south, as far as thirty miles in seven hours despite extreme foot problems. He reached Canadian lines on October 21 and flew to North Africa and then to the United Kingdom on November 11.

A third member of the Swanson-Corcoran B-24 crew, waist gunner Sergeant Robert W. Nicholls from Mina, Nevada, was captured shortly after reaching the ground. He, too, left his POW camp after announcement of the armistice to make his way toward Allied lines. Along the way he received a map, food, and civilian clothing from Italian villagers and farmers, including one man he recorded in his E&E report, "who had lived some years in Boston and spoke good English." Once, when he reached a river, he crossed on the back of a horse provided by an Italian farmer. Like fellow evaders in Italy and all across Europe, Nicholls used haystacks for hiding and resting.

First Lieutenant Horace W. Austin, a B-24 pilot from Virginia Beach, Virginia, was immediately captured after being shot down on August 16, 1943. Before he could escape from his Italian POW camp after the announcement of the armistice, Germans took control and loaded the prisoners aboard a train bound for Florence. Austin escaped from his railcar and intended to steal a boat and make his way to the Adriatic. He stopped to sleep when it got dark only to awake the next morning to discover he was almost in the middle of a German 88 mm battery. He slipped away and changed his route to walk south overland.

A friendly Italian farmer provided Austin a dry place to sleep in his stable and then gave him civilian clothes before taking him to town where he purchased the evader a railroad ticket. At the end of the rail line, Austin resumed walking south. He covered as many as thirty-five miles a day until safely reaching British lines on October 18.

First Lieutenant Elbert L. Dukate Jr., a copilot from New Orleans, Louisiana, evaded in Italy for the longest period of time of any American after his B-24 ditched in the Mediterranean on August 1, 1943. An Italian seaplane picked up Dukate in his dingy and took him to a POW camp on the mainland. When he learned of the armistice and heard rumors that Germans would move the prisoners to Germany or shoot them, he escaped. An Italian workman gave him food and led him to a haystack to sleep.

Over the next months, Dukate, who spoke Italian, hid in various farm and village homes, and managed to secure an Italian identity card. In December he took a train to Rome. In May the Germans raided the apartment where he was staying. Dukate wrote in his report, "I maintained that I was an Italian who had been taken to the United States at the age of three years, had been naturalized, and have been repatriated to Italy in 1942." The Germans apparently believed his story but nevertheless detained him in a local jail.

On June 7, the jail guards unlocked the cells, explaining that the Allies were nearby. The next day Dukate joined Allied troops and, on June 18, nearly a year after being shot down, he was taken to Air Force headquarters in Foggia and arrived back in the United Kingdom on June 27.

The longest document in the MIS-X files detailing evasion in Italy includes the story of ten evaders, E&E reports 146–155. Although from several different planes, all were shot down on August 18, 1943. These men met in the POW camp at Bari and escaped together after learning of the armistice. Walking rapidly, and with the assistance of Italian helpers, the ten reached Canadian lines on October 7.

CHAPTER 15

Romania

HEADQUARTERS
EUROPEAN THEATER OF OPERATIONS
P/W and X Detachment
Military Intelligence Service

AN ACCOUNT OF THE USAAF LOW ALTITUDE ATTACK OF 1 AUGUST 1943 ON THE PLOESTI, ROMANIA OIL REFINERIES AS GIVEN BY 1st Lt WORDEN WEAVER, 67th BOMB SQUADRON 44th BOMB GROUP (B-24)

September 10, 1944
On August 1, 1943, after leaving the IP and going into the target the particular group of which I was a member was still together. On approaching the designated target I could see two of the large oil storage tanks burning, each sending up a large column of black smoke. I believe our bombs hit the designated area of the target. Immediately after the bombs had dropped we went through both of the columns of smoke. I believe the heat in the smoke columns threw the plane up to a greater altitude.

On coming out of the last column of smoke, I went to low altitude. Only a short way from the target the plane received a direct hit in the nose, in the nose wheel compartment, probably by a 37 mm projectile. This hit did not hinder the flight of the plane. Following this hit we were hit many more times by ground fire.

Just before rejoining the group the No. 2 engine lost its oil pressure and the oil temperature gauge showed on oil temperature of over 300 degrees c. The engine soon ran up to an exceedingly high RPM at which time the propeller was feathered (or fused to a standstill as the case may have been) and the engine stopped. Believe this engine failure was due to mechanical reasons because the engine's oil tempera-

ture gauge showed a steady decline in oil pressure before the target was reached. At that time, however, it was believed to have been instrument trouble.

Soon after No. 2 engine had stopped, No. 4 engine caught fire. At this time we were rejoining the group formation. Although the No. 4 engine fire stopped temporarily it soon broke out again causing the engine to lose all power and making it impossible to feather the propeller. The wind-milling propeller, of course, set up a heavy air drag.

After rejoining the group formation we were unable to stay with it for more than a few minutes because the aileron controls had been shot out and the plane was gradually losing altitude with only two engines running. During the time we were with the formation, enemy fighters attacked us. I don't believe they did any damage to the plane if they hit it.

Soon after leaving the group formation I gave the order to prepare for a crash landing, realizing that it was impossible to maintain flying speed much longer. We were not much more than 100 feet above the ground at this time so parachuting was out of the question.

I brought the plane down in a large corn field. Everything went all right with the landing until just before the plane came to a stop. At this time the left wing evidently scraped the ground causing the plane to swerve to the left and at the same time the fuselage rolled to the right. On stopping, the nose was partially rolled under the front section of the plane. The bomb bay section crashed into the radio compartment, the top turret falling down on the flight deck at this time.

At the time of the crash landing three officers, 2d Lt Snyder, 2d Lt Sorenson, and myself were in the cockpit; one enlisted man, T/Sgt Schettler, was on the flight deck and one officer and four enlisted men, 1st Lt Reese, T/Sgt Hinely, S/Sgt Breedlove, S/Sgt Brittain and S/Sgt Suponcic were in the tail-section of the plane.

Immediately after coming to a stop, fire broke out in the mid-section of the plane and began to spread rapidly to other parts. I was able to get out by bending forward the already partially cracked wind shield on my side of the cockpit. This turned out to be the only escape passage in the cockpit.

Lt Sorenson, in attempting to follow me through the opened wind shield, was caught in his parachute harness about his waist and was unable to free himself. At this time Lt Reese and Sgt Hinely, regardless of the fact that the plane was almost completely enveloped in flames and the ammunition exploding, came to the rescue of Lt Sorenson and Lt Synder and Lt Reese cut Lt Sorenson's parachute harness with a government issued hunting knife. After doing this Lt Reese and Sgt Hinely pulled both Lt Sorenson and Lt Synder out of the cockpit.

All crew members got out except Sgt Schettler, who I believe was killed in the crash. Sgt Schettler was the engineer and top turret gunner. His guns were in action during the entire fight with the enemy fighters and I believe his efficiently operating of these guns kept the fighters away until we landed.

On leaving the plane a ME 110 circled overhead, evidently reporting our position. Lt Sorenson, Sgt Hinely and myself walked away together, the rest of the crew going in another direction. Lt Sorenson's left leg, side, and arm were burned, the burns were of the second degree type, large blisters appearing on the burned surfaces. Sgt Hinely was not injured but rather than attempt to escape he chose to stay with Lt Sorenson and myself until we reached some place where we could receive medical attention. The day was hot and clear.

Our first stranger was a Rumanian farm boy. By the use of the Rumanian language script given us by the intelligence department we were able to convey the fact that we needed assistance. The farm boy was friendly and proceeded to help us.

After about fifteen minutes walking we reached a small farm on the edge of a village. Here many villagers gathered around us, giving us water and trying to help the burns by administering some sort of oil by use of feathers. On asking for a doctor, the villagers led us toward the center of the village. At almost every gate someone offered us butter milk or something else to drink.

At a street corner we met the remainder of the crew. Lt Synder's hands were burned and Sgt Suponcic had been hit in the back by flak or pieces of his tail turret which exploded on being hit. The others, Lt Reese, Sgt Breedlove and Sgt Brittain received minor burns and scratches.

We were led to an officer (probably military) by a soldier. After staying here several minutes, he took us to a first aid station, several of us riding a straw covered wagon en route. Our wounds were dressed at the first aid station. We were treated kindly and questioned by an English speaking woman. While here a Rumanian colonel arrived with a military detachment.

We were next loaded into the straw covered back of a truck and taken to the town of Gaesti about six miles north and about forty miles west of Ploesti. Here we were put in beds at a small military hospital known as a Lazarett. We were fed well and visited by many of the townspeople who filed through our room. Three hours after arriving, our wounds were treated again. Late in the evening another crew including Maj Yaeger arrived at the Lazarett.

The next day everyone was taken to Bucharest except Capt Ferguson, who had a broken leg, Lt Sorenson, Lt Snyder, and myself. We were removed to a private hospital in Gaesti for further treatment.

Sgt Hinely, being uninjured, was taken to an improvised jail in a garage in Bucharest. Here he, along with some other air crew members, was kept until a prison camp could be made ready.

On August 4, those of us remaining in Gaesti were also taken to Bucharest. Here we received regular medical attention in the large military hospital. We were kept in a large ward along with many other wounded air crew members.

On 18 August all of us in the Bucharest hospital were taken to Military Hospital No 415 at Sinaia. Here we were comfortably situated and well cared for.

After several weeks at Sinaia, the German and Rumanian interrogation officials arrived and proceeded to question us. One of the German officers asked me such questions as "Have you ever seen the Eiffel Tower?" In other words he wanted to know if I had ever made any raids over France. As far as I know they used no forcing means of extracting information.

By 19 November my burns had healed enough to permit me to go to the prison camp at Timnis de Jos.

As prisoners of war we received good treatment. On the whole our food was good. The building was adequate and kept clean. We had plenty of outdoor space for exercising.

Lieutenant Worden Weaver, from Theodore, Alabama, was one of the earliest evaders and prisoners in Romania. He spent more than a year as a POW before Romania changed sides in the war and released Weaver and other Allied captives.

Romania adopted an official position of neutrality at the outbreak of World War II. Germany permitted this stance on the condition that they have a monopoly on Romanian exports including oil and agricultural products. In 1940, the Soviet Union annexed portions of Eastern Romania while Germany and Italy demanded they relinquish Northern Transylvania to their ally Hungry. Fascist elements then assumed control of the remainder of Romania when Marshall Ion Antonescu forced King Carol to step down in favor of his son Prince Michael.

Under Antonescu's leadership Romania joined the Axis Powers on November 23, 1940. When the USAAF began bombing the Ploesti oil fields in the summer of 1942, Lieutenant Weaver and many other Americans became prisoners of the Romanians.

Staff Sergeant Philip A. Rurak, a B-24 waist gunner from Chicopee, Massachusetts, did not find the Romanians as kind as did Lieutenant Weaver. Rurak escaped his POW camp on November 13, 1943, and evaded for three days before his recapture. In his E&E report he wrote,

> When I got caught the Romanian guards started beating me with their fists and rifle butts. They brought me to their guard house and everyone was striking me. One of the guards hit me in the head with his rifle butt and I bled badly. Later their sub-officer came in and hit me with his pistol. I was then ordered into a sweat box. This box is so narrow that a man's shoulders touch the sides. A man can't sit here, there is so little room. Still, they ordered two of us in the same box and left us there all night.

B-24 pilot First Lieutenant Elmer H. Reinhart from Oakland, California, made it eighty miles from the Ploesti oil fields before F-109s forced him and his crew to parachute from their disabled Liberator on August 1, 1943. Taken prisoner, he wrote that he found "Romanian troops were anxious to get out of the war. They liked the Americans as did civilians but would become enraged at us when our buddies bombed their cities and when we tried to escape. They feared the Russians and didn't like the Germans."

Hit by flak over the Ploesti target, the B-24 piloted by Major William H. Yeager Jr. of Hebbronville, Texas, crash-landed into the Romania countryside on August 1, 1943. Despite the fact that the Romanians were ill-prepared for American prisoners and seemed to know little about the Geneva Convention, the airmen in Yeager's crew stated they were treated well, provided medical care and suitable living conditions, and served "excellent" food. Previously, the Romanians, according to Yeager's report, "had only Russians, whom they treated as slaves." Yeager also noted that one of their Romanian interrogators, First Lieutenant Valjuan, had been the minister of finance in the old Royal government until the Antonescu takeover when he had been reduced in rank to a junior army officer.

Yeager and seven other airmen were transported by train on August 15 to Frankfurt, Germany, for further interrogation. When they revealed nothing of use to the Germans, they were returned to the POW camp in Romania.

Staff Sergeant Charles T. Bridges's B-24 crashed in a Romanian cornfield after bombing Ploesti. The waist gunner from Anderson, Indiana, recorded his observations, writing, "Romania was the richest country I've seen for food stuffs I have seen since leaving the USA. Romania was able to supply food stuffs to Germany and still have surplus for her own needs."

Bridges managed to meet high-ranking Romanians and to acquire insights on their thoughts of the war. He reported,

I talked to Queen Helen soon after crashing. The Queen was always our friend and also King Michael her son. Her help and kindness to me were always to be remembered. The Romanians are highly emotional and react at the drop of a hat. They are hospitable, but can also be very cruel. Romania, and I have talked to many people, many are very good friends, fear a revolution of cessation of European war between democratic people and communists. Serbs whom I have talked to fear all the Balkan and Slavic countries will turn toward communism.

Organizations outside the Romanian military provided additional support for the prisoners but conflicts among them hindered aid reaching the POWs. Second Lieutenant Raymond P. Warner, a B-24 navigator from Lexington, Kentucky, parachuted into Romania after flak hit his Liberator, causing it to break up in midair on January 8, 1943. He wrote, "The Romania Red Cross and Blue Cross fought constantly and we thereby often lost out on things. The Blue Cross is a political organization headed by dictator Antonescu's wife. The Blue Cross was always granted easier access to us. It was the Blue Cross that set up our chapel and gave us an organ."

Warner also explained that the food and aid packets from both organizations were often pilfered before arrival. He reported, "The Romanians claimed the Germans did the stealing, but the Romania government shipping orders were wadded up to fill the space created by these thefts."

In the summer of 1944, the Soviets advanced into Romania. When it became evident that the German/Romania army would not be able to stop the Russian advance, King Michael and his supporters overthrew Antonescu and, on August 23, 1944, declared war on Germany and joined the Allies.

A US Military Intelligence Report dated July 15, 1944, stated that there were 543 American POWs in Romania at the time of the regime change. King Michael began immediate efforts to repatriate the prisoners after he assumed power and flew the former POWs to Bari, Italy. Only a few made it to London to be debriefed by MIS-X. None of the reports are lengthy. Most just record the crew lists, how their planes were brought down, and personal data of the evader.

Yugoslavia

HEADQUARTERS
Co B 2677th Regt OSS (Prov)
APO 512 US Army

1 December 1944

SUBJECT: *Report of ACRU Unit—"Halyard"*

To: *Col George Kraigher*
     Commanding Officer, Air Crew Rescue Unit (ACRU)
     APO 520, US Army

1. *Original mission headed by Lt George Musulin, assisted by Sgt Mike Rajacich and Sp(X)2c Arthur Jibilian, USNR, parachuted into Pranjani, Serbia on night of 2/3 August 1944. After preparing airstrip it was possible to land DC-3's to evacuate hundreds of airmen. Col Kraigher, chief of all ACRU missions in the Balkans, sent me into Pranjani night of first evacuation to assist Lt George Musulin and to deliver vital radio material and supplies. I landed on night of 9/10 August 1944. Later in the month of August Lt George Musulin returned to Bari, Italy leaving me in full charge of ACRU-HALYARD mission. Then after Ranger Unit entered Pranjani, Serbia, Sgt Rajacich left ACRU-HALYARD to join Ranger Unit. That left me and Sp(X)2c Arthur Jibilian to take charge of further Halyard evacuations.*
2. *Work Accomplished—Evacuations:*
   a. *Night of 9/10 August 1944 first Halyard evacuation took place, Pranjani airstrip, Serbia. Four planes DC-3's landed. 48 American airmen evacuated.*

b.   *10 August 1944, first daylight evacuation, Halyard, Pranjani, Serbia. 177 American airmen evacuated, 6 British, 12 Russians, 4 French, 8 Jugoslavs, 7 Italians.*

c.   *26–27 August 1944, second night evacuation Halyard, Pranjani, Serbia. 15 Yank airmen evacuated.*

d.   *27–28 August 1944, third night evacuation, Halyard, Pranjani, Serbia. 43 Yanks, 2 British, 4 Russians, 9 Italians, 2 Polish and 1 United States citizen.*

e.   *5–6 September 1944, fourth night evacuation, Halyard, Pranjani, Serbia. 20 Yanks evacuated.*

f.   *17 September 1944, second daylight evacuation, Koceljevo airstrip. 20 Yanks, medical mission plus 1 Ranger (4 persons), 1 French, 1 Italian.*

g.   *1 November 1944, third daylight evacuation, Bunar airstrip. 3 Yanks and Ranger mission of 4.*

h.   *27 December 1944, fourth and final evacuation of Halyard mission, Bunar airdrome. 20 Yanks-the Halyard-ACRU mission, 2 Jugoslav officers, 4 French, 4 Italians and 1 American citizen.*

3. *Sorties:*

a.   *Night drop 5 August, Ravna Gora. Received supplies 6,000 lbs.*

b.   *Second night drop 27/28 August, Pranjani airstrip. Received supplies and equipment 3,000 lbs.*

c.   *First daylight drop, Bunar airstrip, 25 December, Christmas. Received clothing plus food for American airmen.*

4. *Travels:*

a.   *Movements did not start until our airport and evacuation was menaced by approaching Partisans. We moved from Pranjani, Serbia, on the night of 10 September 1944, north.*

b.   *Left Pranjani, 10 September 1944: Teocin, Brajici, Srasla Bukua, Suvoborski Put, Planinica, Pastric Mionica, Lukouac, Krsna Blaua, Koceljevo (new airstrip located), Dragini, Sabac, Clapcauic, Bradouince, Medjasi, Batkovich, D Crnjelovo, Brezovo, Polje, D Brka, D Zabar, Slatina, Tolisa, Kopriuna, Kozuhe, Grabska, Doboj, Bunar (new airstrip found), Kakmus, Vasiljeuci, Stog, Prelog-Slavic, Okgrulica, Nesisi (new airstrip), Stog, Panik, Kakmus and Bunar.*

5. *Who Accompanied us on travels:*

a.   *From Pranjani to Koceljevo Gen. Mihailovich with his staff, guard and his troops, 3 American airmen, 4 medical staff—Dr. Mitrani, 2 Sergeants plus Dr. Maj. Carpenter, 4 Ranger Mission, 2 ACRU.*

b. From Koceljevo to Boljanic—Gen. Milhailovich, staff troops and guard, ACRU Unit 2, Ranger Unit 4 and Yank airmen 3.

c. Bunar to Okruglica. Gen. Milhailovich, troops, staff and guard.

d. From Okruglica to Bunar. ACRU Unit, 7 Yanks, 1 American citizen and 40 Nationals.

6. How We Received Report of Incoming Airmen to our Area:

a. Gen. Mihailovich consented on informing all commanders to send all Yank airmen immediately to Pranjani, Serbia for evacuation. While on the move all commands were informed to send Yank airmen to Gen. Mihailovich Hq. to be evacuated as soon as new airstrip is found.

b. All Nationals in Serbia, Bosnia, Montenegro, Slovenia, Dalmatia and Slovenia were informed by Gen. Mihailovich to save and protect, hide American airmen from enemy troops and send soonest to nearest command and from there through channels to general headquarters.

c. Airmen were delivered usually by guides or if area dangerous for travel by company or regiment.

d. Airmen arrived by foot, carts, horses and even by stretchers.

7. Treatment of American Airmen by Local People:

All airmen were given beds if available, blankets and food. All were taken into the Serbian homes, best of hospitality. People who gave up their beds slept on the floor. Always three meals a day. Very happy to have Americans in their homes. A free loving people who continue to say that America is their hope. They have absolute faith in us.

When leaving the people would fill up baskets of meat, fruits, bread, cakes, etc. for the airmen to eat on their way back to Italy, also brandy to drink. Souvenirs of all kinds were presented to the Yanks, everything from knives, native shoes and trinkets, wood water cans, insignias, everything that Americans usually try to collect. Also when leaving, airmen would be showered with flowers. People would cry with joy. Nothing was too good for our boys and I and every one of them appreciate every moment with these people and will never forget them.

8. Locating Airfield:

Usually information from Gen Mihailovich of possible areas for landing in safe and secure locality. We would then travel to area reported, then local commandant would advise on possibilities in local area. Area would be looked over and checked for possibilities of landing C-47's. Usually trees, ditches, hedges, fences would have to be cleared. Then again holes would have to be filled, also furrows filled. All work would be done by Chetnik Nationals as ordered by

Gen. Mihailovich. We had no difficulty in locating airports for landing of C-47's.

9. *Work in Laying out Airdromes:*
Altitude of area in feet, measured out distance by feet, located best possible direction for landing, level all rough spots and hills, cut tall grass, fill deep spots, holes with rocks, wood, dirt plus covering with grass turf. Cut down trees, all holes after being filled were tampered with crude implements. Usually have to recruit 1,000 Chetniks to level field, 200 carts to haul dirt and sod.

Airport commandant appointed to take care of airdromes, usually a higher ranking person in the vicinity. He was to take care of pylons and other equipment for daylight and night evacuations. I supervised security over flares and fires at night, smoke pots, runway markers, recognition signals, etc.

10. *Total Number Evacuated:*

American	*343*
British	*8*
Russians	*17*
French	*9*
Jugoslavs	*11*
Italians	*24*
Polish	*2*
US Citizens	*3*

Plus evacuation of Ranger mission, medical unit, and ACRU unit.

Total Number that I assisted in evacuation that was before taking full charge of ACRU Unit:

American	*225*
British	*6*
Russians	*12*
French	*4*
Jugoslavs	*8*
Italians	*7*

The total number left in NAT territory is: 15 Yanks, Slovenia, National Headquarters, Hotedrsica, 4 Yanks and 1 British left in Dinar Alps, National Headquarters Command, Pope Djuich.

11. *Communication Set-up Difficulties and Suggestions:*
First and foremost, radio operator was inadequately equipped for the field. He should have voltmeter, spare tubes, condensers, fuses, bulbs, vibrators, sol-

dering kit, tool kit and spare parts for charging engine. At least two batteries which should be replaced every two months as they lose strength after so many charges. A special suitcase, similar to the one we had, should be designed with traps to hold radio in place. Main difficulty on this trip was battery trouble. We went in with three 40 Amp batteries and all three were at times used for a contact for at least one hour. We had to use one battery for five hours. Gas should be dropped frequently about 20 gallons every month, also oil. Gas is very difficult to find in the field as well as oil. Radio equipment is the most difficult and hardest to carry while traveling. It is heavy and fragile. The horse carrying our radio fell down and receiver was badly smashed. We transmitted one message blind before we went to Chetnik radio operator who had an old obsolete English radio set which he had taken out of a plane. Its B.F.O. was shot but by using his receiver and our transmitter we maintained contact with the base. Three batteries were involved in the procedure, two for his receiver and one for our transmitter. I strongly recommend that all radio operators in OSS be given extensive training in how to repair a radio set. On the whole communications were excellent. We received 87 messages. 115 messages were sent.

12. *Physical Status and Hardships of American Airmen while en route to Evacuation Base:*

   American airmen are very hard to move because of their inability to walk. Since they have not done any infantry training, one could easily see why they were unfit for this kind of walking in Jugoslav mountains. They needed constant attention and rested frequently they could not travel for more than an hour at a time and then would rest for at least half an hour. A lot were injured but that was taken into consideration and that was taken care of by putting them on horses, the mission of course would walk.

Nick A. Lalish
1st Lt, Sig. Corps

None of the successful evasions from Nazi-held territory are as complex as the stories of those airmen who returned after being shot down in Yugoslavia. Axis forces invaded the country on April 6, 1941, and quickly conquered the former kingdom. Divergent factions, based primarily on ethnicity and religion, formed resistance organizations that fought against both the Axis and each other.

After the German occupation, General Draza Mihailovich and his Serbian Royalist Chetniks took to the hills to oppose the Nazis. When Germany invaded the Soviet Union the following June, Josip Broz, better known as Marshal Tito, led a force made up mostly of Croatian Partisans into the fight. The Partisans received aid primarily from Russia, but the British and Americans also backed their efforts against the Axis. The United Kingdom and United States also provided some support to the Chetniks but this diminished as evidence surfaced that they were collaborating first with the Italians before their exit from the war and then with the Germans.

Partisans and Chetniks alike shared the same enemies and allies. Both wanted to free their country from the invaders but had vastly different visions of the postwar government. Tito saw a united communist Yugoslavia while Mihailovich envisioned a return of the king and a Royal government. Chetniks and Partisans initially cooperated in their efforts against the Germans until Mihailovich learned of Tito's efforts to communize villages. He asked Tito to cease his efforts, declaring they should act as soldiers and not politicians. Mihailovich said, "Let's drive the Germans out of our land, and then we can worry about the type of government we want."

Tito responded by increasing his promotion of communism. The Chetniks and Partisans continued to fight the Germans but soon their most intense warfare was against each other.

Despite massive bloodshed within the country, including the evacuation and extermination of its Jewish population, the war in Yugoslavia did not merit major attention of the Allies. They remained satisfied with the two groups of local guerillas keeping a large number of German troops occupied far away from the invasion of Italy in the west and the Soviet advance on the Eastern Front.

American airmen began to parachute and crash-land into Yugoslavia when the US 15th Air Force opened bombing operations against Romania's Ploesti oil industry from airfields in North Africa on April 1, 1943. These operations increased in the fall of 1943 from bases in newly secured Southern Italy. Germans captured some of the downed airmen, but the majority were taken in and assisted by either the Partisans or Chetniks.

The British, who considered Yugoslavia to be within their sphere of influence, began parachuting agents into the country as early as January 1944. They successfully made contact with the Partisans and, with Tito's approval, began operations to evacuate Allied airmen. In some instances early in the conflict, the Chetniks turned evaders over to the Partisans so they could be rescued by the Allies. The British severed ties with Mihailovich and avoided direct relations with the Chetniks for two reasons: first, they had determined that the better organized Partisans were likely to gain control of the country after the Germans departed and, second, they believed the Chetniks were receiving aid from the Nazis. As a result, there were no plans to rescue American and other Allied airmen in the custody of the Chetniks.

Elements in the USAAF were unwilling to leave their fellow airmen behind, but the British and Russians vehemently opposed any rescue operations in Chetnik territory. When briefed on the situation, American general Bill Donovan is reported to have said, "Screw the British, let's get our boys out."

Responsibility for the extraction of the evaders in Yugoslavia came under the Air Crew Rescue Unit (ACRU) of the Mediterranean Allied Air Forces commanded by Colonel George Kraigher. Initially, ACRU had neither known locations for the downed aircrews being held by the Chetniks nor any reliable method of communications with them.

In an after action report classified "Secret" and dated August 15, 1944, Kraigher explained,

From reports on parachute descents observed by returning combat crews, and from subsequent radio signals received from General Mihailovich, it was learned that a considerable number of American airmen were in Mihailovich territory. Operation instructions for their evacuation were drawn up on 28 June 1944. This operation was given the code name Halyard.

During July, several radio contacts were made with Mihailovich and several attempts were made to drop a party by parachute. For reasons of incomplete or corrupt signals or weather, the attempts were unsuccessful.

During the last week in July, signals were picked up from an unknown station using the call letters TKO. This station identified itself as one operated by a group of American airmen and through further exchange of signals definitely identified several of their crew members and their units. A code was worked out, using serial numbers of designated crew members, references to nicknames, etc. It was learned that 150 American airmen were awaiting evacuation and arrangements were made for the reception of an evacuation party which was to drop in by parachute.

The "unknown station using call letters TKO" was First Lieutenant Thomas K. Oliver from St. Louis, Missouri. Oliver, a West Point graduate, had parachuted into Yugoslavia after his B-24 sustained crippling damages from flak and enemy fighters while bombing the Ploesti oil complex on May 6, 1944. Helpers moved him to Mihailovich's headquarters at Pranjani where he joined a hundred or more other evaders whose numbers were growing each day as they arrived from other camps.

Oliver observed that food and clothing, particularly footwear, were in short supply. Although the Chetniks generously shared what they had, the evaders remained cold and hungry as they faced the possibility that the Germans would soon overrun the facility. As the senior officer in the camp, Oliver took charge and secured a radio from the Chetniks. Not having a codebook or any other way to transmit confidential information, Oliver had to improvise.

His message stated:

1. Mudcat driver to CO 520.
2. 150 Yanks are in Yugo.
3. Shoot us some workhorses. Ask British about job.
4. Our challenge first letter of bombardier's name, color of Banana Nose Bengino's scarf.

5. Your verification last letter of Chief Lugs name color of fist on club wall.
6. Must refer to Shark Sqn 469 Group for decoding.
7. TKO 0-24855 Flat Rat 5 in lug order.

Intelligence officers at 15th Air Force successfully decoded the message. From their files is the following explanation as later provided by Oliver:

1. My airplane was named the Fighting Mudcat. APO 520 was the 15th Air Force in Italy.
2. The Germans knew this. The 15th Air Force did not; so I felt it just as well to come right out with it. At the same time, sending this message was somewhat controversial among the 150 airmen. Some feared the Germans would pick up the message, home on it, and capture us.
3. The workhouse of World War II was the C-47, of course. We hoped the literal Germans would visualize old Dobbin getting shot.
4. The first letter of my bombardier's name would be known to the 15th Air Force but not to the Germans. "Banana Nose" Benigno was a pilot in our squadron who always wore a white scarf.
5. Col. Munn, who commanded our group, at one time wrote on the wall of our officers' club in Italy, "All lugs in the 459th Group sign here." M. M. Munn, Chief Lug. Considerably further down the list I signed myself as Thomas K. Oliver, Flat Rat 5. My tent mates and I had labeled our tent as being "Poker Flat." There was a red mailed fist painted on the club wall.
6. My squadron had painted sharks teeth and mouths on B-24s—quite a sight to behold.
7. My initials, serial number, and reference to the writing on club wall.

The ACRU radioed Oliver and the Chetniks, "Prepare reception for 31 July or first clear night following."

During the night of August 9–10, the first evaders were evacuated to Italy from a crude airstrip at Pranjani. Over the next days and weeks, more and more evaders made their way with assistance of the Chetniks to Pranjani and other airstrips. By the end of September, five hundred

Americans as well as more than one hundred additional Allied soldiers and civilians had been rescued from Yugoslavia. Many of the Americans left boots or shoes behind for their Chetnik helpers. The Operation Halyard planes not only took out evaders, but also, they delivered supplies and a team called Operation Ranger that unsuccessfully negotiated a surrender of remaining German forces.

Missions on November 1 and December 27 removed the last of the evaders. When Halyard officers tried to convince Mihailovich to accompany them to Italy, he refused saying, "I prefer to lose my life in my country, than to live as an outcast in a strange land. I'll stay with my soldiers and my people to the end, in order to fulfil duty that my king gave to me. For King and Fatherland—Freedom or death!"

Evaders who escaped Yugoslavia were not debriefed by MIS-X. Instead, they were interrogated by staff of the 15th Air Force upon their return to Italy. These reports were briefer than those conducted in London and most were written by the interrogator rather than in first person by the evader. Each report contained a paragraph, stating, "Never in enemy hands."

The most common complaint by the evaders from Yugoslavia was that their preflight briefings had not distinguished the differences and conflicts between the Partisans and Chetniks. One such comment represents many, reading, "There is insufficient briefing in escape procedures as regards the Chetnik situation." Returned evaders also noted the purses in their escape kits had held Italian and French money but not currency easily used within Yugoslavia.

Typical of the reports was that of B-24 crewman Staff Sergeant Robert H. Knowlton from St. Olean, New York. His report states,

While on a mission to Ploesti on June 6, 1944, plane was hit by flak over the target and after the rally was attacked by fighters. Due to the flak and fighters, the aircraft lost the power in Nos. 1 and 2 engines. On the return to base No. 4 engine was lost.

Crew bailed out midway between Cacak and Pozega and landed within a two-mile radius. Upon reaching the ground

Chetniks from Mikhailovich's Headquarters picked up the crew and took the crew to Headquarters. They remained there until the evening and then traveled in a northeast direction to Prejina. We remained in the immediate vicinity of Prejina until evacuated by C-47 transport on August 10, 1944.

Sergeant Robert L. Hooper, a B-24 gunner from Everett, Washington, was another evader rescued by Operation Halyard. On the return leg from bombing Ploesti on April 5, 1944, Hooper and five fellow crewmen safely bailed out after being hit by flak. He reported that the plane "disintegrated in the air." Met on the ground by Chetniks, the six evaders were taken to the vicinity of Solt and "were treated excellently," according to Hooper. The Chetniks moved them toward the Adriatic coast where they joined another 169 Americans. From there, on August 10, he was on one of the first C-47s that flew evaders to the Bari airdrome.

B-24 nose gunner Staff Sergeant Leon W. Hoadley, from Deposit, New York, was also assisted by the Chetniks and evacuated by C-47 after being shot down following a bombing raid on Vienna on August 22, 1944. Partisans and Germans both pursued and fought pitched battles with his Chetnik helpers during his evasion. During one battle, Allied planes dropped supplies to the Partisans, causing Hoadley, according to his report, "quite some worry as to the Chetnik reaction," but they continued to provide help to the aviator.

While evading with the Chetniks, another B-24 nose gunner, Staff Sergeant Karl Clive Smith from Springville, Utah, was pursued and fired at by both Partisans and Germans after being shot down on November 17, 1944. Finally, he moved by horseback to a Halyard airfield and made it aboard one of the operation's final C-47 flights on December 27.

P-38 pilot Captain Charles King from Tucumcari, New Mexico, suffered burns and a broken back when he crash-landed on November 7, 1944. Chetniks picked him up and disguised him as a wounded comrade, at times traveling on the main roads with the Germans, King explained in his report, "to avoid the Partisan troops." King also reported that the Chetniks treated him well and shared their meager food. He met General Mihailovich before being evacuated on December 27.

Evaders who were helped by the Chetniks found other avenues than Operation Halyard to escape Yugoslavia. P-51 pilot First Lieutenant Richard L. Grose from St. Joseph, Michigan, avoided a German search and joined the Chetniks after crash-landing on September 2, 1944. He then left the Chetniks and made his way to Romanian authorities in Orsovo and then to the Soviets. After a brief stay with the Russians, he rejoined the Romanians who secured him a flight back to Italy on September 15. In his debriefing, Grose noted that the Chetniks were grieved because London radio gave propaganda and information that turned all people in Yugoslavia against them. He said the Chetniks were friendly toward the United States but hated the English and that both Chetniks and other Romanians believed the United States would help rebuild their cities after the war. Grose reported that the Russians, who were often drunk, mistreated the Romanians. Rape was common, causing them to want the United States to come in and police the country. He added that the only good equipment carried by the Russians was what they had secured from the Americans.

First Lieutenant Lewis M. Perkins, a B-24 pilot from Utica, Kentucky, went down on July 28, 1944, after his plane was damaged by another Liberator blowing up in midair. His experiences with the Chetniks showed the inconsistencies in their treatment of evaders. They shot at him while he was still in his parachute and then treated him more as a prisoner than as an evader. He reported, "During the time in Chetnik hands, there were constant battles with the Partisans. The Chetniks seemed to be allied directly with the Germans, and were receiving supplies from the Germans." On September 15, Perkins ran from the Chetnik camp to join the Partisans who, according to Perkins, "took charge and started him off for evacuation the next day."

Second Lieutenant Robert L. Eagan, B-24 copilot from Chicago, Illinois, joined several other Americans with the Chetniks after being shot down on April 15, 1944. The group was moved several times, often being chased by Germans. Finally, after several months, with shoes and clothes missing or worn out and with little food, the Chetnik commander told them to stay behind and join the Partisans. They did so and were eventually evacuated through Russian lines.

Aviators who fell into the hands of the Partisans generally received good care, particularly medical. Partisans, however, had a rather "cold attitude" toward the Americans and often told them about the greatness of the Soviets. Some evaders complained that the Partisans stole their personal items.

Second Lieutenant Seymour L. Rosenthal, a B-17 navigator from Pasadena, California, crash-landed on November 22, 1944, and was met by a boy "wearing the Partisan red star." Loaded on an ox cart, Rosenthal was taken to Sanski but, as he noted in his report, all his possessions were stolen along the way. In Sanski he joined about sixty Allied airmen in what they called the "guest house." According to Rosenthal, their beds were straw-invested with fleas and lice, parachutes were used as covers, and the food was bad and in short supply.

Partisans did their best to evacuate evaders as quickly as possible. Sergeant Gene C. Nelly from Livermore, Kentucky, was picked up by Partisans soon after bailing out of his B-24 on October 7, 1944. According to his report, the Partisans moved him by ox cart and treated him "nice" and "food was best Partisans could provide." A colonel even provided his quarters to another evader. Partisans turned Nelly over to the English mission, and Russian pilots flew him to Bari six days after he landed in Yugoslavia.

B-24 tail gunner Sergeant Theodore C. Schaetzle Jr. from Akron, Ohio, spent only five days as an evader before his evacuation to Bari by a C-47. Civilians and Partisans moved him by boat to the British mission who arranged his flight to Italy. In his debriefing he said he was "well treated."

Major Horace A. Hanes from Bellflower, Illinois, provided some of the most detailed information about the Partisans after being shot down on January 7, 1944. He reported, "Partisans always gave the best they had but didn't have much. Germans seem to be able to take any areas they decide upon except the hills." Hanes estimated that there were 300,000 active Partisans. He observed, "Officer personnel seemed pretty good. Many of them trained in Russia and there were many high ranks from the old Royal Yugoslav army." Hanes was evacuated on March 20.

Mihailovich and the Chetniks continued to fight the Germans, Russians, and Partisans until their final defeat on May 25, 1945—seventeen days after the surrender of Germany. Tito's Partisans, now in charge of the country, captured Mihailovich on March 13, 1946, and placed him on trial on June 10 for "high treason and war crimes." A group of American evaders who had been helped by the Chetniks established "A Committee for the Fair Trail of General Mihailovich" but their lobbying efforts to Congress and requests to testify at the trial were not successful. Mihailovich was executed on July 17 and buried in an unmarked grave. His final words were, "I wanted much; I began much; but the gale of the world carried away me and my work."

CHAPTER 17

D-Day and the Maquis

SECRET
HEADQUARTERS
EUROPEAN THEATER OF OPERATIONS
P/W and X Detachment
Military Intelligence Service

E&E Report 828
Evasion in France

Date: 13 July 1944

Name: French M. Russell
Rank: 1LT
Unit: 406th Bomb Squadron, 801st Bomb Group (B-24)
Hometown: Stillwater, Oklahoma
Target: Central France
MIA: May 6, 1944
Arrived in UK: July 9, 1944

Other members of the crew:

Pilot	2LT	Murray L. Simon	E&E #704
Co-Pilot	1LT	French M. Russell	Narrator
Navigator	1LT	John A. Reitmeier	MIA
Bombardier	1LT	John B. Mead	MIA
Radio Operator	TSGT	Phillips B. Latta	MIA
Top Turret Gunner	TSGT	Leo F. Dumesnil	MIA
Waist Gunner	SSGT	Homer G. Collier	MIA
Tail Gunner	SSGT	Graham S. Hasty	P/W

I landed in a wooded area, pulled my parachute down from the trees, and hid it and my Mae West under some scanty brush. My first impulse was to look for Lt Simon to whom I had yelled on the way down, but I did not want to attract attention by yelling for him. I headed northwest to get away from the plane, sticking to fields close to woods, as I had been told in S-2 lectures. It would have been faster on roads and I think just as safe since I landed at night. I walked cross-country until about 0430. I was wearing worn out oxfords, so that I had to keep on my flying boots. I could hardly have walked in anything worse. At daybreak I lay down in a field close to a dry lake bed, well surrounded by trees, and tried to go to sleep but could not.

I rested until 0600. I examined my escape aids and hid some of my flying equipment and my boots under brush. I put on my green shirt inside out, scuffed up my shoes as I had heard in S-2 lectures and stuffed my escape equipment into the pockets of my flying jacket. At 0715 I walked to the first farmhouse, where a Frenchman was milking, and whistled from the road. I had in the meantime studied the phrase list enough so that I was able to explain that I was an American flier. The man took me to his wife and I had my first encounter with that impossible problem of trying to get a drink of water in France. The Frenchmen offered to feed me, but I was still too excited to eat. I sat there hoping that these people would take me to an underground group, but I could see that I was not making much headway. When I showed my map my host pointed out where I was and told me to go west because there were a lot of Germans toward the east.

I was so tired that I did not think that I could last more than another hour. I went to a village café where I saw a couple of men drinking wine. The proprietress asked me what I wanted, and knowing nothing else to do, I pointed to a wine bottle, which I paid for with the smallest French bill I had. I knew that I could not walk far in the shoes that I had and that I should look for help early. But for the shoes I would have struck out on my own long since. When the proprietress was alone I showed her my crash bracelet and told her that I was an American flier. She fried some eggs for me and called in everybody who came along the street, just to show me off. I ate my eggs while half a dozen or so people watched. A little girl who was supposed to know English came in with a dictionary. I showed her my phrase card and explained that I wanted civilian clothes. She declared that the gendarmes knew that I was there and were coming for me, but I was hidden in an upstairs room, and a woman brought me civilian clothes.

Later I was given a jug of wine, a loaf of bread, and some cheese, put on a bicycle, and told to follow a woman at some distance. We started out in the direction that the old peasant had warned me against going. We came to a main road and the woman left. I saw a couple of men up ahead and followed them. Soon they motioned for me to join them. One of them seemed to know who I was. They took me to a couple of cafes for wine, at one of which a young fellow who spoke a little English took me out in the alley and asked me what I wanted to do. I was a bit startled by the question but I explained that I wanted to go to England. When he asked me how I wanted to go, through Spain or by the Maquis, I was not certain what to say. There had been a rumor at our group that if we got in with the Maquis we would get out quicker than by heading for Spain on our own, so I indicated interest in the Maquis. At another café a German officer and civilian were sitting at a table talking. The Frenchman told me that the civilian was a German from the United States. Some disturbance occurred outside and the Germans went out to see what was happening. My friend went over to steal a cigarette for me from the pack they had left on the table. The German officer returned just then and saw what he was doing. But the German had had enough drinks to be rather happy, so the Frenchman talked himself out of the difficulty, and the German gave him the cigarette. The German officer saw me smoking the cigarette and my friend with a self-rolled one and came over to see what was going on. My friend gave another long explanation to cover this situation with the result that the Germans wanted us to come over and play cards with them. I nearly dropped through the floor at the suggestion and to my dismay my friend seemed rather willing to go over. I told him that it was absolutely out. The German was insistent that we play, but the Frenchman finally talked him out of it. By the time that we had left I was in a cold sweat. I was thankful that these people talked so much with the hands, for my French was almost non-existent.

I was then taken to a place from which my journey was begun. I was moved to a number of places without making much progress toward Spain. Finally I was told that all the people who were keeping me were going to the Maquis, and no one was left who could give me shelter. I decided then to go to the Maquis myself. When we arrived at a town in Maquis territory and the people heard that Americans were there the whole town turned out for us, singing Tipperary and other songs and piling us with souvenirs. There I met Lt Cater (E&E Report No. 827).

There was great excitement when we heard of the Normandy landing. A few days later we heard rumors of imminent German attacks against the Maquis in our section. Late the evening of 10 June we heard that a Boche division was on the road some three kilometers away. We had been told that we would be warned in case of an attack, but we knew that German attacks had taken place before without warning. We had also discovered that the dispersal plans seemed to cover the disappearance of everyone but us. When we got reliable but unofficial news that the Germans were close we thought that we had better be moving. We held a council of war to decide what we would do. The Allied officer who was more or less the senior of our group of airmen knew of a cave and thought that we should hide there for a couple of days and see how the attack progressed, confident that the Germans could not find us there. Lt Cater and I were about the only ones who did not think this plan was a good one. We thought that if the situation was bad enough to require moving our hiding place, which was an excellent one, we had better leave the area entirely. If I left the area I had no intention of coming back. After considerable discussion a couple of men went over to take a look at the cave, and decided that it was unsuitable. The whole group of us packed up our stuff and left this Maquis section early in the morning of 11 June.

We saw some villages burning in the section which we had left. After we had walked some distance and were well out of Maquis territory we had another conference. Most of the men did not know what to do and were inclined to stick with the senior Allied officer, whose plan was to wait in the woods for a couple of days, living on the country, and then to move back into the Maquis section when things quieted down. I wanted to leave on my own, and a couple of RAF men wanted to do the same thing. Lt Cater had already decided to go also, so the four of us left together.

We found supper, bed, breakfast, and a map at a farmhouse. A friendly gendarme told us that no Germans were in the town which we were near. On another occasion a woman with the help of a little boy who spoke English showed us where to go. Once we hid from a truck, only to run into the drivers in a café in the next village. They turned out to be friendly and wanted us to join a Maquis group toward which they were heading. By that time we had had enough of the Maquis, but we thought that we might go along and try to get bicycles from them, the better to be able to continue our journey on our own. We were taken to a very friendly group, but after a couple of days we learned by chance that they had no real connections. Things also did not seem to be going too well for the Maquis and we decided that we had better leave. By that time we decided that four men traveling together were much too conspicuous, so we left the two RAF men.

We walked a considerable distance, taking great pains to keep well separated while going through towns. We went by train to one town looking for people with whom I had stayed before. We were unable to find the people and were sheltered by some farmers. We took a train to another place and approached a house at which I had stayed, taking care not to give the people away or to get into the wrong hands if the people were gone. My friends were still there and were once again most helpful. They got identity papers for Lt Cater, laid out a route for us, and gave us sug-

gestions for travel. They also gave us a paper saying that we were deaf and dumb and wanted a ride, and told us to stop cars and show this note. We knew that cars with gasogene equipment were very unlikely to be German. Parading as deaf and dumb, however, seemed to us likely to attract too much attention. We were taken to a hotel for the night and the next morning were put on an early train which we were told had no control. Some militia man, however, came through checking papers, and we passed this test all right.

After a long ride on a slow train which stopped at nearly ever station we set out on foot again and crossed a large river at a bridge without any trouble. After considerable distance we took another train. When we got off we noticed every-body rushing up to get some sort of a pass from a controller, apparently because the Maquis were active in the section and strangers needed a paper to certify to their genuineness. It seemed just a routine operation, so we queued up, but about the time that we reached the controller he started asking questions. That seemed too difficult, so we left and took the shortest way out of town. After a considerable distance we found shelter at a farmhouse where we were told that we were again in a Maquis section. This group did seem to have some connections, so we decided to stick around. For a number of days we lived comfortably in Maquis controlled towns, well entertained as Americans. Ex-collaborators wanted to show that they were good for something and opened up their stores of wine, which we spend a good deal of time drinking. From there we were taken to a place from which the rest of our journey was arranged.

Evading capture by crossing the Pyrenees into Spain largely ended in the summer of 1944. For one thing, by that time Germans had infiltrated and shut down most of the lines, either executing or imprisoning its members. But the main reason the torturous route became irrelevant, however, was the Allied invasion of France on June 6. With friendly forces now on the continent and spreading their control toward Paris, evasion efforts became easier. Instead of facing long journeys across Europe and the mountains, now all the evader had to do was find a hiding place and wait to be liberated by the advancing Allies. Despite the dangers, numbers of French, Belgian, and Dutch civilians remained willing to assist the down aviators by providing shelter and substance.

English-speaking Gestapo agents, dressed as Allied aviators, infiltrated the lines and then tortured members to reveal the identities of other helpers. The Germans also offered bounties to collaborators for reporting neighbors who assisted evaders. By the spring of 1943, both the O'Leary and Comet Lines had been compromised. Only the Shelburne Line remained secure. Segments of the Comet and O'Leary organizations, as well as smaller lines, continued to guide evaders to Spain over the next year, but most of the original helpers were either dead or in German concentration camps.

Before the Germans infiltrated the lines, help for downed airmen were readily available. B-17 navigator First Lieutenant Gilbert T. Schowalter of Milwaukee, Wisconsin, was brought down on December 12, 1942. In his report he stated, "We were in the hands of three organizations before we got into this last one and finally caught up with an organization that got people out of France. It seems that the entire population of France is an Organization. It is their duty to help us, to feed us, and get us out of France."

By the spring of 1944, the situation had drastically changed, as noted in a MIS-X comment to the report of Second Lieutenant Roy W. Carpenter Jr., a B-24 bombardier from Chicago, Illinois, shot down by flak over France on March 2, 1944. The amendment stated, "In several instances lately helper organizations have broken down in last stages due to interference by the enemy. In such cases the evaders have been given the choice of holing up indefinitely or attacking the Pyrenees on their own. At this time of the year the latter course is feasible, it the evader is in good condition."

P-47 pilot First Lieutenant John Zolner from Ravena, New York, was shot down on his fifty-fifth mission over Holland on March 8, 1944. He reported, "On April 20, we were told that the organization line to Spain had been broken so we would have to be taken to Switzerland."

A comment attached to the report of B-24 navigator Second Lieutenant John B. Wood from Utica, New York, who went down in France on June 2, 1944, noted that he was "probably the last man to come out by the old Burgundy Route." Wood arrived in Spain in late August.

Resistance groups formed in France, Belgium, and the Netherlands immediately after the German occupation. In addition to the "lines" organized to assist the evasion of Allied airmen, underground cells published anti-Nazi newspapers, provided intelligence to the Allies, conducted sabotage against German facilities, and assassinated enemy soldiers.

Within Belgium, about 5 percent of the population actively participated in the underground. This resistance was fragmented by political and regional divisions with no countrywide organization. The Dutch resistance, composed of Communists along with various religious and independent groups, focused primarily on hiding those wanted, including Jews, by German authorities. In addition to assisting evading airmen, the Dutch underground gathered and provided intelligence on their occupiers.

France had the most active and effective resistance against the Nazis in occupied Europe. Formed initially by young men who escaped to the countryside to avoid conscription as forced laborers for Germany, these rural resistors were known as Maquis. With much of the world looking at Vichy France as collaborators, if not allies of Germany, the Resistance offered patriotic encouragement to the belief that the country would once again be free and independent.

The Resistance organizations of the three occupied countries of France, Belgium, and Holland became much more formal and effective upon the Allied invasion of France. With support from advisors, communications equipment, arms, and ammunition were parachuted into remote drop zones, and Resistance organizations took on a more active role in the liberation of their own countries. By far the most active was that of the French Resistance, which was organized as the French Forces of the Interior after the D-Day invasion.

With lines mostly neutralized and the Allies advancing, it was a natural progression for evaders to hunker down and remain in place until they could be liberated. Some, however, became inpatient and began walking toward the sounds of battle and friendly lines.

Staff Sergeant Waldo W. Shows, a B-26 radio operator from Taylorsville, Massachusetts, went down over France on April 13, 1944. He followed the advice of helpers, who told him the escape lines were mostly broken up and to hide until the anticipated invasion. He wrote in his debrief, "On June 15, we heard the first American guns." Shows began moving toward lines. He encountered a military policeman who looked at his dog tags and said, "If you are American you will be treated OK." The military police turned him over to an Air Force liaison who had Shows flown to the beach and then on to the United Kingdom.

American airmen delivering paratroopers and glider infantry in advance of the Normandy beachhead also were shot down and became evaders. C-47 navigator Second Lieutenant John H. Hendry from Jamaica, New York, successfully delivered nineteen paratroopers to Normandy on June 6, 1944, before being shot down near Cherbourg. A French farmer hid and fed him until he was rescued by an American unit on June 21.

First Lieutenant Wilbert G. Laird from Pittsburgh, Pennsylvania, piloted a glider on D-Day. In his report he wrote, "We left our base on June 6 at 0200 in a glider carrying a 57 mm gun and three airborne men. Our mission was to land and fight with the paratroopers. Over the French coast we ran into a smoke screen and broke away from the towing plane."

Laird crash-landed and his group evaded for six days to the east before running into a young German soldier ("aged about 16") who was on a bicycle. The German recognized the Americans and went for his rifle, Laird related, "but I stopped him with my bayonet. He burst into tears and begged for his life, telling us about his mother. He was so young and I did not know what to do with him so I took his gun and left him. I told him if he talked I would come back and cut off his ears." Laird soon reached an American unit.

Those Americans captured by the Germans while evading also faced post–D-Day changes. On June 18, 1944, MIS-X staff wrote in a comment, "It may be well to note here that immunity from punishment for being caught evading in civilian clothing, even with dog tags, can no longer be assumed, now that the invasion has begun."

In France, the greatest change to those evaders who avoided German capture after D-Day was the Maquis assuming the responsibility for their safety and repatriation. This had begun even before the Normandy invasion because of the breakdown of the escape lines. Many of the evaders volunteered to fight alongside the Maquis while waiting for advancing Allied units.

The Maquis were not alone in their battle against the Germans and in providing help to evaders. Private First Class Grover C. Lawrence of the 30th Infantry Division from Mattox, Virginia, was freed from his German captors by the Maquis on August 26, 1944. He wrote of his experience, "In charge of them were a 21-year-old British sergeant major, a 25-year-old French lieutenant, and another British lieutenant. All had been dropped in by parachute about a week before with arms and ammunition, and they seemed to be organizing the resistance."

B-17 pilot First Lieutenant James C. Cater from Maspeth, New York, bailed out over France on April 28, 1944, and was immediately assisted by the Maquis. Cater remained with the underground fighters for two months before reaching Allied lines and returning to the United Kingdom on July 9.

Lieutenant Colonel Holt at MIS-X added a comment to Cater's debriefing noting, "The adventures of LT Cater in the Maquis are typical of irregular troops anywhere. Lack of responsibility and organization, some banditry, and a general happy-go-lucky attitude should not, however, lead one to conclude that such forces are not to be taken seriously."

In addition to sheltering evaders until they were liberated by advancing Allied units, the Maquis also took great risks to assist some in reaching the Pyrenees to cross into Spain. First Lieutenant Joel W. McPherson, a P-47 pilot from Lakewood, Ohio, bailed out over France after his fighter ran out of gas on January 29, 1944. After evading for a week, he joined a Maquis unit that raided wealthy homes for supplies on the pretext their owners were collaborators. A few days later Germans overran the Maquis and captured McPherson.

McPherson escaped two weeks later and joined another Maquis unit who escorted him and a group of refugees to the mountains. Before they could cross, a German patrol killed the Maquis helper and the local guide who were to take them to Spain. McPherson reported what happened next, writing, "A few days later a guide was found and we reached Spain."

In a comment to McPherson's report, Lieutenant Colonel Holt wrote,

An increasing number of evaders are bound to fall in with the Maquis, where free ways, lack of discipline, and recklessness may be a shock to us. This story is a fair example. Before condemning the Maquis for a lot of brigands we must remember that for four years they have been hunted, tortured, and shot—which tends to break down notions of the sacredness of property. They are apt to treat wealthy farmers and owners of chateaux as their natural enemies, as indeed, is the case. But the Maquis are on our side.

In addition to helping evaders reach Spain or protecting them until the arrival of the Allied advance, the Maquis also evacuated airmen by other means. Second Lieutenant Flamm D. Harper, a P-38 pilot from Ogden, Utah, crash-landed in France on July 15, 1944. French farmers gave him civilian clothes and hid him in a cave before taking him to a large Maquis camp where he was told it was now impossible to evade to Spain. Harper remained with the Maquis for three weeks before he was evacuated to the United Kingdom on a British transport plane that landed in a farm field delivering supplies to the Resistance.

It was not always easy for evaders to reach the Maquis. The B-17 on which Sergeant Robert P. McPherson from Sedalia, Missouri, served as the tail gunner, collided with another Fortress. In his E&E report, McPherson gave his account, writing,

I came down somewhere in Luxembourg on July 9, 1944. I had heard in PW lectures that Luxembourg and the lower part of Belgium were mostly pro-German so I hid in the woods until dark and then moved west. I walked for five days through woods and then I came through some small villages. My clothing was a pair of fatigue pants and a heated jacket. I didn't seem to draw much attention in the small villages. When I came to the Belgium and France border I was stopped by two custom officers for my papers. I mumbled a few words and pointed back the way I came and turned around and started walking back. They made no effort to stop me. I went around them through the woods and came on west. I got a loaf of bread from a French woman that day, the first I had eaten in 11 days except for what was in my escape kit. The next day I stopped in a café in St. Laurent and there I got some food and clothes. I stayed there for 11 days and then I was turned over to the Maquis who sent me to a small village in France were I stayed unit the American troops came in.

Maquis gave little quarter to captured Germans. P-51 pilot Major Archibald W. Thompson from Walton, New York, went down near Strasbourg on August 28, 1944. He reported that, once on the ground, he "spent one night giving first aid to 10 Germans captured and shot by Maquis."

The Germans were even more ruthless in their treatment of the Resistance fighters. B-17 pilot Second Lieutenant Murray L. Simon from New York City joined the Maquis after being shot down on May 6, 1944. He summarized his experiences, stating,

One year is considered the average working time for a member of the resistance organizations before being caught. In St. Etienne when the Gestapo caught resistance people they were tortured to reveal names and addresses. One such man had his eyes gorged out and another was submerged in freezing water until unconscious, revived, and beaten, and the process continued until the man talked or died. In any case these men are killed whether they talk or not. Also in this area the Germans had, after capturing certain members of the Maquis, hung their bodies on a bridge at the edge of town.

Second Lieutenant Joseph A. Lilly, a P-47 pilot from Brooklyn, New York, escorted B-17s on a bombing mission on Berlin on April 25, 1944. In his debriefing he reported, "We got lost returning from our escort mission, thought we were in England and came into land at a field only to discover that it had been bombed and that German fighters were on it. The Germans opened up on us, but we managed to get away. Later flak got me over Lorient." French farmers guided him to the Resistance shortly after he landed. Gestapo agents later overran the Maquis camp, captured two resistance fighters, and kicked them to death. The Germans denied locals the decency of burying the bodies.

A MIS-X comment added to Lilly's report stated, "This new chapter of our adventures among Resistance groups is sufficiently grim, one would think, to dispel any illusions about German treatment of their enemies."

After the D-Day invasion, the Allies increased their airborne efforts to drop arms and supplies to the Maquis. Nazi fighters shot down Second Lieutenant Edward Tappan, copilot of a B-24 from Tucson, Arizona, while he was dropping supplies to the Resistance on July 5, 1944. His plane exploded in midair; he was the only survivor. The Maquis unit he was resupplying assisted him until American ground forces liberated him on September 13.

Maquis units often harbored large groups of evaders before the arrival of the advancing Allies. B-17 pilot Second Lieutenant Andrew Clayton from Glasgow, Virginia, went down over France on April 25, 1944. On June 26, he joined about fifty evaders in the Maquis camp. Another member of Clayton's crew, bombardier Staff Sergeant Charles D. Middleton, from Huntington Park, California, made his way to another Resistance camp on May 27 to join150 evaders.

Evaders generally received good care in the Maquis camps. Captain William M. Davis, a P-38 pilot from Leesburg, Florida, found the Maquis "well organized" after going down on July 7, 1944. He included in his report that one camp even had a miniature golf course.

Along with their praise for the help of French civilians, evaders expressed their confidence in the Maquis. According to Technical Sergeant Dirvin D. Deihl, a B-17 top turret gunner from Long Beach, California, who went down on May 30, 1944, and stayed with the Maquis for more than three months, "I was in the hands of the organization all this time and never doubted for a minute that I wouldn't be brought back to safety."

Another consequence of the D-Day invasion and the Allied advance across France was the relocation of MIS-X from London to Paris after the liberation of the city on August 25, 1944. In a letter to an evader, now back in the United States, Captain Dorothy A. Smith wrote on December 15, 1944, "Do write us sometime and tell us about yourself. We are all here in Paris with the pleasant job of saying thank you to all the boys' friends (helpers)."

CHAPTER 18

Airborne and Infantry Evaders

HEADQUARTERS
EUROPEAN THEATER OF OPERATIONS
P/W and X Detachment
Military Intelligence Service

E&E Report No. 2077

Questionnaire for service personnel
Evading or escaping from enemy occupied countries

Name:	*William E. O'Brien*
Rank:	*SSGT*
Unit:	*82d Airborne Division*
Home address:	*Huntington Park, California*
MIA	*June 7, 1944*
Arrived in UK	*June 31, 1944*

July 5, 1944

Take-off time from our marshalling area at Saltby was scheduled for 23:38. Our plane was 2R-U, the crew had flown paratroops into Sicily and Italy without error and so we, being a lead plane, had a navigator so all in all we felt pretty secure in the hope that we would hit our "DZ" on the nose.

We took-off at 23:38, assumed our place in the steadily growing formation as lead ship of the left element. We left the coast of England near Lands End at 01:14 and dropped down to about 300 ft.

The formation was perfect over the water, in the plane we tried to crack jokes to keep our minds off of the task that lie ahead of us, but it was impossible. I have always been fairly religious but I think I became more devout in a few minutes up there than I possibly could have done in several years under ordinary circumstances.

We approached the coast of France from the west flying over the Iles of Jersey and Guernsey, we received our first unquestionable welcome over these islands. Small arms fire came up at us from everywhere looking like a million fire-flies on a summer evening. As we came over our land-fall the small arms fire became increasingly thicker and the ship began to dance around as the result of the flak barrage.

We took our "Mae Wests" off and gave ourselves a final check to be sure that everything was SOP. We had crossed the coast at 02:01 and got the "Red" light at 02:02. It was very difficult to stand up in the plane due to the flak and now the fog made it impossible to see the ground.

We checked equipment and sounded-off, and the captain jump-master called back, "2 minutes." I turned to Capt. Slanina and said, "I'll see you on the ground." Just then we got the "Green light" and the jump-master hollered "Let's go men." The stick began to move and it became harder and harder to stand up, as I approached No. 3 position my right ankle buckled on me and I fell. The Capt. walked on top of me and by the time we could regain our feet we were too far past the "DZ" so the Pilot made a circle and I stood in the door.

When I got the green light I jumped out and the Capt. followed me. When my chute opened I saw a "T" of fire under me and explosives were going off from the "T." The tracers were coming up at me and I heard some bullets popping through the silk of the canopy. I saw the Capt. drifting to my right over a road. I landed pretty hard in an orchard about a half mile from the road.

I heard "Jerries" hollering all around me and the explosives were still going off from the "T" that I thought at the time was ours. I started out in the direction I thought was south in order to meet up with the rest of the stick. I had only gone about 200 yards when I was fired on. I tried to circle around them but I couldn't so I decided to make my way back to where I left my chute. I went past that point to try and make contact with the Capt. but there were Germans on the road, so I crawled back to my chute until 0700 when some Frenchies came over and told me that the Jerry had gone and that there were other Americans a half mile away. They took me past the town to a road junction where I formed up with the rest of my stick. We found from the Frenchies that we were at Magneville, about 10 or 12 miles NW of our "DZ."

Capt. Dawse, the jump-master, had injured his right ankle on the jump and he decided to remain with the equipment while the rest of us, less one man with the Capt. as guard, headed out east in an attempt to reach our lines. We left Magneville at 11:15, there were 15 of us in the party, we stuck to the hedgerows and had scouts out in advance and a rear guard. At 13:30 two of the boys had to fall out because of injuries sustained on the jump. The rest of us moved on south by east. At 15:15 we were sighted by 8 Jerries on bicycles We backtracked about 3 miles, during the run we lost track of 3 men. Then the 10 of us started out again this time due south.

At 16:50 we came to a town in which there was a Luftwaffe rest camp, so we had to hit the ground and crawl out of the area. During the retreat the Capt. and 2 men became separated from the rest of us. We formed up again about 20:00 hours when we meet an infantry major and Lt with about 10 men. Now we had 24 men, we figured out position as "Rayan," north west of Orglandes.

So at 23:00 we split up into 3 squads and traveled south east in an attempt to reach our lines. The first opposition we met was at Biniville where the first squad was fired on from the church steeple and grave-yard. We retreated to high ground above and to the rear of the town and left a rear guard of 5 men at that point.

The others went back into the town to try and force their way through. At 04:15 they did not return as scheduled and since we had heard firing when they entered the town we sent a scout into the village to check on them. He returned and said the men were not in the town. We heard machine gun fire south of the town so we decided that they had made the break and couldn't wait for us.

We checked our position and planned to move onto Orglandes (est. 3 miles). At 10:00 we met 4 more troopers, one of them a medic. We were now 9 strong so we continued moving toward the town. At 12:10 we sighted the church steeple and moved on since we figured the Americans were on the outskirts of the town. (We had heard small arms fire all morning, evidently other small groups of troopers.)

We were moving between two hedgerows when the scout reported some Jerries on the hill to our left. We didn't want to draw any fire so we started back when they opened up on us with their machine pistols. We started firing back and we could see them running back and forth along the ridge. Our rear guard let a Jerry close in on us and one man was killed and two of us wounded. The rest were captured without harm.

The Germans were out of the 91st Div. They had been on the Russian front for 2 years and were hopped up both on morphine and cognac. We had walked into their battalion "CP" area. There were about 200 Germans on the hill. They were pretty abusive and couldn't understand why we were over here fighting them!

*They also wanted to know how the war in Africa was going and became very
angry when they were told that the Americans and British were in Rome.*

*The majority of them were young men, the rest were old and quite a few wore
glasses. Many had been wounded by our fire. They were poor shots! The one who
wounded Pvt. Young and myself wasn't more than 10 yards away from us to the
rear—and we were completely exposed from the rear, trusting our guard to wan
[sic] us of danger. Mistake #1!*

*The Germans took all of our equipment, personal as well as GI. The first-aid
packets seemed to be the best prize to them. The ones of us who were not wounded
received some rough treatment (and later were marched to a PW stockade), but
we two who were wounded were taken along with some Jerry wounded, in an
ambulance to the field hospital at Orglandes. There were at least 15 wounded
Jerries to each American there and after receiving more treatment for our wounds
and having our names taken as Prisoners of War we were taken to the hospital at
Valognes that night.*

June 8th—D + 2
*Valognes had not been bombed or shelled prior to our coming but the hospital was a
wreck regardless. Then every night Jerry would bring "88's" up near to the hospital
and from that point he would shell our troops. With the early dawn he would
move the guns and our artillery (having a position "fix") would start to shell the
area. P-47's, P-38's, and P-51's began to work the area over with dive-bombing
and strafing methods. The German wounded were kept in an underground shelter
but we had to stay in the second story wing of the "H" type building. Every morning at 06:00 we were awakened by dive-bombers going after flak towers and 88
positions within 800 yds. of the hospital along the RR track.*

June 13—D + 7
*Reveille as usual and as an added attraction shelling of the immediate area, one
shell hit the opposite wing starting a small fire. About 13:00 25 B-26's came over
to lay some eggs on the RR bridge near us. One stick came too close, two of the
bombs "bracketed-in" on the hospital "H." The building shook so much that it was
impossible to even kneel down. We were all digging-in in the straw that served
as our beds. That was the first time in my life that I was actually terrified! From
then on I seemed to have lost my nerve, I found myself jumping at the slightest
sounds.*

Jun 14—D + 8
The Germans came through checking for walking cases, 32 of them were marched to Bricbec to be sent back to Germany.

June 15—D + 9
The grave-diggers (German) have finished with the 140 Germans and 4 Americans. They were buried in the garden behind the hospital in a common plot. Rumors about being evacuated, which have been circling around for several days, have at last been realized. Our main fear being the thought of our being sent to Germany. We were transported from Valognes by ambulance to the Marine Hospital at Cherbourg. On the way out of Valognes we noticed that the town was utterly demolished except for the few buildings adjacent to the hospital! Our faith in our dive-bombers was increased 100 fold.

The Marine Hospital at Cherbourg was operated by the Luftwaffe. It was a huge affair, the largest on the Continent, so we were told; we had the best food ration here of any since our capture. At Valognes we were given German rear-line rations which consisted of: Breakfast, 1 slice of sawdust bread with jam and ¼ cup of weak coffee. Dinner, 1 bowl of noodle soup. Supper, 2 or 3 slices of bread and a small piece of liverwurst. This was the regular ration for the non-German soldiers in the rear lines, the labor organization, and any French civilians which may be working with them. They also received 3 cigarettes a day, which we prisoners also received. Front line troops got 12 cigarettes a day and much better rations of food.

At the Marine Hospital we had comparative peace and quiet since our troops were 12 to 14 miles away, and the Allies wanted to keep from destroying the city and docks as much as possible. No bombers.

June 16—D + 10
All men who needed casts, operations or amputations were taken care of in the many rooms of the building. The equipment was very good. Dr. Adams (Capt.), American medic did all of the work.

June 19—D + 13
Today the German Army Catholic chaplain came through the ward and gave confession and communion to those of the faith. A protestant chaplain visited the other men.

The German colonel in charge of the hospital came through inspecting the wounds and made up a list for transfer to the PW camp, taking only walking wounded. 35 of us left the hospital at 13:20 by bus, and true to our previous experiences the driver became lost. We toured Cherbourg with P-47's above us working on road installations at random. (More prayers.) We finally arrived at the Tourlaville (4 miles from Cherbourg—east) PW Camp at 16:40, there were 8 Americans at the camp when we arrived. They had not been wounded, but the peninsula had been cut-off by the Americans and the Germans couldn't evacuate any prisoners into France proper or Germany. We were taken to our quarters, a regular wooden barracks with double-decker bunks and straw ticks. The ticks were full of fleas, a factor that caused us to forget our other troubles for a while.

June 20—D + 14
Reveille again; this time to the tune of 155mm shells cracking in the area. We ran for cover with the air-bursts spraying the camp with shrapnel, the only cover was a ditch but it looked good to us then. While we were laying there we remembered the small evil deeds of our life and tried a one minute repentance in a hurry.

June 21—D + 15
Reveille as usual, and by now our guards are even beginning to show signs of strain and they hadn't been in the Valognes area! The unter-leutnant, who was in charge of the camp, went into Cherbourg to see his captain to try to move us to some caves in the face of the cliff about a quarter mile above us.

At 17:30 we marched up to one of the caves that was being used to house some French laborers who were suspected of underground activity. We got along too well with them and at 01:30 of the next morning they took us back to the "Barrage-Barracks" of the PW camp.

The unter-leutnant had arranged to take us to a "safe-spot," at 09:00 of June 22 we left the camp and marched into the shell-rocked city of Cherbourg. Our artillery was concentrating on the intersections so we had to pick our way along the road sometimes. The French slyly gave us the "V" for Victory sign from bomb cellars and doorways. Occasionally a package of French cigarettes came sailing out of an upstairs window, the guards didn't seem to notice this sign of allegiance and several times during the trip allowed us to stop in front of some house where the women would bring out wine and bread to us.

As we left the suburbs of Cherbourg on the west, we passed a hill to our left that had an 88 battery on it. This battery was shelling the Americans south of the town. Our artillery got a fix and began to fire on the battery. We took cover about 300 yds. from the battery and crawled along as our shells registered-in on the target. The first shell had hit in the road to the rear of us, we hit the ditch in a hurry.

At 14:20 we reached Tourlaville about 7 miles west of Cherbourg. We were in the country and thought that at last we were away from the base-plates of the 88's —until they opened up! We were in a battalion CP with 88's all around! At 15:10 we were situated in a barn adjacent to a house which was a block away from the CP when two P-38's came over at roof-top level to strafe the CP.

We hit the straw and were just getting up again when the 500 lbs. delayed action bomb exploded, we were all knocked down, the doors blew in, windows broke and the roof caved in. We dug into the straw deeper! The 38's came over three more times and each time the ack-ack cracked in our ears. We thought surely these would be our last precious minutes, when they zoomed overhead we would pray that the bomb wasn't under us. We waited the 4 or 5 seconds and heard the explosion, felt the ground shake, looked around to see if everyone was still OK. Some of us actually prayed out loud during the wait between the time when the plane went overhead and the bomb exploded!

The Germans decided to take us away from the town to a cave at an old rock quarry about 1 mile away, on the way out of town we had to bypass the ruins of the CP. The bombs had made direct hits!!

June 23—D + 17

We stayed at the rock quarry only a few minutes, then off again to another "safe-spot." This time we were holed-up in an unfinished "Rocket-Bomb" cave. It was relatively quiet except for an occasional outburst by the 2 batteries of 88's 300 yards away on top of the hill. The food was the same menu, the cigarette ration had been bolstered by our numerous trips through Cherbourg. Smoking became our main diversion from our ever-present plight. We knew it was too good to last. All day the 88's had their fun, then at night our artillery began to range in, in fact it was too accurate.

June 24—D + 18

Everyone is sweating out his time to go to the "latrine" outside our cave. Our guns have been busy all day, and we have coined a new phrase, "Boom Boom, No Chow." But there was more truth than poetry about it. At 19:10 we were moving again. (After the usual "counting-off" in the open during a barrage!).

This time we went past the Marine Hospital and turned left towards the Marine Arsenal, our stomachs turned a flip. Here were two dangers: 1. Evacuation by sea. 2. A last ditch stand (which [put] us in the middle again!). And having experienced our own artillery and bombers we really began to sweat. First we went to Fort du Homet which was a fort in every sense of the word, literally bristling with guns.

Our nerves on edge after so much travelling and exposure to danger, we began to demand more safety. And luckily we had a mild-type German officer in charge of us. He finally had us taken to an underground shelter below one of the docks, we were 26 ft. below street level and all solid concrete. We slept easily for the first time in weeks.

June 25—D + 19
We were due to leave our shelter to move back to the fort at 12:00 but as the first 5 men ran the 25 yds. to the side of a building 3 shells landed around our area. We decided to wait until night-fall, but the Arsenal commander wanted to blow the docks so we left. The first 25 yds. were the hardest, every time we poked our noses out we got a 105mm in return.

Finally we all arrived in a submarine pen, an oval-roofed structure with an 18 ft. roof. Some shells bounced off the roof while we were in there. The next 600 yds. were in the open. Running 15 yds. at a time and ducking behind some ruins on the way we finally made it without casualty, after many more prayers.

Now we are in a "Bunker," an 8-roomed shelter above ground. The walls were fairly thick but we knew the roof couldn't withstand a direct hit, so we still sweated out the idea of the fort, (300 yds. north of us), making a last desperate stand.

We can hear small-arms fire in the city now and our hopes run hand in hand with the many rumors. The guards are treating us better as time goes on. They went into the fort to draw their ration of cognac and must have taken more because they shared it with us, and some even managed to get drunk. In return we consoled them with the thought of good treatment when they were captured, (the fact of their capture being accepted long ago).

June 26—D + 20
Another day, a million more rumors, two new prisoners; they were captured in the outskirts of the city the day before. Small-arms fire is closer today. The marines are blowing up everything that our guns and bombs haven't hit. Some oil reserve was hit this morning and the fort is obscured by the billowing clouds of black smoke.

Some of the guards are promising their pistols to some of the men, it is common to see prisoner and guard sharing cigarettes and alternating on bottles of wine. Our artillery has been very active, again it becomes a test of one's will power and nerves to answer nature's call.

June 27—D + 21
A terrific explosion that rocked the bunker woke us all at 06:15 and the speculators
began their day's work of issuing rumors. At 12:40 we saw our first free Ameri-
cans, two officers and about 30 men entered the fort under a "white flag." The
guards eager to be our pals gave us their guns and stood around like a bunch [of]
sheep. The officers with us went over to the fort and talked to the men who had
lined up the last of the defenders against the wall. The captain in charge of the fort
refused to surrender until he saw his men had already quit.

We were formally liberated at 12:57, and a good thing. At 1300–14 battalions
of heavy artillery and 100 heavy bombers were due to hit the fort. It's great to be
an American!

Airmen who avoided being shot down by enemy fighters or flak and did
not suffer collision with other planes or mechanical problems returned
to their bases where they had warm barracks, hot meals, and perhaps
a woman waiting for them at the local pub. Officers and enlisted clubs
offered strong drink, more food, and entertainment.

The infantrymen who went ashore or parachuted into France on
D-Day did not have such luxuries. They slept in water-filled foxholes, ate
out of tin cans, and hoped to survive another day. The pay for foot soldiers
was less than the airmen and there was no such thing as a free trip home
after twenty-five or thirty-five successful missions.

In many of the E&E reports, airmen readily admit that they joined
the air corps specifically to avoid the infantry. There were only two significant advantages for the infantrymen. First, unlike the killers from the
sky, foot soldiers got to go through the pockets of dead enemy. Also, with
months, and sometimes years of experience of training and marching,
ground soldiers did not acquire the blisters that lent their name to their
air comrade evaders.

There was little love lost between the air and ground forces. Infantrymen rightfully thought that the Air Corps received accelerated pro-
motions, higher pay, and led a leisure lifestyle when not flying. Some
ground troops, after seeing their friends blown apart by errant bomb
runs or strafed by confused fighter pilots, looked at all aircraft as hostile.

Bad feelings were enhanced by the public and media back home that portrayed the airmen as chivalrous knights of the air. This enhanced the imagination of the American public about the "boys in blue" and provided a relief to the bloody meat grinder of ground combat. Regardless of their prejudices, however, once airmen separated from their planes and soldiers lost contact with their ground units, they united as Americans to evade capture by the Germans.

Paratroopers along with regular infantrymen made up more than 10 percent of the evaders interviewed by MIS-X. This included about 130 airborne personnel primarily from the drops on D-Day and the later Operation Market Garden. Infantrymen from units advancing across France and forced to evade numbered nearly three hundred. Some of these paratroopers and infantrymen were forced to evade after becoming disoriented or otherwise cut off from their units. The vast majority, however, did not begin their evasion until being captured by the Germans and either escaping or having their prisoner of war camp overrun by advancing Allies.

Nearly all the airborne and infantrymen reports are post-D-Day with their evasions occurring in France. The first two infantry evaders, however, escaped enemy captivity fully a year before the Normandy landings. Germans captured Private Sylvio N. Derosier of the 1st Armored Division from Lewiston, Maine, and Private Rene O. Bertrand of the 1st Infantry Division from Lowell, Massachusetts, at the Battle of Kasserine Pass in North Africa on February 17, 1943.

The next day the two soldiers joined more than a thousand other American and British prisoners as well as thirty French detainees. They learned that, while the Americans and British were to be transferred to POW camps within Germany, the French prisoners were to be returned to France and demobilized. Derosier and Bertrand, who both spoke French, made friends with several of the French detainees and evacuated with them first to Italy and then on to Marseilles.

The two then made their way to Olette from where they crossed the Pyrenees into Spain. They arrived at Gibraltar on May 18, 1943, and the United Kingdom ten days later. Their E&E reports, numbers 34 and 35, are among the earliest of all evaders.

German armor overran Corporal Raymond B. Sarant's 168th Infantry Regiment on February 16, 1943, in Tunisia. He evaded for four days before being captured and evacuated by air and rail to Stalag 7A in Moosberg, Germany, on March 21. Three weeks later he was transferred to Stalag 5B in Willengen from where he made his first escape on May 20. Recaptured a short time later, he found himself transferred to Stalag 3B in Furstenberg.

Sarant escaped for the second time on September 19, hopped a freight train, and made it close to the Belgian border before being caught once again. Weeks in solitary confinement followed each unsuccessful escape attempt. Undaunted, Sarant once again escaped from Stalag 3B on October 24. Again, hiding on a freight train, he successfully made his way to France where he met helpers who assisted him in his journey to arrive in Spain on February 1, 1944.

Sarant's E&E report number 451 is the thickest file in the MIS-X archives. In addition to the usual report, his folder includes a section labeled "Part II: Prison Camp Conditions" where Sarant lists fellow Americans he met while in captivity; his descriptions of life in the POW camps include medical aid, food, and morale and detailed drawings he produced of the camps where he had been held.

Sarant is modest and straightforward throughout his report. He makes no great claims of personal bravery or his defiance of the risks in his three escape attempts, or the fact that he was one of the few to evade from a prison camp deep within Germany. He elaborated in his report, writing,

Escape mindness was growing in the camp but it had far to go. Most of the men who had been out once were not eager to go again; a few were though, however. I made a tour of the barracks before my final escape and made talks on escape, telling the men as much as I knew about preparations and planning. I left behind two friends who had been on my first escape and who knew the details. In all of the camp there was much talk about waiting until spring before trying to escape.

Private First Class Edward P. Jones of the 80th Infantry Division from Augusta, Georgia, was captured on October 27, 1944, along the Moselle River near Metz. His captors moved him to a POW camp near Stuttgart, Germany, where, Jones observed in his debriefing, "Two men obtained a bucket of paint and brushes from the new building being erected and started to paint a line down the main thoroughfare until they reached the gate. There they paused while the sentry opened the gate for them and they continued to paint on down the road and were never seen again."

Two weeks later, while outside the camp unloading a railcar full of ammunition on December 12, Jones watched an American plane strafe the rail yard. He and several others escaped amid the confusion. On December 28, Jones reached American lines. A staff comment to his E&E report stated, "Recommend that PVT Jones be given an appropriate award for his courage and fortitude in making his escape. He was also able to provide much military information which has been forwarded to proper authorities."

The number of American infantry evaders greatly increased during the airborne invasion behind the beaches of Normandy on D-Day. Many planes failed to reach their drop zones, and paratroopers individually and in small groups were spread across the countryside.

Typical of the paratrooper evaders is the story of Second Lieutenant James J. Wilson of the 82nd Airborne Division from Douglaston, New York. In his report he wrote,

On the 6th of June 1944 I was taken prisoner by the German army near St. Mere Eglise. I had made my jump, and having landed outside the drop zone, I collected a small group of men and attempted to reach the battalion assembly area. We were surrounded and captured by German infantrymen. I was placed in a POW enclosure for one night, where I was searched. I then went to a POW camp near St. Lo, where I was interrogated by German intelligence officers. I gave them my name, rank, and serial number only. After five days, a group of prisoners were marched off. While on the road, US aircraft strafed our group and on jumping into a ditch to avoid being hit, I broke my left knee. I received first aid from the Germans and was transported by truck to the POW hospital at Rennes, France. On the 2nd of August 1944 I escaped and made my way to the American lines on the 5th of August.

Unlike airmen, successful evasion by paratroopers and infantrymen did not merit a ticket back to the United States or an easy assignment in England. Rather, as soon as physically able they were returned to their units and combat. Wilson recovered from his knee injury in time to jump into Holland as a part of Operation Market Garden a month after his escape. He was wounded, hospitalized, and after healing once again returned to his unit on December 11.

Sergeant Willis L. Whitman from Rogers City, Michigan, also of the 82nd Airborne Division, had similar experiences. Captured west of St. Mere Eglise shortly after landing on June 6, 1944, he escaped on June 13 when P-47s strafed his POW column. He evaded to American lines and, after being hospitalized in England, returned to his unit in December in time to drop into Holland later to suffer wounds at St. Vith and was again captured. Whitman was sent to a hospital about which he wrote in his report, stating, "The treatment during my stay with the Germans was pretty rough. The German captain in charge had been an SS trooper." Whitman was later liberated by advancing Allies.

Still another 82nd Airborne paratrooper, Sergeant Edward J. Morrissey from Canton, Massachusetts, also fell into German hands on June 6, 1944. Captured soon after landing in the rear of the Normandy beachhead, he escaped two days later when US planes strafed his column. Germans again captured him on June 21 as he attempted to reach American lines. He received fair treatment by his captors, one of whom is mentioned in his report. He related details about a particular German interrogator, writing that "he had taken a lot of trouble to learn English because he liked Americans, but we were a pain in the neck politically. If we would just break away from Roosevelt and Morgenthau and the Jewish bankers everybody would be happy." Moved to confinement in a school, Morrissey took maps from textbooks, escaped, and headed for friendly lines. With help from the French, he made it.

The Germans feared the American paratroopers. Staff Sergeant Clyde Tinley of the 101st Airborne Division from Akron, Ohio, became a prisoner five days after he jumped into Normandy on D-Day. He escaped and reported on his E&E report, "German soldiers all firm in belief that all American paratroopers were ex-convicts recruited from prisons."

Germans captured Private First Class Leon E. Keene of the 82nd Airborne Division from Plant City, Florida, three days after he parachuted into France near St. Mere Eglise on June 6, 1944. Over the next weeks he escaped, was recaptured, escaped again, was recaptured, and finally escaped once more and made his way to friendly lines.

American infantrymen were more prone than the airmen to physically fight their captors. Private First Class Arthur L. Mullins from Shelbyville, Indiana, was captured with others two days after jumping into Normandy on June 6, 1944. The Germans began moving them toward POW camps in Germany. Mullins wrote in his E&E report, "We were passing through a small village 5–6 miles south of Bricquebec when we were strafed by four P-47s. They flew over us several times and we thought they had recognized us as American PWs, but later they came back and made a sweep down the road, machine gunning us from about 350 feet altitude. Twenty-three Americans and seven Germans were killed and 47 Americans seriously wounded."

A few days later Mullins escaped. "The Germans moved us onto a road between two hedges and began to count us. Another man and I zigzagged through the crowd and killed two German guards then hopped the hedge and ran about 500 yards to a wheat field nearby and were then hidden by Frenchman. We continued to hide in the woodshed at the farmer's house. Twice the Germans came there and searched for us, but as we now had weapons taken from the German guards we had bumped off, we easily disposed of them, too."

An unusual MIS-X comment accompanied Mullins' E&E report likely because of his killing several of his captors. "Should not be returned to duty in France."

Most infantry evaders were not as fortunate as Mullins. French Forces of the Interior (FFI) troops freed 30th Infantry Division Private First Class Grover C. Lawrence from Mattox, Virginia, from his German captors on August 26, 1944. Upon return to American lines, he was sent back to his unit where he was wounded on October 18 and evacuated to a Paris hospital.

Private First Class Anthony J. Da Cunha of the 79th Infantry Division from Lowell, Massachusetts, was captured at La Haye du Puits on July 13, 1944. He escaped when Allied artillery hit his prison camp and he made his way to US lines whereupon he was immediately returned to duty. On October 10, 1944, he once again fell into German hands. Although wounded, he escaped and again evaded to US lines. This time he was evacuated and interviewed by the MIS-X. They were not, however, all that interested in his story as his entire report is only two paragraphs in length.

Some evaders rejoined their old units on their own. Germans captured Private Rene P. Morasse of the 28th Infantry Division from Lawrence, Massachusetts, near Evreux, France, on August 19, 1944. He reported,

> With 30 US PWs I boarded an open truck, we had gone about two miles when Allied bombs started to fall. The driver and two guards jumped and ran. Several of us jumped and ran too. The guards fired at us. I ran a block, ducked into a house and asked a French woman to hide me. She hid me for a couple of hours and then got a man who took me to his barge at the Pont-de-Neuilly. I stayed there until August 26 when I heard the Americans were in Paris. My helper directed me to the Arc de Triomphe and there I ran across my old outfit, sitting in the road waiting for the victory parade to start.

Captain James C. Snedeker of the 1st Infantry Division from Columbus, Ohio, accomplished the most unusual evasion by an infantryman. Snedeker departed England on December 18, 1944, aboard a Royal Navy steam gun boat for Antwerp where he planned on joining his unit. German patrol boats attacked the craft, sinking it and knocking him unconscious. Snedeker woke up on a German boat, he was taken to shore, and then he was trucked inland before escaping after being strafed by a Royal Air Force (RAF) fighter. He found help with the Dutch Resistance and, along with three RAF airmen, was taken to the beach on January 2. He reported, "We were put on a motor-sailboat that night, and the next night we contacted a British patrol boat which permitted us to pass. We arrived somewhere south of Yarmouth at about dawn on January 3. The crew of three men pushed off at once to return to Holland."

Captured on October 9, 1944, Sergeant Max Morgenstern of the 80th Infantry Division from New York City attacked and killed a German guard and escaped, taking the German's boots and pants.

Ten Germans held another infantryman, Private First Class Agaton J. Godlewski of the 30th Infantry Division from Philadelphia, Pennsylvania, after capturing him on August 6, 1944 near Mortain, France. Godlewski convinced the Germans to surrender to him and then led them to Canadian lines.

First Lieutenant Henry J. Chiarini of the 9th Infantry Division from East Boston, Massachusetts, escaped from the Germans. FFI helpers took him on August 13, 1944, to a village near Saumur that expected Americans to arrive anytime. Chiarini reported, "They had American and French flags up all over the place, and the streets were crowded with people. Then in the afternoon, a rumor started that there was a German motorized column approaching the town. Immediately all the flags came down and the streets deserted."

Private Walter R. Gochnour of the 145th Combat Engineer Battalion escaped his captors near Sarralben, France, on November 27, 1944, and began evading toward Allied lines. He came across an American sleeping in a foxhole. Fearful of being shot, he put the man's rifle to one side, woke him up, and revealed his identity. Gochnour returned to his unit.

CHAPTER 19

Atrocities

E&E REPORT NO. 2669
ATROCITY REPORT

T/5 Michael T. Sciranko

B Btry, 285th Field Artillery Observation Battalion
Hometown: Bedford, Pennsylvania

At 0800 hours 17 Dec 1944, our whole battery left Duren for St. Vith. There were 20–30 vehicles in the convoy. We went through Malmedy at about 1430, headed south on the main road. About twenty minutes later, after we had gone a couple of miles and had just passed a road junction, we were stopped by intense shelling and machine gun fire. Everyone got out and took cover in the ditch.

At about 1500 some Tiger tanks came out of the side road that we had just passed, and started down the main road towards St. Vith. As they went by, the Germans jumped off and told us to put up our hands. Then they marched us back up the road towards Malmedy, and at the road junction, lined up about 50 of us in two columns and started to search us. They took all the valuables that they could find; such as rings, watches, and money. All that they took away from me was a letter from my wife that I had in my overcoat pocket. When they spotted the six stripes on M/Sgt Lacy of our outfit, they took him off down the road with them for questioning. As they finished searching us, they put us in a bunch in a field about 25 yards back from the road. There were already some other PW's there from another outfit. Meanwhile the Tiger tanks kept going by. I should say that there were about 75 of them in all, moving at about 12–15 mph, and with an interval of about 75 yards between each one.

After we had been standing in the field for about 20 minutes, one of the Tigers stopped in the road and pointed his 88 at us. For a moment we thought we'd had it, but then we did not think such a thing possible. They played around with the 88 for about five minutes, and then the tank started off down the road again. As it began to move, one tanker stood up in the turret and with his pistol picked off two guys on each end of the bunch. One of them was Cpl. Lester, a guy from my outfit. Right after that, the Germans on the same tank opened up on us with their machine guns, and we all hit the dirt. Some because they were dead, some because they were wounded, and the rest for protection.

After that, every tank that came down the road opened up on us with machine guns, burp guns, rifles, and pistols. Sometimes the Germans would jump off their tanks as they were moving, and come over into the field to finish off anyone they thought was still alive. They were laughing and yelling among themselves. After they had shot anyone who breathed or moved, and fired a few extra rounds for good measure, they would run back and climb on their tanks again and continue on their way. There was no one acting as a PW guard or trying to save us. It was just one big shooting gallery.

I kept my head flattened into the mud and blood as much as I could. However, at the same time I could see that the Germans were wearing black uniforms, with the lightning bolt insignia of the SS. Some wore camouflaged coveralls. Most of them were wearing black visored field caps, but some had helmets.

As I was lying there, I felt something pierce my butt, and from then on I was waiting for the one that would finish me off. Everyone around me was screaming and hollering. I heard someone on my right gasp and say, "I can hardly breathe anymore." Another on my left got up and tried to run away, but he tripped over my feet and fell next to me. One guy was praying out loud, but a German soon noticed him and gave him the works. All the time the bullets were whizzing around, and I could hear them hitting the steel helmets.

At about 1630, after we had been there for an hour and a half, the tanks had all gone by, and we did not hear any more coming. We looked around, and everything seemed fairly quiet. Someone yelled, "Let's go," and five of us jumped up and got away from there as fast as we could. As we were running across the field, a machine gun opened up on us from another field across the road. No one got hit. We ran like hell for about a mile and a half across fields, hedgerows, and barbed wire. Then we came to the Malmedy road, and just after we had crossed it, a jeep came along down from Malmedy with an Ordnance captain in it. He picked us up and took us to an aid station in Malmedy. Then, as his outfit was moving out, he took us along with his.

A fellow battery mate of Sciranko related his account of the same atrocity to MIS-X debriefers.

E&E REPORT NO. 2907
ATROCITY REPORT

SGT Kenneth F. Ahrens

Btry B, 285th FA Observation Bn.
Hometown: Erie, Pennsylvania

Sgt. Ahrens's battery was on 17 December 1944 moving along the road Malmedy–St. Vith. At 1330 hours they were intercepted by a column of German Tiger tanks and captured.

The head of the battery column was stopped at the crossroads. The Tiger tanks covered them until the arrival of the armored infantry (Panzergrenadiere). When the Panzergrenadiere arrived, they marched the Americans in small groups down the road to a small field. On the way they stopped them frequently to search and plunder the prisoners, taking watches, rings, billfolds, and anything else of value or interest to the Germans. With this frequent halting, it took twenty minutes to arrive at the field, not more than half a mile down the road. During that time, the Germans had captured about twenty more Americans who had been proceeding unsuspectingly along the Malmedy–St. Vith road.

When the prisoners arrived at the small field they were told to stand in a group in the middle of it with their hands up. However, a medic was allowed to bandage one of the men who had been wounded during the bombardment, and then both medic and wounded man were returned to the group. For twenty minutes, the prisoners stood in the field with their hands raised looking at each other and wondering what was going to happen. Then several tanks and half tracks with a number of foot soldiers pulled up on the road alongside the field. A young officer emerged from one of the tanks and stood on the turret. He pulled out his pistol, aimed at the group of prisoners and fired one round. Ten feet from Sgt. Ahrens a man fell to the ground shot through the head. The officer fired again and another man fell shot through the head. Then all the tanks, halftracks, and infantry opened fire with machine guns, rifles and pistols. Sgt. Ahrens fell to the ground and dug himself into the mud. He felt a burning sensation in the back from a flesh wound and lay there as though dead. The shooting went on for fifteen minutes to half an hour. Vehicles continued to pass by on the road and each came abreast of the field fired into the group of prisoners, now groaning, screaming and praying. Then six or eight Germans moved among the group, kicking the bodies to see if they were dead and shooting anyone in the head who showed signs of life. They laughed and joked throughout. Sgt. Ahrens heard them pass fifteen or sixteen times while he lay among bodies riddles with bullets, his own back covered with blood. Eventually the Germans left and he heard the vehicles move away.

All was quiet for a while, then someone said "Let's go." The ten or twelve who lived jumped up and ran and some who were too badly wounded had just enough strength to rise, say "Don't leave me here," and fell again. When he reached the road, a machine gun fired on them, apparently from a German rearguard and some of the men ran into a house for cover. Later the house was burned and those who ran out were shot. Sg. Ahrens and four others, all of his battery, and an MP headed into the woods and ran north, their only thought was to get out of that area. They met Americans four or five miles from the scene. These American soldiers took the men to an aid station and from here they were taken to the 28th General Hospital at Liege.

Evaders provided the most accurate account of the German massacre of American soldiers at Malmedy. It was not, however, the only atrocity reported in their E&E reports. These included the execution of American soldiers as well as their civilian helpers. German soldiers were well aware that American bombers targeted their hometowns and that many of their families had lost their houses and lives to air attacks. They also were themselves targets of bombers and fighters while in convoys and on the railroads. Some sought vengeance.

Second Lieutenant Joseph E. Wemheuer, a B-17 bombardier from Los Angeles, California, went down in France on May 13, 1943. He reported, "While in France I was shown a typewritten page that said the following US airmen had been shot by the Germans. I also was told these men had been captured, shot and buried near Doullens. A large number—several hundred—French people came to the funeral, which irritated the Germans. The coffins were not marked, but a French sister drove nails in the top of the coffins, one for the first name on the list, two for the second, etc."

Six of the executed airmen were from Wemheuer's crew, three more from another aircraft. MIS-X interrogators obviously took such reports seriously. Attached to the E&E report was a note, "Can you verify the above and if so how and why they were shot?"

While some of the atrocity reports were based on hearsay, others were from direct observation. Second Lieutenant Douglas J. Eames Jr., a B-24 copilot from Hyde Park, Massachusetts, witnessed German machine gunners shooting airman in their parachutes on June 22, 1944. A French doctor also showed him photos of Germans burying Russian prisoners alive.

The E&E reports further reveal that the Germans were more likely to commit atrocities against infantrymen than airmen. Staff Sergeant Clyde Tinley, an infantryman in the 101st Airborne Division from Akron, Ohio, jumped into France on D-Day. He reported that there was a special German unit that executed captured paratroopers behind lines. The Germans called them swine, hung them by their heels, and cut their throats.

Flight Officer Donald F. O'Hora, a glider pilot from Buffalo, New York, was captured shortly after crashing in France on D-Day. Before being freed from a German hospital by advancing Americans on June 15, he observed,

> Outside Amfreville on June 9 saw a group of patients marched off with their hands clasped behind their necks in the usual position for prisoners. For no apparent reason a German guard shot one of them in the back with his rifle. The man dropped and died by the roadside where he was left. The German's uniform had green piping. Wounded paratroopers told of having seen other paratroopers hanging in a barn. They also told of a man who had been so injured in landing that he could not get out of his harness. A German slit his wrists and left him to bleed to death."

Despite these incidents, generally American aviators were not treated badly, even if captured wearing civilian clothing. Treatment got even better when captors turned them over to the German Luftwaffe who managed their own prisoner camps. French, Belgian, and other civilians who aided evaders, however, were not well treated. Civilians, as well as their families, captured assisting evaders were at best sent to concentration camps and at worst lined up and shot.

First Lieutenant Milton V. Shevchik, a B-17 pilot from Ambridge, Pennsylvania, went down on February 8, 1944. During his evasion he met a woman who told him, "The Gestapo had caught up with a family who had hidden a US flyer in their house outside Beauvais. They had been shot. She claimed to have intercepted several letters exposing other organization members to the Gestapo."

Second Lieutenant William H. Reese, a P-51 pilot, crash-landed in France on August 17, 1944. Assisted by the Maquis, he reported that he observed Germans execute thirteen old men and children and rape several women near Precy. Reese also stated in his E&E report that the Maquis captured and executed a young woman who helped the Germans.

CHAPTER 20

The Germans

HEADQUARTERS
EUROPEAN THEATER OF OPERATIONS
P/W and X Detachment
Military Intelligence Service

E&E Report No. 521
Evasion in France

26 March 1944

Name:	*Robert V. Laux*
Rank:	*2LT*
Unit:	*532nd Bomb Squadron, 381st Bomb Group (B-17)*
Target:	*Frankfurt*
Home address:	*Pittsburgh, Pennsylvania*
MIA:	*11 Feb 1944*
Arrived in UK:	*24 March 1944*

Other members of the crew:

Pilot	*2LT*	*Robert V. Laux*	*Narrator*
Co-Pilot	*2LT*	*Donald G. Harrer*	*MIA*
Navigator	*2LT*	*Phlemon T. Wright*	*E&E #522*
Bombardier	*2LT*	*Judson F. Doyle*	*MIA*
Radio Operator	*SGT*	*Abe A. Helfgott*	*E&E #524*
Top Turret Gunner	*SSGT*	*John E. Holton*	*MIA*
Ball Turret Gunner	*SGT*	*Richard C. Hamilton*	*E&E #526*
Waist Gunner	*SGT*	*Rudolph Cutino*	*E&E #525*

Waist Gunner	*SGT*	*Thomas J. Glennan*	*E&E #523*
Tail Gunner	*SGT*	*Henry R. Barr*	*MIA*

We met moderate flak over the target. Before long five or six fighters coming in from the tail blasted number three engine and shot up the plane. We fell out of formation and some P-47's covered us. At about 12,000 feet an FW 190 shot out number two engine, set it on fire, and started a fire in the bomb bay. I rang the alarm bell and told the men to get out. After all the men had cleared the ship, I pushed the two detonators. I jumped with my leg straps unfastened, but I had no trouble with my parachute.

I landed hard in a field. Before I could get out of the harness, some Frenchmen were helping me. They motioned for me to run to the woods, and they took care of my equipment. I found a deep gully, pulled brush over myself, and lay there for a couple of hours. I heard a number of shots from Germans trying to scare us out. Many automobiles passed on the road, but I was not bothered by searchers.

When things quieted down I started walking through the woods. I hid as a number of civilians passed. That evening I found an abandoned house and slept in it.

Next morning I started walking at 0530 and kept to the woods as much as I could. I heard a woodcutter and approached him. He started to run when he saw me, but when I told him that I was an American, he came back. By means of my phrase card I explained that I was hungry and thirsty. After he brought me food, I asked him for civilian clothes. He brought me a coat and a pair of trousers which I put over my OD's, keeping my GI shoes. The boy gave me a beret and told me that I was going to Spain. I started walking south by compass. When I got hungry I stopped a farmer and showed him my phrase card. He brought me food.

At a cross roads a German motorcyclist stopped, raised his hand, and shouted, "Halt!" I thought that he was saluting me, so I gave him a Hitler salute back. A number of truckloads of Germans passed, and I saluted all of them. They returned my salute.

I knocked at the back door of a farm house and frightened a couple of women so badly that they had dropped a pail of milk. Before they could give an alarm I ran over to them, explained that I was an American, and asked to sleep in the barn. A farmer brought me blankets, let me milk his cow into my water bottle, and made me comfortable for the night.

Early the next morning the farmer woke me up, saying "Garcon! Vite!," gave me some food, and put me on my way. As I was about to look at a road sign at a cross roads, a German staff car full of heavily armed MP's pulled up. I was still carrying my flying jacket to use at night. I thought to myself, "Here goes," and walked right on. A German got out of the car, motioned to me to come over, and said in French something that I did not understand. I looked dumb. He repeated slowly with gestures asking whether to go this way or that. I pointed down the road, and the car drove off.

Some distance down the road, I showed a woman my phrase card. She stood and looked at me for a few minutes and then took me to her house. From that place my journey was arranged.

In addition to blisters, hunger, adverse weather, and fatigue, evaders faced another impediment to their escape—the Germans and their collaborators. The meetings with the enemy by Lieutenant Laux were not unusual. While the evaders did their best not to encounter the Nazis and their supporters, it was inevitable that their paths would cross. We only know the stories of those evaders who successfully handled these meetings as those who were not successful spent the remainder of the war as POWs and never completed an E&E report for MIS-X. Unlike the massacre at Malmedy, atrocities were the exception rather than the norm when evader met German.

The odds definitely did not favor successful evasion by Americans. The reasons for such a low success rate are many, one of them, however, was the fact that British airmen assumed the duties of night missions while American bombers and fighters operated primarily during daylight hours. A plane or parachute descending from the sunlit sky was easy to see by ground observers.

Spread across occupied France, Belgium, and Holland in June 1942 were twenty-three German infantry divisions and three panzer divisions with an authorized strength of nearly 400,000 men. There were also thousands of Nazi sympathizers on the ground and other civilians who welcomed the opportunity to turn in American airmen for the German offered bounties. France, Belgium, and Holland combined are about the same size of Texas—268,000 square miles. Within this territory at the beginning of World War II was a population of about sixty million people. Throughout the three countries were more than 600,000 miles of local, secondary, and main roads and highways. An efficient railroad system, most of which remained operational throughout the war, criss-crossed the area as well.

Much of the contact by evaders with Germans did not result in any confrontation. In most cases the Germans did not anticipate encountering an American and the evader wanted to make the meeting as brief as possible.

Second Lieutenant James A. Schneider, a B-17 bombardier from Mobridge, South Dakota, was shot down over France on December 31, 1943. He wrote in his E&E report,

> I walked into a German soldier leaning with his bicycle against the trunk of a tree. I was beside him before I saw him. For a second we stared at each other and then, because I had an unlighted cigarette in my mouth, I asked him for a light in English. He looked puzzled and said something I could not understand as I pointed to my cigarette. After he struck a match and lighted my cigarette I turned and walked away from him without looking back. I was wearing my heated suit, green coveralls, electric shoes and carrying one flying boot. The German was armed, middle-aged and looked stupid. I cannot explain why he didn't stop me except that after the first second of surprise I tried to carry off the situation naturally.

First Lieutenant Dale R. Sandvik, a P-47 pilot from Palmer, Alaska, was downed by flak on March 18, 1945, near Erfweiler, Germany. When challenged by a German soldier, he answered, according to his report, "Ja, Ja" and was allowed to proceed down the road. Three days later he made it to Allied lines.

B-17 tail gunner Staff Sergeant Lawrence H. Templeton from Wausau, Wisconsin, landed in France after his plane collided with another Fortress. He described what happened: "I had been walking for almost an hour when I rounded a curve in the road and saw a German soldier approaching on a bicycle. There was no time to get off the road.

I was dressed in O.D.s and had not washed the blood off my face. There was nothing to do but brave it out and he rode by me without a glance."

German fighters shot down Second Lieutenant James J. Robinson from Portage, Wisconsin, in his P-47 over France on July 24, 1944. He began walking south. He reported, "That afternoon a German soldier stopped me and asked me what time it was. I held up my wrist watch for him to look at and then turned from him and walked on my way, fighting down my desire to hurry."

First Lieutenant Charles H. Freeman from Tampa, Florida, was knocked unconscious when he crash-landed his P-47 in France on June 11, 1944. French helpers took him to a farmhouse and then escorted him on his evasion south. When a SS trooper stopped them on the road, the helper claimed Freeman had been bombed out of this home at St. Lo during the D-Day invasion, had been injured in the blast, and had lost his papers. The soldier allowed them to continue their journey.

Major Paul E. Gardiner, from Cherokee, Oklahoma, also landed in France after his P-47 was shot down by flak on June 18, 1944. French farmers hid him in a farmhouse. He recounted his experience, stating, "On the morning of July 26 a German soldier walked by as I was looking out the window. He got a good look at me, and to keep him from being suspicious, I came out and set a ladder up against the wall. I acted then as if I were trying to fix the roof. He stopped several times to look back at me, but he never returned."

B-17 tail gunner Staff Sergeant Clifford Hammock from Pitts, Georgia, was shot down over France on December 6, 1943. On his E&E forms he recalled,

> I stayed in a barn for seven days, receiving food from my helpers. Then I was told that the Germans were coming back from the front line. I was taken to a house in which a German soldier was staying in the room below me. From here I was taken to another house where a German soldier was staying. One day by mistake he saw me around the house dressed in my khaki trousers, OD shirt, and flying boots. He apparently thought nothing unusual about my appearance.

Second Lieutenant Robert B. Andrews from Elmira, New York, had a similar experience after crashing on May 25, 1944. He was hidden in the attic of a home in Belgium that had a German soldier billeted below.

B-24 waist gunner Staff Sergeant Frank Digiovanni from Brooklyn, New York, was shot at by machine guns as he descended into France on July 24, 1944. He wrote, "I hid in a hedgerow near a muddy road, thinking that no one would come through there and that I could continue the next night. When it began to get light I found my hiding place was close to a German dugout. I could almost touch ten Germans as they walked by me."

Not all Germans soldiers were dumb, nonobservant, or unconcerned. Many airmen were captured by attentive, dedicated soldiers. Unfortunately, there are no postwar debriefings of former POWs to reveal just how and why they were captured. From the E&E reports of successful evaders, we do know, however, the stories of some who were temporarily in the hands of the enemy. Some were abused while others were treated under the provisions of the Geneva Convention.

B-26 radio operator Technical Sergeant Fred E. Conder from Capitan, New Mexico, was shot down over France and captured on August 7, 1944. He later escaped and reported, "I was never interrogated by the Germans, but my watch and rings were taken and not returned. When the Germans searched us, they cut open the soles of our shoes to see if we had anything hidden in them."

At times German searchers took extra measures to capture downed airmen. The Germans used dogs to track B-17 top turret gunner Technical Sergeant Bruno M. Gallerani from Longmeadow, Massachusetts, after he landed in Belgium on August 17, 1943.

Second Lieutenant Jack E. Ryan from Minneapolis, Minnesota, was the copilot of a B-17 when he was shot down near Paris on August 16, 1943. He immediately discarded his parachute, flying boots, and Mae West and hid in nearby brush. German soldiers and civilians soon arrived and found his gear. He overheard the leader of the soldiers say that "he would give them to the person who found me." The soldiers also offered tobacco to the adults and candy to children if they helped in the search.

Paratrooper Private Norman F. Welsh from Rochester, New York, of the 82nd Airborne Division was captured near Etienville, France, on June 21, 1944. Welsh reported,

> They took me to their battalion command post where I was inter-rogated. They asked me the usual things—name of CO, unit, and so on. When I refused to answer they called a young fellow who pulled a Mauser on me and told me to come outside with him. He marched me a short way into the woods, then stopped and said in English, "I'm supposed to scare hell out of you." After a while he took me back and said I wouldn't talk. Later they gave me some good food and cognac and tried to gain my confidence.

Welsh escaped a few days later and returned to American lines.

B-17 bombardier Second Lieutenant Eugene Sydlowski from St. Louis, Missouri, went down in France September 5, 1944. He reported,

> One of our flyers was killed in the following fashion. His name was 2LT Dean N. Post, a P-51 pilot who was forced to bail out. He was captured by the Germans and was brought to Gerardmer in a car under guard. A SS non-com came out of a restaurant across the street picking his teeth and spotted LT Post. For no reason he pulled his pistol and walked across to the car and shot LT Post. The French buried him near Gerardmer and covered his grave with flowers. The next day the Germans tore off the flowers and took turns defecating on the grave.

Second Lieutenant Thornton Bline, a B-17 copilot from Hortonsville, Pennsylvania, was shot down June 25, 1944. Two Gestapo agents dressed in American uniforms came to where Bline was being hidden by a French family. The Frenchman, thinking the US advance troops had reached their village, let them in and welcomed them. They took Bline prisoner, burned down the house, and executed the Frenchman and his family.

Evaders also used harsh countermeasures against their German pur-suers. B-17 copilot Second Lieutenant Archibald L. Robertson from

Auburn, Alabama, was shot down over France on July 10, 1943. He found refuge in a barn after he showed the owner his blistered feet. When he continued his walk, he encountered a single German whom he knocked unconscious. The German fell into a drainage ditch, but Robertson pulled him to the bank "so he would not drown."

Staff Sergeant Jack W. Carrol from Coronado, California, began his evasion after his B-26 was shot down over Holland on August 17, 1944. He was straightforward in his report when he wrote, "During the time I traveled alone I was stopped three times by the Germans. One I killed with my .45."

Fighters shot down B-17 tail gunner Staff Sergeant Dale Markland from Ogden, Utah, on February 16, 1943, over France. Markland reported that once on the ground helpers had told him that two of his crew members "had stumbled into collaborationists. The collaborators had pretended to shelter them but after they were asleep the Germans were notified." The helper promised that the collaborators would be "taken care of."

In the months after D-Day, some evaders found the Germans weary of war and realizing theirs was a lost cause, treated them well. B-24 co-pilot Second Lieutenant James M. Ackerman from Paterson, New Jersey, suffered severe burns to his face when he bailed out near Reims on June 23, 1944. French civilians took him to a German hospital for treatment. The German "soldiers were nice to me," he later reported. Ackerman remained in the hospital for sixty-seven days until August 29, 1944, when the Germans evacuated and left seriously wounded POWs behind to be liberated by advancing Americans. During his hospitalization, Ackerman received French and American Red Cross parcels every two weeks. Weekly he received a clean shirt and towel. He reported that the food was adequate, and he was issued three cigarettes a day. There were armed guards, bars on windows, and doors were locked. No religious services, even for the dead, were held.

The Germans shot at top turret gunner Technical Sergeant Ernest W. Furfaro from Brooklyn, New York, as he descended by parachute into France after his B-17 was struck by flak on August 2, 1944. Unable to evade because of a flak wound in his ankle, he was captured by the Germans and taken to a hospital where he was operated on. He wrote, "I received the best of care." He was then moved to a French home and "given the best of everything before liberated."

In some instances, German soldiers saved evaders from mistreatment or even death. Second Lieutenant Grover C. McKinney from Lake Charles, Louisiana, was wounded in the thigh and leg while fighting with the 3rd Armored Division in France in November 1944. His German captors gave him immediate first aid. McKinney had a German P-38 he had captured in an earlier battle and some of his captors wanted to shoot him. A medic interceded and saved his life. The medic told McKinney, according to his report, "If this had happened a year ago in Africa, you would have been shot, but we don't do that anymore."

Second Lieutenant Norman N. Wolf, a B-24 navigator from Cleveland, Ohio, was captured shortly after landing in France on July 25, 1944. His captors accused him of being a spy despite his dog tags because he had managed to change into civilian clothing. When the Germans began retreating, Wolf and others overpowered their guards, took them prisoner, and returned to American lines. In his E&E report Wolf stated,

> I am anxious that the two guards whom we captured and took to the American lines get good treatment. Both Karl Peeters and Walter Sabisch saved our lives on several occasions, I'm sure. When some of the retreating Germans wanted to kill us, these two guards would tell them that we were special prisoners of the division. Peeters told all the retreating Germans that I was an infantryman and not an airman. I'm sure I would have been killed had it been known that I was an airman. The German soldiers were so angry because they were being strafed that I don't think they would have hesitated to kill me in cold blood.

Upper Montclair, New Jersey, native First Lieutenant Robert T. Howling of the 30th Infantry Division had a similar experience after being captured in ground combat in France on June 24, 1944. In his report he cited two German soldiers because they "saved our lives at least a dozen times" by preventing other soldiers from shooting them.

Evaders also took Germans, both willing and unwilling, as prisoners and brought them back to friendly lines. P-51 pilot Second Lieutenant Walter O. Costello from Atlanta, Georgia, crash-landed forty miles southeast of Avranches, France, on July 20, 1944. Farmers immediately came to his aid, hid him in a barn, and advised him to wait for the American advance. While Costello hid, a German came to the farm well for water and Costello captured him and held him prisoner until the next morning when he joined advancing American tanks and turned his prisoner over to MPs.

Sergeant Louis P. Gorglione from White Plains, New York, was captured with several other Americans while fighting with the 2nd Infantry Division between Vire and Tinchebray, France, on August 14, 1944. A GI who spoke German attempted to convince their guards to surrender to them. One German confirmed he had received letters from his brother in a US POW camp that Americans treated POWs well. After being promised that their wounded would be cared for, the Germans surrendered.

When his fighter was downed by flak on March 18, 1945, Lieutenant Walter R. Johnson from Fountain City, Tennessee, hid the first night and then began walking toward the sounds of American tanks. Along the way he encountered two German soldiers who asked, "American pilot?" He answered in the affirmative but told them they were nearly surrounded by US troops; if they surrendered to him, he would see that they were well taken care of. They threw away their weapons and became his prisoners.

As the Allies advanced toward the German heartland, airmen began to successfully evade from Germany itself. Staff Sergeant Byron T. Johnson, a B-17 waist gunner from Cincinnati, Ohio, went down near Coblenz on September 19, 1944, and evaded to friendly lines. He wrote, "Advice on getting out of Germany: Avoid civilians and open fields. Go across country, stay off roads. Sign posts have been taken down. Travel after dark unless in forests."

In one instance even German civilians gave aid to a downed aviator. P-47 pilot Second Lieutenant William W. Donohoe Jr. from Long Island, New York, was shot down near Aachen, Germany, on October 14, 1944. He finally sought aid at a German farmhouse. In reporting his experience he wrote,

The family that helped me were Catholics. They had no Nazi emblems in their house, though they had pictures of several relatives and friends in uniform. They seemed to like the US and Americans, and were relieved when I answered "No" to the question, "Are you an Englander?" These people seemed to have no resentment against Hitler, or against the Allies. They were just tired of it all, and anxious to have the war over with.

American infantry evaders also had contact with the enemy dressed in American uniforms. Captured on January 11, 1945, near Houffalize, Belgium, by Germans wearing American uniforms, 90th Infantry Division soldier Private First Class Louis W. Cappello from Danville, Illinois, managed to escape within hours and return to American lines.

Private First Class Edward R. Snyder of the 82nd Airborne Division from Akron, Ohio, had a similar experience on December 26, 1944, also in Belgium. He wrote,

At about 2000 hours while returning to Manhay I met seven soldiers in American army uniforms. I asked them where they were going. They said they were headed for Manhay. Suddenly, one of the soldiers stepped behind me and placed a US .45 caliber pistol in my back and told me to follow. I realized then that these soldiers were Germans in American uniforms. The other six Germans were armed with US M-1 rifles, four of them spoke excellent English, and they even seemed to know most of our slang words.

His captors took him to an SS headquarters where he was interrogated and put to work in a kitchen. In captivity, Snyder observed more Germans in American uniforms along with American jeeps and rations. Snyder escaped on January 4 when US tanks approached.

Germans also posed as American airmen to oppose the bombing missions. Several fighters, three B-24s, and at least one B-17 were repaired after crash-landing in occupied territory. Kampfgeschwader 200 (KG 200, or in English Combat Air Squadron 200) operated captured

American planes to infiltrate formations and report their positions and altitudes. They had little success as American formations quickly developed standard identification procedures to detect infiltrators. The KG 200 planes faced dangers from their own forces. German flak brought down one of their B-24s on April 6, 1945, on a ferry flight from Hidesheim to Bavaria.

B-17 waistgunner Staff Sergeant Elton F. Kevil, waistgunner from Ballinger, Texas, reported an unconfirmed encounter with fake German planes on October 8, 1943. He wrote, "About one minute after our navigator warned us to be on the lookout for the escort of P-47s we would pick up on the way to the target, we saw what looked and acted like our escort except for the fact that the planes did not tip up their wings. They had USAAF insignia on the side. They flew along us for 45 seconds or a minute and then pulled past us and started attacking from the nose at 12 o'clock high."

Just the thought that Germans might be flying American planes endangered aircrews. Staff Sergeant James L. Berry, a B-17 top turret gunner from Bliss, New York, came down in Belgium on August 17, 1943. He later stated in his E&E report that a bullet hit the number two engine. He continued, "The navigator said it was a .50 caliber bullet which hit us. I thought that some of the other planes might have fired on us, thinking we were a B-17 which the Germans had captured and were using against American formations. Our plane was a brand new one and was used on this raid because every available plane was needed. We did not have the customary triangular marking and we did not even have the group letter yet."

CHAPTER 21

Humor and Religion

SECRET—AMERICAN
MOST SECRET—BRITISH

HEADQUARTERS
EUROPEAN THEATER OF OPERATIONS
P/W and X Detachment
Military Intelligence Service

E&E Report No. 448
Evasion in France

March 3, 1944

Name:	William L. Olson
Rank:	2LT
Unit:	578th Bomb Squadron, 392nd Bomb Group (B-24)
Home address:	Chicago, Illinois
Target:	Ludwigshaven
MIA:	December 30, 1943
Arrived in UK:	March 2, 1944

Other members of the crew:

Pilot	2LT	James H. Sibley	MIA
Co-Pilot	2LT	Leonard Volet	MIA
Navigator	2LT	William L. Olson	Narrator
Bombardier	2LT	Edward M. Boyle	MIA

257

Radio Operator	SSGT	Peter Garris	MIA
Top Turret Gunner	SSGT	Nicholas M. Carusone	E&E #415
Ball Turret Gunner	SGT	John L. Sullivan, Jr.	E&E #345
Waist Gunner	SGT	Everett F. Satterly, Jr.	MIA
Waist Gunner	SSGT	Frederick M. Wald	MIA
Tail Gunner	SGT	Fred T. Schmitt	E&E #344

On the 30th day of December, 1943, I was sailing blithely along in my B-24, returning to base in England, I thought, after a successful bombing on Ludwig-shaven, Germany. Right after the bombs were released and we were turning off we ran through a thick series of flak bursts, some of which undoubtedly hit our ship although it was unnoticed at the time. About 20 minutes after leaving the target, the engineer, who was manning waist gun, called the pilot on interphone inform-ing him that oil was escaping from No. 1 engine. Pilot noticed oil pressure had dropped considerably and feathered engine OK. About 20 minutes later No 2 had oil leakage and cylinder head temperature had risen and it was necessary to feather No 2 which was not as successful as it windmilled very slowly at times.

By this time we had dropped a mile or so behind the group and had lost con-siderable altitude, dropping from about 24,000 feet to 19,000 with No. 1 out and after both were out the group went out of sight. Pilot asked me to figure amount of time left for flight from time plane was at about 10,000 feet losing altitude at rate of about 900 ft. per min. and it developed that we would be compelled to ditch a short way off French coast or bail out.

Knowing how a 24 ditches we decided to hit the silk. Pilot gave warning over interphone and by emergency bell. I helped Bombardier out of turret and followed him to bomb bays. He finally jumped out of bay after gentle persuasion and I fol-lowed. This was at about 1500. There was an under cast so I opened chute almost immediately getting a juicy jerk and losing escape kit in my flight suit as well as helmet which was knocked off of my bean by straps flying up as they do in RAF chutes.

After breaking thru under cast I saw I was floating over town (Louviers) which I thought I was to land in. Due to a high wind I landed about 2 kilos south —my feet first hitting a nice cow which was peacefully munching some grass then flying into a barbwire fence which was torn down and inflicted a bad cut in my cheek as well as numerous scratches (I'm bucking for the Purple Heart). Aforemen-tioned cow went galloping across the countryside at about 40 MPH losing at least a month's supply of milk.

I finally managed to disentangle myself and by that time numerous French peasants had galloped up from nearby areas. I didn't stop to chat with them but gathered up my chute and Mae West and stuck them under some bushes. As many people were running up from all directions I thought it best to take off cross country and while looking for a suitable place to hide a French girl motioned for me to follow her. As she was fairly pretty I did so without hesitation.

She led me to a cottage but almost immediately her husband came rushing in excitedly yelling what I gathered to be the Germans were coming in droves. I immediately took off but spying a nice plot of grass in her back yard plunged into that and lay motionless, using my silk glove as a compress to stop the flow of blood from my cheek (Same Purple Heart).

Some German soldiers immediately went into the house and putting guns to the heads of the peasants demanded to know where the American was. They said they did not know but think I ran down a road alongside the house.

After a bit I heard them leave but still lay motionless until dark meanwhile taking enjoyment out of watching the heads of Germans going down the road looking for me. (I only saw their heads and tops of their guns due to a hedge which hid the rest of them).

At last when night fell (boom) the girl, named Aimee, and her hubby took me into their house and gave me a pair of trousers and cape and I then walked with them to their house in the town of Louviers. The house in the country belonged to Aimee's mother. I stayed there that night—Dec 30—and they informed me that they would give me some money and a rail ticket to Paris for the next AM where I would travel all alone and would make my way as this outfit was not connected with any organization in any way. However, later that night I was informed that the other persons had found out of my presence and that I would be flown back to England the next night.

In the meantime they filled me full of wine and Pernod and I slept very well. The next night I was picked up by a lady who led me to a car where her husband drove me to her home a bit on the outskirts of town. Woman's name was Jeanne and the husbands name Rene—name and address unknown. Husband was a forester or something and cut down trees. They were fairly well to do and had many chickens, etc., which they killed off rapidly so that I would be well fed. As that was New Years Eve we got properly stiff and retired. I stayed there four days and talked to Mssr. Verny, 2nd chief cook to Prince of Wales at Buckingham palace in 1909, who spoke a bit of English, and who was eager to have his name mentioned to Intelligence.

On Jan. 3, in the afternoon, I was picked up by an ex French Army officer in his car who drove me to his home and gave me a very nice suit and two cognacs after which he drove me to a town called Vefnon and took me to the house of Madam Fournier. That evening I met there Sgt. Carusone, S. Sgt. Peter Garris and Lt. Edward O'Boyle, gunner, radio operator and bombardier respectively on my crew. We had identity pictures taken and cards made and the following day were taken by her husband to Paris by train.

At the station in Vefnon we also picked up a so-called Polack who had supposedly escaped from a German labor camp and who accompanied us. Name Alex, blond, age 19 and a bastard.

We got to Paris at about 2100 that evening, Jan. 4, and were met at the train by a French Gendarme, Monsieur Bernard, who took us to a tavern where we dined and there we met Mssr. Robert Thiriet, our blessed benefactor. He was an ex French soldier who had lost both legs at Dunkirk but who had more than enough guts to make up for it.

At about 11 PM that evening a flock of females came to the tavern, one for each escapee, and we left with them making it appear as if we had just come from a party. Among them was Paulette Echeroux (with me) and her girlfriend Germaine or something like that with Carusone. We split up, the four of us going to Paulettes apartment where Carusone and myself were to stay—address 19 Rue Bridaine. Paulette, incidentally was the sister of Robert who was running the show.

From this point on Carusone and myself saw very little of the other crew members and Alex who were staying over some tavern address unknown. We were marvelously wined and dined, going out to taverns, theatres, subway riding and parties with Paulette, Robert, Bernard and friends.

About four days later, Robert took C and myself for a train ride—it was a Saturday Jan 8 or nearby. We left on a 7:45 am train for Bordeaux. Incidentally we had more photos taken for new identity cards in Paris. We arrived in Bordeaux at about 1800 that evening where we walked around for a couple of hours waiting for a train for Dax.

First train ride was uneventful. It was loaded with German soldiers who traveled 1st class (we went 3rd) and we ate in the diner on train with a flock of German pigs as dining mates.

We left for Dax about 7 PM arriving there at about 9:30. Upon arrival Robert took us immediately to family there who fed us and put us up. Next day—Sunday —Robert and wife of this bloke went to theatre and this fellow (name unknown to me possibly C knew it) took us for a most miserable bike ride to Pyrohadade and return, distance 48 kilos round trip after which C and self were in a state of near exhaustion.

The following morning were awakened by Lt. McDanal and Sgt. Ross and we were all taken for a ride in an old beat up charcoal burning truck to a large house about 30 kilos south of Pyrohadade accompanied by Robert and friends of Mc and Ross. We stayed in this house until the following night, Jan 10, when we were met by a guide at about 2100 who was to start our walking tour over the Pyrenees.

We walked through loads of mud and rocks and about four kilos from the house we met another guide and the two of them walked the whatyoucallit off of the four of us and at about one AM the next morning they poured us into a barn on top of a high hill with assurances that we would be met that night by more guides. (Robert paid off the man at the last house and gave us a few hundred francs for expenses or something.)

That morning a woman brought us a jug of wine and some bread which we put away quickly and we then spent a boring day mostly rubbing our feet.

That night were met by another guide who was also a fast walker and a few hours later another guide relieved him who could walk faster, especially up hill. That night we also slept in a pile of hay and the entire next day we sweat it out without food or water until late that evening when we were brought some bread and wine.

A little later we were met by two more guides, one French and one Spanish, who walked us right out of France into Spain, leaving us at the frontier. All of the guides took our name, rank and serial numbers. They told us to walk a couple of hours more and we would come to a hotel where we would get ham and eggs and a nice bed.

We finally came to the "hotel" and after a couple of miserable cold hours in another hayloft without food we set out again, arriving at about noon of the 14th in a little town called Orbaceits. There we inquired and found out a bus left for Pamplona on the 17th.

The Spanish military police finally picked us up in the town and turned us over to a good little joe named Geronimo who owned a small general store. After some persuasion we convinced him that the consul would take care of him and he arranged for real beds for us to sleep in and gave us food. (I have his card in my envelope, also pictures of Robert and Paulette.)

On the morning of the 17th we took a bus to Pamplona accompanied by two armed soldiers. They took us to the Cibil Gobierno (civil governor) where we were fingerprinted and given a card to fill out with place for names, addresses, way we got into Spain, etc. We only gave our names and rank and put USA as home and left other spaces blank.

Enlisted men were given identity cards, officers none and we were all taken to Fonda Pascuelana who was in pay of consul. Officers, Mc and self, were taken to some soldiers headquarters, where Spanish officer gave us a long list of hooey to fill out, including 18 questions on French morals, airports, airfields, etc. which we did not answer merely drawing a line after the questions or putting no information down. Mc and I were taken back to Fonda from where we called consul in Bilbao, Mr. Wannamker, who saw to it that we had clothes furnished, cigs, and everything else.

That same day enlisted men, C and B, were taken by train to Lecumberry—about 12 kilos from Pamplona—and Mc and I were left there. We stayed in Pamplona almost three weeks. We were free to do as we liked and ate pastries, chocolates, went to movies (in Spanish) with Senoritas and generally had a pretty fair time. We called the consul often for money and smokes and generally drove him crazy.

A few weeks later we were picked up, including all enlisted men and a few new arrivals, by a Spanish Lt. in the air force and taken to Zaragoza, arriving there late on a Sat. night. We tore loose in Z for a day or two and left on the following Monday by air force bus for Alhama de Aragon. We were very well treated there and were picked up about 12 days later by Col. C. E. Cousland, Military Attaché, who took us to Madrid by car (Jan. 18). There were 26 of us by that time. We left that same evening for Gibraltar and arrived there the evening of the 19th. We were issued uniforms—to some extent—and after about 9 days in Gibraltar left by plane for England and here I am.

Lieutenant Olson's use of humor, irony, and sarcasm is an absolute outliner of E&E reports. MIS-X interrogators sought the facts and only the facts. Some of the draft reports in the files show efforts at humor to be redacted. Just why Olson's unredacted draft report made it into the final files is unknown. Whether it was on purpose or by accident, it is revealing of the sense of humor shared by many of the evaders.

There was no official written regulation on the inclusion of humor in the E&E reports but the unofficial policy made it clear that humor should be omitted. Second Lieutenant James H. Walsh Jr., from St. Louis,

Missouri, was shot down while piloting a B-24. According to his report he managed to get on a train where he randomly approached Frenchmen for assistance. Fortunately for him none were collaborators. In comments to Walsh's report, MIS-X commander Lieutenant Colonel Holt wrote on June 24, 1944, "His approaching people in the train is the type of idiocy that requires divine protection."

A note attached to the comment, signed simply DEE (likely MIS-X staff officer Captain D. E. Emerson) states, "Just for the record it may be pointed out that this comment represents the type to which we have for some time objected. A great number of the exclusions also are what we refer to as the omission of amusing detail." The note also is evidence of the openness that Holt had with his subordinates.

Young men in times of hardship and difficulty have always found humor, often of the gallows genre, in adverse situations. They laughed at what they considered military bureaucracy and red tape. Even situations that were frightening at the time were found funny when retold later. Olson's report is the only one to include humor throughout, but other evaders also managed to include humorous accounts.

Much of the humor in the reports involved direct contact with the Germans and certainly must not have seemed funny until much later. Second Lieutenant Edward C. Miller, from Brooklyn, New York, was the copilot of a B-24 when shot down over France on January 7, 1944. Assisted by the French Resistance, he evaded to Paris where he did some sightseeing. He wrote,

> When I was in Paris I was taken to see the Arc de Triomphe. While I was looking at the tomb of the unknown soldier I felt a heavy hand on my shoulder. I turned to find myself face to face with a German soldier. I thought that I was already on my way to Dulag Luft and did not know what to say, but it seemed the German just wanted to take a snapshot of the tomb. I stood there holding his rifle when he took his snapshot. The German thanked me and left. When I rejoined my helper he was in stiches at the sight of me standing there holding the German's rifle. I could just begin to see something funny about the situation.

B-17 radio operator Technical Sergeant Kenneth P. C. Christian from Kansas City, Missouri, was shot down on February 8, 1944, and began walking south. While on the road, he was approached by three German soldiers. He raised his arm and shouted "Hail Hitler" and walked on. The Germans returned the salute and did not question him.

Technical Sergeant Walter L. House, a B-17 radio operator from Bowling Green, Kentucky, shot down on September 6, 1943, had an encounter with unalert Germans. Assisted by helpers, he and other evaders began making their way to Spain. House wrote,

> At one time a group of us were riding along on bicycles, strung along the road like a convoy. One sergeant with us could not ride a bicycle at all, and while he was making an attempt he wobbled right across the road in the dark and ran into a couple of German soldiers on bicycles. We thought we had lost the sergeant and would be lucky if the rest of us did not get taken. But these German soldiers picked the sergeant up, placed him on his bicycle, and helped him get on his way again. As if this incident were not nerve-racking enough, later we were walking along in pairs, pushing our bicycles. A couple of German officers in a staff car stopped our lead pair to ask them for road directions. While they were talking away, the rest of us passed them, pushing our bicycles along two by two. What they thought we were doing I could not imagine. The only solution was that they did no thinking.

David G. Prosser from Scarsdale, New York, joined the Royal Canadian Air Force before transferring to the USAAF as a flight officer in 1941 when the United States entered the war. On September 3, 1943, he was the navigator aboard a B-17 shot down over France. He began his evasion. In his report he wrote, "When I reached Nevers, I found it full of Germans. I was very hungry and tried to find a small restaurant, but saw only large ones, so I sat in a rather large one. A civilian I noticed sitting next to me wore a Nazi eagle pin, so I decided not to have much conversation with him."

Staff Sergeant Harry H. Horton Jr., a B-17 waist gunner from Ashville, North Carolina, was shot down over France on August 17, 1943. Helpers assisted his evasion. Recounting in his E&E report he wrote,

> When we were in Paris, we went to a café and enjoyed a most delicious meal. A number of German officers were sitting around, some of them quite close to me. While we were waiting for desert, we started smoking cigarettes and held them in our hands. Our waiter remarked to us amiably, "Messieurs smoke cigarettes during the meal just like Americans do." We could hardly get rid of the cigarettes quickly enough.

P-51 pilot Second Lieutenant Elmo H. Berglind from Seattle, Washington, had an even closer contact with German soldiers after being shot down over France on March 18, 1944. After a month of evading, he joined a helper who had had too much to drink in a cafe. From a nearby table the helper heard a German soldier tell his companions how well he spoke English. The helper told the Germans that his friend spoke English very well. When the German asked for a demonstration Berglind reported, "I spoke as poorly as possible and threw in all the French I knew. I tried hard to be funny and told him he was the only Englishman I had ever liked; whereupon he put his arms around me and gave me three packages of cigarettes."

Airman encounters with civilians on the ground sometimes resulted with humor. Some things were funny by what did not happen. Staff Sergeant Louie F. Weatherford from Samson, Alabama, was a radio operator on a B-17 that crash-landed in a freshly mowed hay field on September 6, 1943. He noted, "A farmer, standing 300 yards away, ignored our arrival completely."

Second Lieutenant Harry E. Roach Jr., a B-17 navigator from Philadelphia, Pennsylvania, was shot down in France on May 1, 1943. His civilian helpers took good care of him but still found time in the midst of danger to make jokes. He reported the humor, writing, "I was well fed and when I left in the morning they said, 'Hurry up, American.' They also asked me to bomb their house with chocolate sometime."

One evader found that the Germans also had a sense of humor. Technical Sergeant Joseph F. Dogle, an infantryman in the 30th Infantry Division from Kansas City, Missouri, was captured near the Belgian border on August 27, 1944. Dogle wrote, "The interrogator's first question to me at the Regiment CP was, 'Have you read Tom Sawyer?' I was so surprised. I said I had. Then he said my position was like that of Tom when he was captured by the pirates. He went on joking and telling the others about the book for quite a while. Then he got down to business." Dogle managed to escape and successfully evade to friendly lines.

Evaders also encountered animals. Staff Sergeant Robert G. Neil from Providence, Rhode Island, was a B-17 ball turret gunner shot down on May 17, 1943, and began his evasions moves immediately. He recounted his story, writing,

> Just before nightfall we started looking for place to sleep, like good tourists. I came to a haystack and started to make myself comfortable for the night. I disturbed a dog which had already established itself in the haystack, and he began a furious barking. Five or six more dogs came to help him express his indignation at being disturbed, so I left in a hurry before someone came along to find out what all the fuss was about.

With all the danger and death that came with each mission, religion played an important role in many aviator's means of coping. Prayer before, during, and after missions were routine with most airmen. However, like humor, almost no mention of religion made its way into the final E&E reports. Numerous reports did acknowledge that Catholic churches and priests generally provided sanctuary and assistance, but little was included about individual prayer and religious influences.

French civilians assisted Second Lieutenant Raymond J. Murphy, a B-17 navigator from Des Moines, Iowa, after he was shot down on April 28, 1944. He wrote, "After they had discovered that I was a Catholic they gave me a note to a priest and directed me to a town where I could find him."

First Lieutenant James G. Shilliday, a B-17 navigator from Pittsburgh, Pennsylvania, who went down over France, managed to get thoughts into his E&E report shared by many of his fellow aviators. He wrote,

In the chilly, foggy pre-dawn of September 6, 1943 plane number 30203 was airborne with a full crew aboard. The tanks were full and in the bomb bay were ten dangerous looking 500 pounders labeled Stuttgart, Germany—to be delivered air freight pre-paid. The crew relaxed and prepared themselves for a monotonous two hours of which precedes electrifying moments. We had no false illusions about where we were going or what might happen. If you're lucky Jerry picks on somebody else, if you're not you fight like hell, try to stay in formation, do a lot of praying, and maybe you come home.

Prayer continued on the ground as recorded by Second Lieutenant Jack R. Zeman, a B-17 pilot from Toledo, Ohio, shot down on January 5, 1944, over France. Zeman hurt his leg on landing. In his account he wrote, "For the next two weeks it bothered me to the point that when I wanted to lift my leg I had to pull it up with my hands. I just shuffled, and I shuffled for 25 miles." He used his escape kit compass but also relied on other powers to make a decision when approaching a fork in the road. He continued in his report, "I told myself that if I did not start traveling in a definite direction soon, it would be too late. Praying hard, I took the road to the right." Later, about another junction he wrote, "Reaching fork in the road, I did not know which way to turn. After repeating the line from the 23rd Psalm 'Thou are with me,' which I used whenever I did not know which way to turn. After repeating the line from the 23rd Psalm 'Thou are with me,' which I used whenever I felt things getting beyond me, I took the road on the left."

Despite the hardship and dangers of evading, Sergeant Norman P. Therrien, a B-24 waist gunner from Haverhill, Massachusetts, managed to go to church after being shot down in France on December 12, 1942. He wrote in his report, "The morning being Sunday, we attended Mass."

Staff Sergeant Glen H. Keirsey, a B-17 ball turret gunner from Tonkawa, Oklahoma, found comfort in his Bible during his nearly year-long evasion after being shot down in Northern Italy on August 17, 1943. Captured, he was interred in an Italian POW camp. Shortly after Italy signed the armistice of September 8 that ended their war against the Allies, Keirsey headed for the nearby mountains before the Germans moved in and took over the camp. He found help in a village and hid until June 8, 1944, when he and other evaders met an advancing British patrol and were told to wait for the arrival of more units. He recorded what happened, writing, "We were laughingly told that we had taken care of ourselves for nine months and should be able to continue to do so until the main body of troops moved in." The evaders waited for three days, and then hitched a ride to Rome. Keirsey wrote that while hiding for all the months, "I had a New Testament which I read three times."

German fighters shot down Sergeant Otto V. Roskey, a B-17 ball turret gunner from Chriesman, Texas, on February 4, 1944. In his E&E report he managed to include both religion and humor. He wrote that when he got on ground, he "spent about ten minutes getting religion." With his phrase card from his escape kit, he then went to a nearby house seeking help where "he played Fuller Brush man for a Belgian girl."

Evading infantrymen as well as airmen looked to their religion during their escape. Germans captured Joseph R. Ripnik, a private in the 80th Infantry Division from Phoenixville, Pennsylvania, on September 20, 1944. After being called a "Stubborn American" for refusing to give information, he grabbed a guard's rifle, stabbed him with the bayonet, and according to his own account, "ran for the woods. I hid the next day and was very scared the Germans would find and shoot me. I said a thousand 'Hail Mary's.'"

In addition to the rare mention of religion or humor, E&E reports seldom commented on the evader's reaction to making it back to friendly territory. Comments that did make their way into the reports are very much in the tradition of MIS-X matter of fact reports. Staff Sergeant Frank K. Piechoto, a B-24 ball turret gunner from Crows Landing, California, went down in Holland on June 29, 1944. Assisted by the Underground, Piechoto hid until British infantry arrived the following

November. In his E&E report he simply stated, "We were plenty glad to get out of there."

Technical Sergeant Raymond F. Pencek, a B-17 top turret gunner from Cicero, Illinois, went down in France on January 11, 1944. He successfully evaded and made his way back to the United Kingdom on September 9 where he wrote in his E&E report that he was "a lucky man to avoid the grim clutches."

Fifth Infantry Division soldier Private Floyd E. Fortner of Middleborough, Kentucky, became separated from his unit in France on September 3, 1944. He evaded until October 26 when he reached American lines. His thoughts as recorded in his E&E report are likely those of most evaders, "I was the happiest man alive to see Americans again."

Odds and Ends

HEADQUARTERS
EUROPEAN THEATER OF OPERATIONS
P/W and X Detachment
Military Intelligence Service

E&E Report No. 800
Evasion in Holland, Belgium, France

June 28, 1944

Name:	*Donald K. Willis*
Rank:	*MAJ*
Unit:	*HQ 67th Fighter Wing (P-38)*
Home address:	*None listed*
Target:	*Cover for Bombing Mission of Airdrome in Germany*
MIA:	*April 10, 1944*
Arrived in UK:	*June 28, 1944*

I crash landed on the coast of Holland near the Waalchedrn Islands after one engine had been hit by flak. I put the P-38 down between a football field where a game was in progress and the dikes. A wing struck one of the dikes and smashed the aircraft. Spectators and players were running from the football field when I got out of the plane. At least 500 people were milling about the crash and along the dikes.

I ran to the path where the people had left their bicycles and took one, grabbing with it a long red coat to throw over my flying jacket and green trousers. The coat had ten guilders and a watch in the pocket.

I got in among some cyclists on the path at the top of the dike and pedaled toward the German soldiers who were running from a nearby gun post. The soldiers were busy for the first few minutes trying to keep people away from the plane though several climbed on the dikes and searched the countryside with field glasses. I pedaled beside a woman who kept watching me out of the corner of her eye but she never spoke.

When we rode into a small village the woman turned down a side street. I parked the bicycle by a stone bench and sat there trying to think out my next move. A carload of German soldiers drove in to the village and stopped in front of the church. They got out, lined up in two ranks, and were into the fields with dogs to search. I walked around the town waiting for them to get some distance away before following the route taken by one of the parties. After they had searched a barn I crawled in thinking it was the safest place to hide at the moment. I was seen by the woman who owned the barn and she hurried out to tell me I could not stay there. I had no trouble understanding her because I speak Norwegian, which is somewhat similar to Dutch. She promised not to tell that I had been there unless the Germans came back. I crawled down a drainage ditch to a field of high grass and hid for the rest of the day.

After dark I checked my compass and walked cross-country in a SW direction. It was not easy walking because of the many dikes and fences. About midnight I stopped to rest at a barbed wire entanglement and was just missed by three German soldiers walking along a footpath. I thought they were a searching party and didn't move until I discovered they were the relief for a small gun post that I had nearly stumbled into. I went toward a group of buildings to see if I could find a place to sleep. A young boy and girl hailed me as I started to crawl into a haystack, and after some difficulty I convinced them I was an American airman.

I waited at the haystack while the boy took the girl home. He returned with food and said he would walk with me. He knew the country well and by 0800 hours we had reached Rosendall. My friend turned back then after giving me excellent advice and directions. There were some German strongpoints to be avoided but I was shown how to go around these and I was helped by traffic signs put up by the Germans. I found the road to Antwerp and followed it, keeping to a safe distance in the fields.

Around noon I reached Esschen. I had passed many people but so far had not spoken to anyone. At the edge of Esschen I saw Germans on duty at a control post and stopped an old woman to ask her how I could pass this barrier. She motioned that I should go around the control.

I went into a wood for the afternoon and hid where I could watch the people working in the fields. When they finished work I followed some of them along a small road into the town. There was either no control post here or the workers going to their homes in the evening were not searched. I found the railroad on the other side of Esschen and walked parallel to it until dark, when I made my bed in a stack.

I walked steadily all the next day, avoiding towns and speaking to no one. Twice I ran into German officers hunting in the fields but each time I hid before they could see me. I arrived at Antwerp in the afternoon and tried to get around it before dark but I picked the wrong direction and ran into water. In retracing my steps I walked into a German anti-aircraft battery and the soldiers on sentry duty motioned me away. At dark I crawled into a haystack but couldn't sleep because of the cold. Before daylight I went up to a farmhouse and got the farmer out of bed, but he wouldn't open the door. Finally he said to come back in the daytime. I waited for him to get up because there were no telephone wires to the house and I didn't see how he could notify anyone of my presence. He gave me some food and asked no questions.

I went into Antwerp that morning, having decided to ask someone how to get through the town. I stopped at a store where a man was loafing in the doorway, and after I started talking he asked if I was an American and took me inside. He gave me 230 francs and after assuring me that he liked Americans, told me I could ride a streetcar to the southern end of Antwerp for one franc without too much risk. He gave me good directions for doing this and when I had gotten outside of town I stopped at a roadside café to get some beer. There was a sign advertising "Boca beer," so I put down a franc note and said "Boca." The few people in the café paid no attention to me, but the Belgian who gave me the beer guessed my identity. I was taken into a back room, and given some eggs and bread but not a word was spoken to me. Just as I was leaving the Belgian brushed off some straw that was clinging to the back of my coat and smiled while doing it.

I started to Brussels, following the railroad line but got on the wrong tracks. Because I had more confidence now and felt some desperation about getting help, I went into a small railway station and tried to buy a ticket to Brussels. There was only a porter in the station and he explained that I was following about the only railroad in Belgium that didn't go to Brussels. He wanted to know if I had parachuted and told me he knew an English-speaking person. We went to see this person who said I would be helped, but while I was eating someone came in and said the police had been informed. I ran out the back door and got away from the place without seeing any activity.

I arrived at Boom about mid-afternoon. The railroad and road bridge were controlled by sentries and many people were being checked as they crossed. I was afraid, because only those people recognized by the guards did not have to show papers. Not having found a way to cross by dark I found a haystack to sleep in that night.

The next morning I watched some laborers carrying poles across the bridge. After they had done this several times I saw the guards were not paying any attention to them. My opportunity came when two women stopped to talk to the guards and while their attention was diverted I went up to one of the labor groups and hitched onto the pole they were carrying. The men looked at me but said nothing.

I walked to the woods where the men were stacking the poles and found that their work was directed by a German soldier with a rifle. At first I thought he was a guard, but he was paying too little attention to the workers. I wasn't sure how I could get away without arousing the German's curiosity and was pretending to work when a peddler arrived with an ice-cream cart. I crowded around with the workers, put down a 5-francs note and walked off, while the German was arguing with someone and had his back to me.

In the afternoon I stopped at a small café to buy a glass of beer and was followed out by a man who waited until we were alone before asking if I was not an American. When I admitted it and asked him what he was going to do about it he said he would like to help. From there my journey was arranged.

During my evasion while I was living in a large Belgian city I watched an American raid on a nearby target. I saw a B-17 catch fire and leave formation. Soon after that several parachutes opened above the city and one floated down into the section of town where I was. I had a good view of it and watched this parachutist land in the walled-in garden of a house. Just as he touched the ground a German motorcyclist stopped in front of the house and ran around to clamber over the garden wall at the back. When the German got into the garden the American burst through the front door of the house and hopped on the German's motorcycle and tore off down the street blowing his horn as loud as he could, and was cheered on by the Belgian people. Unfortunately, though I saw the start of his evasion, I never learned how he it made it out, nor did I find out who he was.

Much like Major Willis's story about the airman escaping on a motorcycle, there are many stories of evaders that do not exactly fit in other chapter heading. Within the MIS-X files are "one of a kind" accounts as well as various papers, orders, and other documents of interest that further the story of the evaders in Nazi-occupied Europe.

An air-to-air rocket shot down the B-17 on which Sergeant Herve A. Leroux from Hebronville, Massachusetts, was the ball turret gunner on January 5, 1944. He reported, "At nightfall I set out due south by my compass. I passed through a field full of debris from our aircraft. A piece of armor plate from behind one of the pilot seats had been driven two feet into the earth. It looked like a gravestone and I was at first afraid to pass."

Not all the dangers were from flak or German fighters. Second Lieutenant William E. Middledorf from Detroit, Michigan, was the copilot on a B-17 over France on August 15, 1943. "Returning from target our aircraft was struck by the propeller of another B-17."

While some E&E reports went on for multiple pages, some were extremely brief. This is likely because of the number of evaders that had to be debriefed at the time, the fact that the war was nearing an end, or simply because there was not much of a story to tell. First Lieutenant S. C. Williams, a P-51 pilot from Kansas City, Missouri, crashed-landed in France on September 2, 1944. He wrote, "I bellied in 30 miles south of Angars and was immediately taken into town of Aubigne-Briand by a FFI man on a motorcycle. The next day I was taken to Angers where I contacted the American troops."

Among the shortest of reports was that of Staff Sergeant Paul F. Dicken, a B-24 waist gunner from New Orleans, Louisiana, shot down over France on December 30, 1943. He summarized quickly, writing,

I was the right waist gunner of Lt. Schafer's crew and when he ordered us to bail out I left the plane at 1100 hours at 20,000 feet. I blacked out and came to at 5,000 feet, heading for a village. I guided my fall and landed at a crossroad. My chute got caught in a bush and I was unable to disentangle it. I discarded my Mae West and walked north. I met a woman and a boy but could not make myself understood so I went on. I avoided a farm where many dogs were barking and reached another farm near the woods. I knocked, walked in and explained I was an American. From there my journey was arranged.

Dicken returned to the United Kingdom on March 20, 1944.

Another short report was that of B-17 radio operator Staff Sergeant Herbert W. Dulberg from Chicago, Illinois, who was shot down over France on September 16, 1943. The report that noted Dulberg's return to the United Kingdom on February 5, 1944, is only one-third of a page, double-spaced. It states that the airman was shot down and was immediately surrounded when he reached the ground by French farmers who arranged his journey.

E&E reports were widely distributed to various headquarters, including the 8th Air Force, MI9, Royal Air Force, and MIS Washington, after their approval by Lieutenant Colonel Holt. There they were studied for their intelligence value as well as advice and guidance that could be passed along in preflight briefings to aircrews. Evaders were also of interest to ground commanders after their units began to liberate their hide places in their advance across Europe.

Flight Officer Thomas A. Matassa, copilot of a B-17 from Glendale, California, was shot down over France on August 10, 1944. After only two days of evading, the Maquis assisted him in reaching American lines. While being evacuated from the front, General George Patton learned of his journey and invited him to his headquarters and, according to his report, "asked him for his whole story."

General Patton also personnally debriefed B-17 pilot First Lieutenant William J. McKeon from Rockaway Beach, New York, and asked him about the tactical situation he observed during his evasion to American lines. McKeon had been shot down by flak while returning from a mission over Augsburg on July 19, 1944.

P-47 pilot Second Lieutenant Robert J. Clees from Arlington, Virginia, was shot down over France by a FW-190 on June 24, 1944. Clees successfully evaded and, with the aid of French farmers, remained hidden until he met advancing Americans on August 20. Accompanying the unit was writer Ernest Hemingway. Clees reported, "We had a very good time together."

Flak downed the B-17 that Staff Sergeant Kenneth N. Hougard from Portland, Oregon, served as a waist gunner over France on his twenty-fifth mission on May 8, 1944. Hougard evaded until liberated by an advancing US unit on July 4. Before evacuation to England, he was sent to army headquarters were he met General Dwight Eisenhower, the Supreme Allied Commander in Europe. On July 7, the BBC broadcast,

> At Corps Headquarters the General met SSGT E. Hougard of Portland, Oregon. He had just come through enemy lines. Hougard was a gunner in a Flying Fortress which was shot down over France on May 8th. Members of the French underground saw him parachute to safety, they took charge of him, they fed and clothed him, told him later about the invasion, and finally they passed him through to the American lines. He had just arrived and General Eisenhower promised to advise his commanding officer that he was safe.

Hougard's report is not unique just for his meeting with General Eisenhower. His became the exception to the protocol of awards being approved only through men's units. Even MIS-X could only recommend awards and forward the recommendation to the airman's unit—a procedure they rarely enacted. But Hougard received a special commentary rather than the typical endorsement that read, "For distinctive evasion from enemy territory, displaying courage, initiative, determination, and intelligence." Within his E&E report is a recommendation dated July 6 for an Air Medal for Hougard's display of

> courage and initiative in evading capture by the Germans after bailing out of his plane on May 6, 1944. He risked his own capture by German troops on four occasions by helping an infantry officer and a glider pilot who were hiding from the Germans in a barn near St. Nicolas de Pierre Pont in the La Haye du Puits area. He preferred to risk his own life under shell fire from American

troops in order to get back to his unit; whereas he could have been evacuated along with his French helpers.

The lengthy E&E report, dated July 16, 1944, was also professionally printed, unlike the regular forms for appendixes B, C, and D, as well as having a new cover sheet. Also, an additional designation, IS-9WEA—and a series of numbers based on the date—followed the E&E number. A new section of appendix B provided space for each part of the report to be evaluated as "Reliable, Creditable, Questionable, or Undetermined." Subevaluations for "Observation, Hearsay or both" were also included.

Another MIS-X exception was P-47 pilot Second Lieutenant Rudolph Augarten from Philadelphia, Pennsylvania, who was shot down over France on June 16, 1944. MIS-X recommended him for an award "for successfully escaping from a German prison camp and successfully evading the enemy until he reached American lines."

Recommendations for awards also occasionally came from the evaders themselves. Second Lieutenant Harry A. Hawes, a B-17 bombardier from Kansas City, Missouri, landed in France on September 3, 1943. He reported,

> Just as the navigator jumped, I saw the copilot looking out the bomb bay. His head was bleeding. While I was in the nose by myself, I checked my chute. Then I raised myself up to the cockpit to see how the pilot was. I looked back in the ship and saw Sgt Hamblin in the radio room helping the radio operator out. I think Sgt Hamblin should be recommended for the Silver Star or DFC for his action. Although he was wounded and dazed, he realized that the radio man was wounded, and in spite of the danger to himself, he assisted the radio man in getting out of the plane.

Hamblin (E&E No. 210) also successfully evaded.

Some of the E&E reports are rather fatalistic. Second Lieutenant Arthur J. Horning, a B-17 navigator from Cleveland, Ohio, successfully evaded with assistance of the Belgian Resistance after being shot down on October 10, 1943. One of his fellow crewmen was killed, the other eight captured. In his report, Horning noted that the Fortress had flown only one previous mission and had aborted because of cylinder heat. The plane had not been air checked by the maintenance crew before being sent out again. Horning wrote, "When we took off on October 10, we knew we were flying a coffin, and would never come back, but we also knew that we could not abort as they believed we were fakers."

Sergeant Thomas S. Geary from Woodhaven, New York, was acting as bombardier aboard his B-17 over Holland when it was damaged by flak and then downed by fighters on February 22, 1944. Geary was not supposed to be on the mission. The Fortress's regular bombardier was "ill at base, I took his place," Geary wrote.

Reports also occasionally included details on the deaths of fellow crewmen. Tail gunner Staff Sergeant David Butcher from Oak Park, Illinois, was the only survivor when his B-17 went down over France on July 4, 1943. Butcher reported that he later observed the graves of his fellow crewmen buried by the French. His report was verified by a British officer and fellow evader.

Bomber crews were carefully briefed on their responsibility to destroy their bomb sights and other classified material before bailing or after crash-landing. Most reports note compliance with these instructions, but B-17 copilot Second Lieutenant Dewey C. Brown Jr. from Mathis, Texas, went into extreme detail. After being heavily damaged by enemy aircraft on August 17, 1943, Brown's crew prepared for a crash-landing. As they descended, they threw their bomb sight into a river, destroyed the top turret gun sight, papers, and radio, and threw out parts of their machine guns. They did not stop after successfully crash-landing, as they tried to destroy the remainder of the Fortress with incendiary bombs.

The Germans also made reports on each downed Allied aircraft, but only one made its way into the MIS-X files. On May 6, 1944, B-17 pilot Second Lieutenant Murray L. Simon from New York City was shot down over France. The Office of Strategic Services intercepted the German report of the incident and provided it to Advance Headquarters "A" Force, a unit established by the British to coordinate deception efforts. The "A" Force forwarded the translated document to MI9 who in turn passed it along to MIS-X.

The document, dated May 15, 1944, states,

On May 6, at about 1 a.m. an American Bomber, probably a
four engine plane, crashed in flames in the woods of La Barthe
(4 kms south of Mably). After having warned the Feldgendar-
merie (the Wehrmacht unit responsible for policing the areas in
occupied territories), the Roanne Brigade (a local unit) proceeded
to where the plane had crashed and ascertained the aircraft had
been almost completely destroyed as a result of fire and of two
successive explosions that were heard after the crash. It appears
that the plane was shot down by a night fighter as machine
gun fire was heard a short time before the crash. The aircraft
was loaded with leaflets "L'Amerizue de Guerre" No. 99 dated
26/4/44 which were destroyed or badly damaged. A detachment
of "T.O." is guarding the wreck and making enquiries. One of
the crew members, severely wounded, was taken to the E. F. S.
hospital in Roanne and immediately operated upon. No bodies
having been found, it is thought that the other crew members
parachuted to safety. They are being looked for.

Airmen were briefed not to carry any written materials that might
be of intelligence value to the enemy and also not to keep notes of helpers or details of their evasion. Staff Sergeant William E. Shuster, a B-17
ball turret gunner from Wilmington, Delaware, found a way around the
regulation. Crash-landing on July 21, 1944, near Trier after his Fortress
had mechanical problems, Shuster was briefly held prisoner before escaping and reaching Allied lines. When he arrived in London, he turned
over a journal he had kept in pig Latin during his journey. A translation
is included in his file.

Along with the drafts and final statements, appendixes, and various
forms in each E&E report, there are also copies of routine orders maintaining accountability and providing assistance. The Military Liaison
Office of the American Consulate in Gibraltar routinely prepared orders,
stating,

Having reported at this station on (date), you are placed on temporary duty [at] this office. Upon completion of this temporary duty you will precede by first available transportation to London, England, where you will report without delay to the Commanding General, European Theater of Operations, US Army. In lieu of subsistence, a flat per diem of $6.00 is authorized while traveling and while temporary duty this station.

Odd papers in the files also provide insight into how the files were not carefully edited or purged before their transfer to the National Archives after the war. In addition to the multiple handwritten and typed drafts, just about anything remotely, or not even remotely, related to an evader's story found their way into the files. In the E&E report of B-17 navigator Flight Officer David G. Prosser from Scarsdale, New York, who was shot down over France on September 3, 1943, and arrived back in England on December 18, is a single page with the single practice line used by a clerk typist, "Now is the time for all good men to come to the aide of their country."

Little info was added to the files after their completion, and almost none in the years following the end of the war. The documents themselves were not declassified until 1975.

An exception was an inquiry by Pennsylvania congressman Richard S. Schweiker, twenty years after the war, concerning Technical Sergeant Richard H. Krecker, a B-17 radio operator from Pottsville, Pennsylvania, "who was shot down over Augsburg, Germany on March 16, 1944." An interoffice Disposition Form from the Department of the Army Office of the Chief of Information dated December 29, 1965, requested a review by a subordinate office to determine if the still classified E&E report (No. 776) of Krecker could be declassified and released. "The Archives maintain this file as a Secret document, but have authorized a portion of its contents." The DF itself is marked "Secret" and later declassified. The request made it through several other offices before the DA Adjutant General Office approved the release of the report on January 20, 1966.

CHAPTER 23

After Return

SECRET—AMERICAN
MOST SECRET—BRITISH

HEADQUARTERS
EUROPEAN THEATER OF OPERATIONS
P/W and X Detachment
Military Intelligence Service

E&E Report No. 660
Evasion in France

Date: May 21, 1944

Name:	*Charles E. Yeager*
Rank:	*Flight Officer*
Unit:	*363th Fighter and Recon Squadron, 357th Fighter and Recon Group (P-51)*
Home address:	*Hamlin, West Virginia*
MIA:	*March 5, 1944*
Arrived in UK:	*May 21, 1944*

Were you wounded? Yes, slightly. A 20 mm fragment penetrated right hand at joint of index finger.

Three FW-190s came in from the rear and cut my elevator cables. I snap-rolled with the rudder and jumped at 18,000 feet. I took off my dinghy-pack, oxygen mask, and helmet in the air; and then, as I was whirling on my back and began to *feel dizzy. I pulled the ripcord at 8,000 feet. An FW-190 dove at me, but when he was about 2,000 yards from me a P-51 came in on his tail and blew him to pieces.*

I landed in a forest-clearing in which there was a solitary sapling about twenty feet tall. I grabbed the top of the sapling as I passed it and swung gently to the ground. My chute was hung up in the tree, however.

I hid my Mae West and started off to the south-east, for I thought that I was in the forbidden zone. Before I had gone 200 feet half a dozen Frenchmen ran up to me. Some of them got my chute down, and one of the men took me by the arm and led me to a house some 200 yards away. There I was given food and civilian clothes. A gendarme was also approaching the house at this moment, and, I was quickly hidden in the barn. When the gendarme left I was brought back into the house where one of the men who had left the group now returned and gave me a note in English telling me to trust the people in whose hands I was. I was then taken to another house about a kilometer away, and from there my journey was arranged.

Chuck Yeager successfully crossed the Pyrenees into Spain and returned to the United Kingdom and reported to MIS-X on May 21, 1944. Following the regulations of the time the USAAF reassigned Yeager to rear duty in England. Yeager, however, with only one kill before being shot down by three FW-190s on his eighth mission, wanted to be back in the cockpit to have another go at the Germans. He appealed his assignment and requested permission to return to combat.

His appeal went up the chain of command all the way to Supreme Allied Commander General Dwight D. Eisenhower. Supported by the fact there were no longer any escape lines after the D-Day invasion that might be compromised in the event of capture, and the enthusiasm of the young pilot who had such good eyesight that it was said he could "see forever," Yeager returned to the air. By war's end he had shot down twelve and a half (shared kill with fellow pilot) German fighters.

Yeager remained in uniform after the war concluded and became the Air Force's top test pilot. In 1947, he became the first pilot to break the sound barrier. He later served in the Vietnam War and retired from active duty as a brigadier general in 1975.

After D-Day and Yeager's successful lobbying to return to the cockpit, the decision on whether or not to reassign evaders to combat depended upon their experiences with the Germans, their personal desires and those of his unit, and the classic mantra of "the needs of the service." B-24 Second Lieutenant Norman N. Wolf, a navigator/bombardier from Cleveland, Ohio, went down in France on July 25, 1944. Captured a day later he managed to escape and make his way to American lines.

Intelligence officers from the First United States Army sent a letter dated August 3, 1944, along with him when he returned to London on August 4 for debriefing by MIS-X. It stated,

> It is recommended that the following officer, having escaped German hands in France, not be assigned to combat duty in European Theater of Operations after return to his unit. LT Wolf was captured July 26, 1944, after baling [*sic*] out of his plane. Subsequently he escaped from his captors by overpowering his guards, imprisoning them, and delivering them into American hands. Germans have complete record of his name, rank, and serial number. As he was captured in civilian clothes, Germans held him under suspicion of being a spy, prior to his escape.

Some evaders previously sent back to the United States also sought return to combat in Europe. Captain Paul Pascal from Philadelphia, Pennsylvania, shot down while a lieutenant navigator aboard a B-17 on September 3, 1943, wrote to MIS-X on March 25, 1945:

> Since my return to the States I've made a couple of requests to be sent back to the ETO. It seems that most of our boys over here are off the ball. No one seems to know exactly what limitation is placed on those of my ilk. Perhaps you know if I may go back by signing a waver or perhaps I might return under another form of duty? If you know any angle which might allow me to go back to France how about slipping me an earful.

Flak brought down Second Lieutenant Leonard J. Schallehn, a P-47 pilot from Saratoga Springs, New York, in France on June 15, 1944. The Maquis hid him until they were overrun by advancing Americans two months later. Back in the United Kingdom, his fighter squadron sent a letter to MIS-X requesting he be returned. The letter stated that Schallehn was "well liked and fit in well" and that his return "will serve the best interest of the service."

On August 25, 1944, P-47 pilot First Lieutenant Robert L. Dawn from San Francisco, California, bailed out over France. From the comment to his E&E report: "After walking unconcernedly past a German soldier guarding a lock on a canal he received help from a French boy. From there it was the usual story; civilian clothes, shelter, resistance groups until overrun by the advancing American army on September 2."

Dawn returned to his fighter squadron only to again be shot down in October 1944. Although suffering a minor leg wound, he walked through both German and American lines until he reached a US artillery observation post. He wrote, "Went thru chow line and had my breakfast before anyone saw fit to stop or question me. Had already been shot down once at St. Quentin on August 25, 1944 and had been through 63 Brook Street where I saw Lt. Byron. I requested to go back on operations, but now I want to go back to the States."

B-17 tail gunner Ivan L. Schraeder from Peoria, Illinois, was shot down in France in 1944, and with assistance from the French underground evaded to Spain and returned to the United Kingdom where he rejoined his bomber squadron. With only days left in the war, his plane was shot down, killing him on April 20, 1945.

Paratroopers and infantrymen, with few exceptions, were returned to their units and combat after reporting to MIS-X. A comment to the E&E report of Private First Class Richard Vatalaro of the 101st Airborne Division from Akron, Ohio, stated, "While in the hands of Swiss authorities the soldier claims to have made a signed statement to the effect that if he was released he would not fight again in this Theater. . . . The soldier is now performing duty with the 506th Parachute Infantry Regiment."

Other than the few repeat successful evaders, the Office of the MIS-X's primary contact with the airmen after their debriefings concerned returning money and personal items and passing along messages from former helpers. Captain Dorothy Smith took care of much of this correspondence. These letters show that the MIS-X personnel and the evaders often formed strong bonds and affection despite their short time together.

P-38 pilot Captain Paul S. Miller from Los Angles, California, ran out of fuel and crashed in France on March 4, 1944. He successfully evaded and made it back to the United Kingdom twenty-two days later. Captain Smith wrote Miller on February 5, 1945, saying that twenty-seven pounds "we believe belong to you" had been sent from the consul office in Spain and that she would forward a money order to him if he sent the correct address. Smith concluded the letter, "What's it like to be back in the States? We envy you. Write us sometime."

Captain Smith also forwarded money "found to have never been sent to you" to Second Lieutenant Carl H. Bundgaard, a P-51 pilot from Withee, Wisconsin, downed on July 4, 1944. In the closing paragraph she wrote, "Did you have a good trip home and find the USA all that you had been dreaming of? Write us sometime and let us know what happened when you got back."

On December 14, 1944, Captain Smith forwarded a money order for French francs to B-24 top turret gunner Staff Sergeant Arthur S. Meyerowitz from the Bronx, New York, who had been shot down on December 31, 1943. Meyerowitz responded on January 9 with a thank you, information on his promotion and hospitalization from his injuries, and a request for return of "the small gun which is a very highly prized possession of mine." He concluded, "I hope the buzz-bombs haven't been bothering you folks too much over there."

Smith replied on March 13, "We can't send a gun through the mail. We don't know how or when it will get to you, but don't worry about it because we fully appreciate your attachment to it. At present, it is in the major's desk—as he is the only one of us with enough rank to have a desk with drawers—and there is a big label tied to it giving your name and home address." She added, "We were all very pleased to see that you had made Tech. Sgt. We often worry about what sort of a deal you boys get when you get home. Do you run into one another often? There must be a lot of you home now."

On April 30, 1945, Sergeant Arden N. Brenden, a B-17 waist gunner from Starbuck, Minnesota, was shot down by fighters. On March 16, 1944, he wrote to MIS-X,

> I am writing you to let you know how much I appreciate the fact you wrote me the address of Mrs. Legeune. I have not as yet received a letter from her but am in hopes I will soon. I was recently discharged from the army so I am now taking life easy. I am traveling as a representative for a cement company. Again I wish to thank you for sending me the address of a family which did so much for me while I was in that country.

On January 4, 1945, MIS-X wrote to Second Lieutenant Robert T. Conroy, a B-17 navigator shot down by German fighters on July 14, 1943, at his Burlington, New Jersey, address, saying,

> Recently we met some friends of yours—Mme Lionel Henry and M. Lucian Duquesne. They were interested in your present whereabouts which we were unable to give them but we explained that you had returned to America. They were very pleased to have this news and stated that they would write you a letter. We promised Mme Henry that we would tell you of her second child—a girl—whose middle name is Roberta. This daughter was born on July 15, 1944. Mme Henry remembered that she and her husband had had the pleasure of meeting you on July 15, 1943. This information is passed to you in the event you should care to write Mme Henry.

B-17 top turret gunner Technical Sergeant James E. Tracy from Holyoke, Massachusetts, successfully evaded for more than five months after being shot down in France on October 14, 1943. He wrote in a letter to MIS-X from the United States on August 16, 1945:

> I wish to express my thanks for the information you sent me. I was very glad to receive Mr. Bruxelle's address. I wrote to him

immediately. He is one of many who aided me in my trip thru France. Perhaps thru him I will be able to contact others who have helped me. Thanking them is the least I can do. Many of those who helped me were killed and it is very nice and makes me quite happy to know that at least one of them escaped the jinx of helping me.

First Lieutenant Stanley J. Wolczanski, copilot of a B-17 that went down near Paris on June 14, 1944, managed to have a letter smuggled from France to the United Kingdom from where it was posted to his sister in his hometown of New Hartford, New York. A report on the letter from the UK Postal and Telegraph Censorship Office eventually made its way into Wolczanski's MIS-X file. By that time the airman had been liberated by advancing American infantrymen and had been interviewed by MIS-X personnel on September 14.

The Censorship Office report stated, "An Allied serviceman, who is apparently being concealed by French civilians, writes to his family in the USA." It continues under "Copy of the letter" to relate, "If this letter reaches you as I hope it does you will know that I'm safe at the moment from the enemy. I'm feeling fine and am in good health and hope that you are all the same. If you got this letter it will be good news to what you have received in the past." This is likely in reference to a telegram of his being listed as missing in action after his Fortress went down.

The letter continued, "The French are treating me well and I hope that after the war we can help them. Give my love to everyone, Dad and Mom for your sake I hope this goes thru. Please give my love to Wanda. In closing I ask you to keep this secret only with the immediate family and Wanda as its knowledge to anyone else can mean my capture. Please don't tell anyone."

Not all ended well even for airmen who successfully evaded. P-47 pilot First Lieutenant Harry W. Hohl Jr. crash-landed in France on June 8, 1944, and made his way back to England to be debriefed by MIS-X on August 28. He returned to duty and was shot down and killed the following January.

On May 23, 1945, MIS-X received a letter from Harry W. Hohl Sr., stating,

> Yesterday I received an envelope containing several snapshots, French money with addresses written on it and two other lists of names and addresses written in French and German. This envelope was addressed to my son, LT Harry W. Hohl, Jr., who was reported "killed in action'" on January 2, 1945. I would be grateful if you would give some explanation of these papers. If possible where they came from, and why they were sent to my son.

MIS-X responded on June 21, reporting,

> In June of 1944 your son, when on a mission, was shot down over France. He evaded capture by the Germans until August when the territory in which he was hiding was liberated by Allied Forces. At that time the souvenirs he had collected were held by our office for security reasons. When those security reasons no longer existed the souvenirs were returned. The snapshots and names with addresses must be people who helped your son while he was hiding from the Germans. The officers of this detachment met your son at the time he was liberated and it is with deep regret that we receive your news.

P-51 pilot Second Lieutenant Joe M. Randerson from Austin, Texas, crash-landed on September 3, 1944, after being shot down by small arms fire. He suffered severe burns in the crash and Chetniks transported him in an ox cart to a barn where Nada Mihailovich, wife of General Mihailovich, treated his injuries. After he recovered, the Chetniks moved him to several safe houses before turning him over to a Russian major on November 5 who took him to Belgrade, then to the American consul.

Following his recuperation, Randerson returned to his fighter squadron and completed forty-nine combat missions before the war in Europe ended. After he returned home, Randerson, in gratitude for Nada saving his life, sponsored her and her children, Vera and Dan, to come to

America and become citizens. His parents helped support the Mihailovich family as they adjusted to their new lives. The children went on to
complete their college education at the University of Texas and became
successful in business in the Houston-Galveston area.

CHAPTER 24

News

UNDERGROUND ESCAPE
By Jim Douglas
(Boeing News, Vol. 14, No. 6, June 1944)

The hero of this story is called Sgt Joe Morgan. That is not his name. His real name must remain a military secret. Apart from the use of fictitious names for Morgan and his crewmates, this story of the sergeant's adventures in the Underground has been altered only with respect to details which might conceivably aid the Nazis in establishing the identity of his plane or the vicinity in which it was shot down.

They were going to walk back from this raid. The crew knew it even before the pilot's cool command came over the B-17's intercom: "Prepare to abandon ship!"

With the number three engine afire and number four running away, the Fortress was going down. Nazi fighters knew the ship was doomed, too. They broke off the fight and went streaking after the rest of the Forts that were heading for targets in Festung Europa.

Aboard the crippled bomber, the guns grew quiet. The engineer gave up trying to put out the fire that was already eating into the wing. The bombardier released his bombs on a barren field. That way they couldn't kill innocent farm folk.

Crew members hurriedly worked their way toward the escape hatches, trying to get out before the bomber exploded. Sharp questions were flashing through their minds.

If they survived the bailout would the Nazis be waiting for them, or would the natives be on hand to help them get away? Would they be in a mood to help? After all, they were being bombed by the Americans. Tech. Sgt Joe Morgan was thinking of that as he stood awaiting his turn to jump.

When the bomber was at 18,000 feet, the first men dove out into the blue. Over the intercom Morgan could hear the navigator and the bombardier helping the wounded co-pilot out. He saw the chutes open below. Then it was his turn to find the answers to his questions. He jumped.

There were no Nazi planes overhead. Just the blazing Fortress and swaying chutes in the air. He watched the bomber racing away, then heard an explosion. The plane had blown up within half a minute after the last crewmen escaped.

Morgan bumped to earth in a plowed field. Men came running toward him, from nowhere, it seemed. He had a moment's indecision, then he started for some nearby woods. There was no time to ask questions, just make a get-away.

As he raced over the broken field he stumbled momentarily. He regained his balance, and saw more men—directly in front of him. The men shouted at him— in a strange tongue. They waved their arms, gesturing frantically. They were, he soon perceived, just farmers and villagers.

The men pointed out where the radio man, Sgt Harry Foss, and the ball turret man, Staff Sgt Mike Sweeney, had come down a couple hundred yards away from Morgan. He hid his chute and ran over to join them.

WOUNDED CO-PILOT

The three airmen stood in the middle of the field, bewildered. A score of peasants gathered around them, staring and talking excitedly. One villager stepped forward. Speaking in English, he told the three another crew member was in a nearby field, badly wounded. They knew it was the co-pilot.

When they reached the co-pilot they found him too dazed even to notice them. It was evident he must be put under a doctor's care immediately. The villagers assured the flyers they would see that a doctor was called, and advised them to hide in a hollow in the field. As they started for the hollow, the English speaking villager stepped forward again and pleaded with the flyers to turn themselves over to the Nazis.

"The war will be over in three weeks," he said, "so why endanger the lives of all of us? If you escape we will be killed as hostages, and you will gain only a few weeks' freedom."

The others seemed to understand and they growled their disapproval at the speaker. It was certain they didn't agree with the man. They led the flyers through the falling twilight to the hollow, not bothering to argue.

"Wait up, you guys," Foss called as Morgan and Sweeney walked on ahead. "I got a piece of flak in the heel and it's slowing me down."

Morgan and Sweeney stopped and waited for Foss. They hadn't noticed his limp before.

HIDE AND PLAN

They stripped off the shoe and sock. The flesh was cut and bruised, but the wound wasn't deep. The men knew it was going to be slow going; but when Foss suggested they leave him, they said, "Nuts."

They lay in the warm darkness of the night, watching a full moon creep across the sky, and made their plans for an escape to neutral territory. It would be necessary for them to leave this particular area quickly, for the Nazi troops were thick here, and in the habit of stopping civilians to examine passports.

About midnight some of the farmers came out to the hiding place with civilian clothes and food. In broken English they told the flyers the best path of escape.

Just before dawn Morgan crept from the hollow to some nearby woods and cut a forked stick for Foss to use as a crutch. The wounded foot was bothering him.

As the first traces of sunlight came in the eastern sky, they started out, keeping well off the roads. As they crossed fields they watched the farmers harvesting their crops. Occasionally they stopped to steal fruit from trees, or drink from a stream.

For nine days the men kept up their never-ending hike, always working their way in the general direction of neutral territory. Some nights they slept on farms, sometimes they were turned away.

QUIZ SESSION

The days went by. They were getting a little desperate now. At last, at one farm house [sic] they stopped and asked for aid. They were met by English-speaking natives who asked them in.

Morgan, Foss and Sweeney stepped into the drab room. The frizzled old man who seemed in charge thrust his head into another room and spoke lowly to someone unseen. Then he returned to the men and sat down at a rough-hewn table. Two younger men came from the adjoining room and looked the flyers over critically.

The Americans felt cold sweat standing out on their foreheads. Why didn't someone speak?

The old man broke the silence. "You are Americans?"

"Yes," Morgan replied cautiously.

"You're airmen? Where was your plane shot down?"

"We landed over a week ago," Morgan said.

"What squadron were you in? What was your base?"

The questioning continued for nearly an hour. Morgan knew the old man was trying to trick him into a wrong answer. The other farmers seemed to be making a mental note of all the flyer said.

Morgan nudged Foss, who was standing beside him. The two edged toward the door.

The old man smiled then. "It's all right, lads," he said. "You have just stumbled into the Underground."

IN FRIENDLY HANDS

The younger men smiled warmly and then disappeared into the next room, to reappear with food and wine. The flyers sat at the table and relaxed for the first time in nine days.

They were able to do a lot more relaxing, for their stay at the farm home stretched out into days. During the stay, the men could never go outside in daylight. Even the persons on adjoining farms didn't know their neighbors were members of the Underground. Morgan and the others had to sit inside, reading English books and playing cards. It wasn't until night that they could walk out and stretch their legs.

So thoroughly was the Underground working that it had means of checking the flyers' records. There were no chances taken here.

Days later the men were given travel orders. They were seeing Nazis now. They walked on the same streets with them. After a few brushes with them, the flyers realized the Nazis seldom speak to civilians. Always the flyers were told where to go. Sometimes they stopped in little villages, other times in cities. They ate and slept in the homes of the rich and poor alike. Young and old—all kinds were in the Underground.

YANKS—HOT GOODS

For months the slow process of working to a neutral country kept on. Sometimes the men sat at a house for days, waiting for the next move to be plotted. If the going was hot in some spot, they were abruptly rerouted.

After months of travel the men were safely outside enemy territory. From there they went to England, arriving in mid-winter.

Upon reaching England, the men were sent back to the States. They will not be allowed to return to the European theater for action again. They know too much about those who helped them, to risk being recaptured and forced to talk in Nazi torture chambers. And according to international law, if they are grounded in enemy territory a second time the men could be shot as spies.

Morgan and his companions learned this in their travels of Europe: the Underground is ready to rise up and fight the Germans when the first invasion troops are put ashore. If they are as efficient as Morgan found them to be, Europe will be very unhealthy for Nazis.

Contents of the MIS-X E&E reports were classified. General information received a classification of "Secret" while appendix C, which contained details on helpers and lines, was marked "Top Secret." MIS-X required each evader to read a War Department directive dated August 6, 1943, titled "Amended Instructions Concerning Publicity in Connection with Escaped Prisoners of War, to Include Evaders of Capture in Enemy or Enemy-Occupied Territory and Internees in Neutral Countries."

The directive explained that publication or other communication of accounts of evasion or escape "not only provides useful information to the enemy but also jeopardizes future escapes, evasions, and releases." Details of this "publication or other communication" followed. A second section detailed specific information not to be revealed or discussed.

A certificate concluded the directive where the evader signed and dated that he had read the document and understood "that any information concerning my escape or evasion from capture is Secret and must not be disclosed to anyone other than the agency designated."

The *Boeing News* article was not the first leaked information about evaders, but it did gain significant attention from the chain of command. An undated, unsigned memo from the headquarters of the 8th Air Force to the commanding general US Strategic Air Forces in Europe stated, "Publicity of this sort makes it difficult to persuade evaders of the importance of complete security in regard to their escape and evasion." It then referenced the War Department Directive of August 6, 1943.

There are no surviving documents of the 8th Air Force or other headquarters directing an investigation by MIS-X. A memo to Lieutenant Colonel Holt, likely prepared by Captain Dorothy White, along with the 8th Air Force memo and the *Boeing News* article are in the E&E report of B-17 ball turret gunner Staff Sergeant Joseph M. Kalas from

Bethlehem, Pennsylvania. In addition to Kalas, the memo identifies the other two crewmen as radio operator Sergeant Ardell H. Bollinger from Drexel Hall, Pennsylvania, and waist gunner Staff Sergeant Leonard J. Kelly from Everett, Washington.

According to the memo, "They were MIA September 23, 1943 and arrived in UK January 23, 1944. These men were interrogated by CPT White. The *Boeing News* story agrees in all essential details with their evasion story as published in E&E Reports 335–337. The narrator of the *Boeing News* story is identified by CPT White as SGT Kalas." There is no record of any discipline administered to the three evaders.

Although the *Boeing News* article created the most controversy, other articles preceded it into print. Some reporters, either ignorant of security problems or possibly believing "a good story" was worth risking American lives, did not hesitate to write about the evaders. On February 26, 1943, the *Washington Evening Star* published an article headlined "Lt. Robert E. Smith Awarded Air Medal in London Ceremony: Flyer, Forced Down in France Found Way Back to England."

Smith came down in France on September 23, 1943, and returned to the United Kingdom on January 26, 1944. The newspaper article reported,

> Second Lt. Robert E. Smith, 620 Otis Place N.W., who was forced down in Vichy France, in his RAF Spitfire last fall found his way back to England through France and Spain and is now fighting with the United States Air Forces in England, was awarded the Air Medal at ceremonies in London yesterday, according to an Associated Press dispatch.
>
> Lt. Smith is the son of Frank E. Smith, an engineer with the Chesapeake & Potomac Telephone Co. The father received the news of his son's award at Gallinger Hospital where he is under treatment for a broken ankle received in a fall recently. Mrs. Charles R. Smith of 9115 Providence Avenue, Silver Spring, wife of an uncle of Lt. Smith said, "Bob could come over here and train pilots, but he says he would rather be over there knocking down enemy planes. He is a very brave boy.

Lt. Smith attended Park View Elementary School and was graduated from Central High School. He attended Bullis Preparatory School in Silver Spring and The Citadel military school in Charleston, S.C. After attending George Washington University for half a year he went to the West Coast for aviation instruction. He joined the RAF in December 1941 and transferred to England. Lt. Smith was with a bomber squadron over France last fall when his Spitfire fighter ran out of gas and he was forced down in France. While he was still reported missing, his family in Washington was notified by the War Department that Lt. Smith had been transferred from the RAF to the Army Air Forces. Sometime later American authorities in Vichy reported he had been found and American representatives in Spain subsequently reported he had reached Barcelona. From there he went to England.

First Lieutenant Charles W. Walters, a B-24 pilot from North Tonawanda, New York, parachuted into France on January 7, 1944. He returned to the United Kingdom on February 24 and apparently talked with a reporter from the Associated Press after returning to the United States. On April 11, an AP story, datelined April 10, North Tonawanda, New York, ran in the *New York Times* with the headline "Escape from Reich Described by Flier" with the subtitle "Walters, Ex-Temple End, Says Reaching Britain after Crash Was Lots of Work and Luck." According to the article,

First Lieutenant Charles W. Walters, former Temple University end, who with six other American airmen, trudged through occupied Europe and reached England two months after their bomber crashed in southwest Germany, said tonight that the escape was "just a case of a lot of hard work and a lot of luck."

The 28-year-old former football player, mentioned for All-American honors in 1938, credits "my long athletic background for giving me stamina to get back home. The trip was out of enemy-occupied country was sure rugged and most of it was made on foot," he added. Lieutenant Walters, now resting at home, said the Liberator he was piloting burst into flames after a bombing mission Jan. 7 on the Ludwigshafen poison gas manufacturing center.

"Three of my crew, Second Lieut. J. M. Bickley, copilot, Fort Worth, Tex.; Tech. Sgt. Louis Del Guidice, radioman, New Haven, Conn.; and Staff Sgt. Carl Hite, engineer, Gary, Ind.; landed near me," he explained. "We haven't heard from the other five boys."

The group met three other American airmen shot down in a previous bombing mission "right under the noses of the Germans," Walters declared, but said he was unable to disclose the details. The three were Capt. Peter Hoyt, pilot, of Cleveland; Second Lieut. William Cook, navigator, of Phoenix, Ariz.; and Dan Hanslik, bombardier, of Saginaw, Mich.; Walters said. He identified Cook as a 1940 Colgate University graduate and runner-up in the 100-yard dash in the 1940 national championships.

"Several times we came very close to being capture, had little to eat and were bothered by the cold," Lieutenant Walters said. "We were able to plot our way to England through the use of the escape kit which is part of the equipment on American planes."

The lieutenant, now getting acquainted with his 14-month-old daughter, Judith Lynne, said he would report to the Atlantic City relocation center April 20. Before he enlisted in March, 1943, he played end for the Paterson, N.J. Panthers, farm team of the New York Giants, and was a teacher and coach at the Union, N.J. High School.

Flak brought down B-26 pilot First Lieutenant John B. Hegg Jr. on September 23, 1944. On January 19, 1945, his hometown newspaper the *Detroit Free Press* published "Detroiter's Amazing Escape from Nazis" by Norman Kenyon. The story read,

Capt. John B. Hegg, Jr., 23, of 3410 W. Chicago, never thought he'd be an actor. But when the chips were down, he acted a role for 72 days that won him his life and freedom. Much of the story is locked in the War Department's secret files. The horror he experienced perhaps has helped other Allied airmen to escape the Nazi inquisition.

Capt. Hegg portrayed a Dutch farm character. He is blond and fair, harkening back to his Swedish ancestors—excellent qualifications. But for 72 intense days he was a deaf and mute Dutch rustic. His story started last Sept. 23. As flight commander of a B-28 unit, he was piloting his Marauder on a bombing mission against Germany, just over the Holland border.

Suddenly, five direct hits from a Jerry antiaircraft gun bracketed his ship. Fire broke out in the left engine and radio compartment. Out of control, the bomber plunged to earth. At 9,000 feet, Capt. Hegg ordered his six-man crew to bail out. Capt. Hegg went out at 7,000 feet, a brief moment before the Marauder exploded. He landed safely.

For a week and a half he dodged German patrols before being captured. Then for four more days he was questioned, but the Nazis could only shake their heads. "The Huns have developed the idea that all American fliers are ex-gangsters, paid fantastic salaries to do as much damage as possible," Capt. Hegg said.

Later the Detroit flier fled from the Germans, although handicapped by shrapnel wounds on his face and hips. He went without food three straight days, at other times ate only fitfully. Eventually he reached Dutch territory. "I became a Holland farmer," he related. "I'd never been on a farm in my life, but I watched the others. I learned to let my shoulders sag and to walk with a shuffle." He lived surrounded by German soldiers billeted in the same house.

"The Allied drive had stalled and I was reconciled to spending the rest of my life always fearing the Germans would get wise to me," he went on.

Finally, he reached Washington. He will be sent to a Miami rest camp shortly. He is a graduate of McKenzie High School and a former war plant employee.

On April 11, 1944, the *New York Times* reported on P-47 pilot Major Walker M. Mahurin, with the headline, "Two American Aces Lost on Missions over Europe." The article read,

> Two of America's seven leading aces in the European Theater were shot down in air combat March 27 when powerful formations of American planes smashed nine French airbases the War Department revealed yesterday in messages to the flier's families. They are Maj. Walker M. Mahurin of Fort Wayne, Ind., credited with twenty-one planes. It is believed that Major Mahurin may be a prisoner of war for one of his comrades in the March 27 air battles forwarded information to Mrs. Mahurin that he had seen the ace bail out of his plane. Major Mahurin for months held the title of America's leading ace in the European Theater and added to his fame Dec. 22 when he shot down two Focke-Wulf 190s within two minutes while escorting American daylight bombers to northwest Germany.

The article continued with information about a fellow pilot who became a POW.

Six weeks later the *Times*, under the headline "US Thunderbolt Ace Comes Back" reported "Major Walker Mahurin, Eighth Air Force fighter pilot, who had been missing since March 27, is reported back in England, according to a Fort Wayne, Indiana message from his mother. Mrs. Mahurin has a letter from her son saying he is safe and back here."

A FW-190 shot down Captain Elmer E. McTaggart over France on May 14, 1943. While evading to Spain, his helpers managed to get a message to England that he was safe. This message was relayed to his wife in Virginia. On June 2, under the headline "Flier's Wife Gets News of Safety," the *Richmond Times Dispatch* reported, "A three-word cable from England today was reason for great rejoicing by Mrs. June McTaggart, 24, of 5644 Santa Cruz Avenue, Richmond. The cable, which said 'Mac is safe,' came after her husband Captain Elmer 'Mac' McTaggart, 25, pilot of a P-47, had been reported missing in action. His plane reportedly had been riddled by Nazi planes over enemy territory. McTaggart has a four-month son, Stuart whom he never had seen."

Evasions by ground troops also became the subject of news articles. Tech 6 William J. Barrett of the 4th Tank Destroyer Group from Irvington, New Jersey, captured forty Germans and three half-tracks on September 9, 1944. On December 19, 1944, Earl Mazo reported in the *Stars and Stripes*,

> With Third Army—If Cpl. Bill Barrett kept a diary of his tank destroyer activities in Europe his most eventful 24 hours would read something like this: "Tonight a buddy and I were sleeping side by side when a mortar shell came in killing him and cutting me up a little. I did not want the other fellows to come after me, because the shells were dropping pretty thick and they might get killed, so I played dead and they let me be. Late tonight a German patrol came along, though, and took me in. They put me on a tank which was soon knocked out. So I was carried to a ditch and put alongside a wounded German captain who looked like a sensible guy. He talked English, so I said, 'Look here, Mac, the fighting is over for you birds. You know both you and I would be better off in American hands. He thought about it for a while.' The captain handed me his luger, called to his men to throw away their guns and told me they were all my prisoners. I waved my white undershirt and a bunch of Yanks came over and seemed surprised as hell when I told them that, while lying on my back, I had captured all these Germans and their three half-tracks."

Reporters continued to write and publish stories about evaders much to the displeasure of MIS-X. C-47 pilot First Lieutenant Harvey W. Doering from Wahiawa, Indiana, and his three-man crew were shot down by flack on D-Day after dropping their load of paratroopers. After crash-landing they began moving, with the help of Frenchmen, toward US lines. Before being overtaken by the US 9th Infantry Division, the crew spent two days in a farmhouse under a heavy table as artillery neared. Taken to VII Corps Headquarters, the crew was interrogated in presence of about twenty war correspondents. Colin Wills, a BBC correspondent, listened and wrote a script that he broadcasted the next day.

MIS-X attached a comment to Doering's E&E report:

> Crews should be briefed to resist our own interrogators, correspondents, and broadcasters concerning details of their evasion or escape. By War Department directive such information is to be given only to American military attaches and authorized personnel of MIS. These evaders were improperly interrogated by a field S-2 in the presence of 20 war correspondents, and their story was later put on the air by BBC. To jeopardize the lives of our helpers for the sake of a moment's publicity strikes as a high price to pay.

MIS-X again reiterated this stance in a comment to the report of B-24 waist gunner Staff Sergeant Frank Digiovanni from Brooklyn, New York, who went down in France on July 24, 1944. After reaching American lines, he talked to several journalists. The staffer noted, "The reason for the War Department directive forbidding evaders to tell unauthorized people their story is the protection of helpers. Crews must be briefed not to talk about their evasion, because in the great majority of cases helpers are involved, and they must be protected."

CHAPTER 25

V-E Day and Beyond

HOLLAND OFFICE
6801 MIS-X DETACHMENT
MILITARY INTELLIGENCE SERVICE
UNITED STATES ARMY
APO 887

10 June 1946

SUBJECT: History of the Holland Office of 6801 MIS-X Detachment

The Holland Office was established in June, 1945, for the purpose of investigating the help given by Dutch Nationals to American and British aviators who were forced to evade the enemy in Holland during the war.

*   The end result of the investigations of the Holland Office were to forward for approval of the headquarters unit recommendations for recognition awards to be given to Dutch Nationals who had contributed materially to the escape and evasion of American and British personnel. These recommendations were to be made on the basis of the quantity and quality of the evasion help given, and upon the amount of personal risk in that aid. The recommendations were to arise out of a joint conference of the British and American units to bring both units in accord on the assistance by any helper of Allied pilots. The work was, first, considered to result in a joint award of the British and American governments, with the possible inclusion of the Dutch government, but was later modified to a policy of separate awards, meeting with the approval of the Dutch government. Nevertheless, since no differentiation had been made by underground workers in the handling of evasion personnel of the two governments, helpers were to be recognized for their*

work irrespective of the American or British nationality of the personnel which they had aided.

An additional duty of the Holland Office was to ascertain the existence of any claims which might be outstanding or forthcoming from Dutch Nationals as a direct result of their evasion help. In the beginning it was not clear to what extent there might be persons eligible to file claims against the Allies for difficulties such as deaths and imprisonments that had arisen out of voluntary work done to evade downed airmen. The claims policy itself was in the formative state, and required further definition for accurate application in the region. Minor claims for losses of articles of clothing and food, and vehicles such as bicycles, were settled by following the British precedent of obtaining parcels and bicycles as explained below in the section on claims.

On May 8, 1945, the Allies celebrated Victory in Europe (V-E) Day. To paraphrase a popular song of the time, "The lights went on again all over the world and the boys are home again."

Airmen and aircraft began making their way back across the Atlantic Ocean. Some men with lengthy combat records were discharged; older planes were placed in storage. Other men and their bombers and fighters prepared to join the fight against Japan, but that conflict also ended before many were redeployed.

On May 14, 1945, MIS-X completed their final evader interviews. E&E Report No. 3064 briefly relates the story of Second Lieutenant Carl H. Gooch, a B-17 pilot from Independence, Missouri, shot down by flak over Holland on September 26, 1944. Two Dutch boys took him from the field where he landed to a farmhouse near Leiden where farmers gave him clothes and food. His helpers hid him until the end of the war.

With no more evaders to interview, MIS-X turned their full efforts to recognizing those French, Belgian, and Dutch citizens who had assisted American airmen. As early as December 1944, British authorities established offices in Paris, Brussels, and The Hague to seek out and reward those who had helped Allied aviators. The Americans joined them after V-E Day in these efforts.

The "History of the Holland Office" of the MIS-X detachment in Holland, portions of which lead this chapter, provides excellent insight into their efforts. MIS-X conducted similar operations in France and Belgium, but either no summaries of their efforts were made, or they did not make their way into the MIS-X archives.

The lengthy Holland report is in two parts, totaling twenty-four single-spaced pages. It includes an "Original Organization of the Unit" that covers personal, quarters, and supply. The report notes "Franklin D. Coslett, promoted from 1st Lt. to captain after assignment, was the officer in charge of the unit, and was especially suited to this assignment, having himself been an evader following the forced landing of his plane in Holland in the spring of 1944." Coslett, a B-24 navigator from Wilkes Barre, Pennsylvania, had been shot down on April 29.

"Operations of the Holland Office" explains that they based their initial investigations on information gathered by their British counterparts and upon the E&E reports from MIS-X in London and Paris. There were, however, problems with the E&E reports. The commentary notes,

> Many of these reports were indefinite in their references, and it was only with great difficulty that the majority were traced by investigators. In addition, one of the difficulties experienced tracing helpers from the references in the E&E Reports was the fact that many helpers working with the underground organizations were themselves hiding in a region remote from their actual homes. When located, many were at an address some distance from the place of reference. Also, many of the helpers had made use of assumed names in their work.

The Holland office also sought helpers who assisted aviators unsuccessful in evading and who became prisoners of the Germans. "RAMP Reports" from Repatriated Allied Military Personnel, recorded by the former POWs on standard forms and from personal interviews, also provided leads and read, "The majority of these forms were either incomplete in naming helpers, or were incorrect in their references or the spelling of those references. Nevertheless, he RAMP reports served as an additional important source of names of helpers of pilots." (Throughout the report, aviators are referred to as "pilots" rather than crewmen or airmen. No explanation is provided.)

Former underground leaders assisted in developing lists of helpers. The Holland office noted the names of each helper on index cards and filed them by country province. As more and more helpers were identified and questioned, it became apparent that many, like most civilians all across Europe, were suffering from food and other shortages. The report noted, "Captain Coslett arranged for the acquisition of clothing and food parcels, and other items such as bicycles for distribution to helpers by visiting investigators. In a country where such items were definitely among the scarce and nonexistent materials, these gifts were welcomed as Godsends by these helpers who were deemed deserving of them."

Holland Office investigators did not just wait for helpers to come to them; they took to the field in search of the Dutch who had assisted downed aviators. Captain Coslett led the way by retracing his evasion route to seek out his helpers. Suboffices were also established in outlying provinces.

The report continued, "January 1, 1946, Coslett reported to the Paris Headquarters that the work originally accepted by the American branch was virtually complete and that in some instances even assistance was being accorded to the British office by sending investigators from the American office into the area assigned to the British."

In the second part of the Holland office report, the investigators noted that, despite the redeployment of much of their staff, they were pressured "to complete the greatest bulk of work with the personnel available."

To reach out to helpers not yet identified, the Holland office began a newspaper and radio campaign to further identify those who had assisted American airmen. This generated "a huge volume of letters and postal cards." By February 1946, the Holland office began cash payments to Dutch citizens for their assistance helping evaders.

The Holland office, as well as those in Paris and Brussels, separated helpers into six categories. Grade I contained "those persons who are accredited with having been the chief organizers of large groups operating over an extensive period of time. In addition to their having been the organizers, they should at all times have assumed active direction of operations, and in more than just local areas."

Grade II was given to "those persons who were the chief organizers of small groups operating over only local distances, or were active sub-leaders of large groups." Generally, these helpers assisted fifty or more evaders.

Grade III included those helpers "who transported roughly 30 to 40 pilots over distances, who housed 40 or more pilots for brief periods of time, or who housed a smaller number of pilots, 30 or 40, for longer periods of time." The authors of the report admitted that this was a "variable category" and required "considerable discussion."

The MIS-X investigators assigned Grade IV "for their having done a quantity of transporting or sheltering over an extended period of time, but usually are not leaders of their groups." In their continued efforts to quantify assistance rendered, the investigators included those who "had helped 15 or more pilots, had transported them over local distances, or had sheltered them during a major period of time."

Grade V contained those helpers who had "direct contact with at least one evader involving shelter of at least one night, or personal transport over a distance exceeding about 15 kilometers." This grade was also given to helpers who made initial contact with evaders and assisted in their escape from their landing spot.

"General help given not necessarily involving personal contact" made up Grade VI. This included furnishing ration cards, suits of clothing, and other material necessities of life.

The History of the Holland Office concluded,

> A statistical summary of the cases handled and graded brings out the fact that up to the 30th of June 1946, about 12,000 names had been entered on the files and considered either positively or negatively for recommendation for recognition. Eight persons were recommended for presentation of the Medal of Freedom, Gold Palm; 14 for the Silver Palm; 60 for the Bronze Palm; and 163 for the basic award without palm. Totaling 245 Medals of Freedom recommendation. In the lower categories, 5,353 were recommended for the presentation of the Eisenhower Certificate,

2,123 for the letter of thanks from the Military Attaché to the Netherlands, and 998 were placed in the group to receive definitely no award. The remainder of the 12,000 names have been closed in the files as duplicates under pseudonyms or underground addresses, or have been accounted for as persons who were erroneously reported as having aided airmen.

Except for those investigators seeking former helpers, MIS-X personnel began returning to the States soon after V-E Day. Records and files were transferred to Fort Hunt. By the summer of 1946 all had returned and MIS-X was no more. Colonel William Holt rejoined the faculty at the University of Washington in Seattle in late 1945. Captain Dorothy Smith remained in France to marry French Resistance leader Commandant Pierre Hentie.

Six days after the war in the Pacific ended on August 14, 1945, MIS-X at Fort Hunt received orders through intelligence channels to "burn all your records" and other materials within the next twenty-four hours. It took thirty-six hours to accomplish the orders and when the smoke cleared, there was little remaining to note the accomplishments of MIS-X. The destruction of the records and materials came somewhat from the natural paranoia and mistrust of intelligence officers, in general, about openly sharing their methods and procedures. It is more likely, however, that MIS-X was caught up in the efforts to destroy evidence of MIS-Y's interrogations and hidden microphones that eavesdropped on high ranking German prisoners of war.

More than 3,000 E&E reports did, however, survive the purge because they were still in Europe being used by the offices in France, Belgium, and the Netherlands to identify and reward helpers.

CHAPTER 26

Legacy

To provide at-risk of isolation personnel with the skills and confidence to "Return with Honor."
—US Air Force Survival, Evasion, Resistance, and
Escape School Mission Statement (2021)

American airmen received Escape and Evasion briefings at their stateside training bases before deploying to the European Theater. Prior to their missions over Nazi-held territory, they once again were briefed and issued escape kits and purses. At no time during World War II, however, did standard centralized instruction for E&E exist.

The first effort to establish such training came from the commander, not of European air forces but those in the Pacific. USAAF general Curtis LeMay, a veteran air commander in the European and China-Burma-India Theaters, was an early proponent of survival training for aircrews. When he assumed command of all aerial operations against the Japanese home islands in 1945, he established several survival courses in Canada before consolidating all Air Force survival training into a single center at Fort Carson, Colorado.

In the early 1950s, the Air Force survival school moved to Stead Air Force Base near Reno, Nevada. During this same time the navy, marines, and the army also established or expanded their survival training. In 1952, the Department of Defense designated the Air Force as the executive agent for escape and evasion, meaning they had "specific responsibilities, functions, and authorities to provide defined levels of support for operational missions, or administrative or other designated activities that involve two or more of the DoD Components."

The survival school moved to Fairchild Air Force Base, Washington, on March 15, 1966, when Steed closed. Today, it continues to be the executive agent for survival training by the other services while also operating separate schools for tropic, desert, and artic survival at other locations. By the 1970s, training became known officially as Survival, Evasion, Resistance, and Escape, or SERE.

Today's Air Force SERE training lasts for nineteen days. The Fairchild AFB center also provides a five and half month specialist training course that teaches service members on how to teach SERE techniques.

Official guidance for the actions by service members while in combat or captivity came with Executive Order 10631 signed by President Dwight D. Eisenhower on August 17, 1955, which stated, "Every member of the Armed Forces of the United States are expected to measure up to the standards embodied in the Code of Conduct while in combat or in captivity." This Code of Conduct, with slight word changes by President Jimmy Carter in 1977 and President Ronald Reagan in 1988, remains in effect today.

Central to the code is that it prohibits surrender except when "all reasonable means of resistance" have been exhausted and that "certain death the only alternative." It encourages captured American service members to "resist by all means available" and to make every effort to escape and aid others." The code also affirms that under the Geneva Convention prisoners of war should give only "name, rank, service number, and date of birth."

Returning MIS-X staff and evaders contributed to the early work to establish survival training schools. Former evaders also strived to maintain the comradery of being veterans of the Winged Boot and Blister Clubs while also recognizing those who assisted their evasion.

Many evaders maintained contact with their European helpers after they returned home. It was not until two decades after the war, however, that evaders formally organized as the Air Forces Escape and Evasion Society (AFEES) with the stated purpose "to encourage airmen who were aided by Resistance organizations or patriotic nationals of foreign countries to continue friendships with those who helped them."

AFEES held its first reunion in Buffalo, New York, on May 15–16, 1964, and over the years increased to a membership of nearly 1,000 evaders. Activities include annual reunions and visits to Europe to thank their helpers.

After their first meeting, the AFEES saw the need for a symbol or logo for their organization. All agreed the unofficial "winged boot" pin they had worn on the inside of the lapel of their uniforms during the war should be included. Using the winged boot as the central theme, they added generic wings with the shield of the United States of America above the letters AFEES on top. At the bottom they added the Latin phrase *Pro Libertate Ambulavimus*, which translates to For Liberty We Walked.

In 1992, the AFEES published *Air Forces Escape and Evasion Society*, which contains evasion stories and a list of members. Clayton C. David, president of the society, wrote in the dedication,

> This book is dedicated to our "Helpers," the thousands of foreign nationals, who risked their lives to come to the aid to the Allied fliers shot down over enemy occupied countries. It is dedicated to the hundreds of brave men and women of the Resistance who were tortured and executed by their occupiers, because they were Helpers. It is also dedicated to those of our Helpers who survived long periods of detention and torture in Nazi prisons and concentration camps.
>
> The penalty for aiding Allied airmen was well known, but this did not deter our Helpers from taking the risks. We, the survivors, salute those who paid the ultimate price. We vow to make known to future generations that these brave men and women made the supreme sacrifice to insure our freedom, as we fought together for the freedom of all.

The passing of the years has thinned the ranks of the evaders and their helpers. Old age has finally stopped the movement of the "wing-footed" evaders in a manner the Nazis and their collaborators never could. Their legacy lives on, however, through the training of modern airmen and airwomen at SERE schools and in the hearts of everyone who believes in never giving up regardless of the circumstance and danger. Today, AFEES activities are mostly conducted by the children and other family members of the original evaders.

Appendix I

American Aircraft

B-17 FLYING FORTRESS

The Boeing Company flew the first B-17 bomber in 1934. Upon seeing its large number of machine guns, a Seattle newspaper reporter labeled it the Flying Fortress, a name that forever remains associated with the aircraft. Boeing shared production with Lockheed, Douglas, and Vega to manufacture 12,730 B-17s prior to and during World War II. Over the years the original B-17 went through more than a dozen adaptations and models, with the G model the most popular with nearly 9,000 taking the air. B-17s delivered 44 percent of the 1.5 million tons of bombs dropped on Nazi Germany and its territories—more than any other type of aircraft.

General

Crew: 10 (pilot, copilot, navigator, bombardier/nose gunner, flight engineer/top turret gunner, radio operator, waist gunners (2), ball turret gunner, tail gunner)

Length: 74 feet 4 inches

Wingspan: 103 feet 9 inches

Height: 19 feet 1 inch

Empty weight: 36,135 pounds

Gross weight: 54,000 pounds

Max takeoff weight: 65,500 pounds

Powerplant: 4 × Wright R-1820-97 "Cyclone" turbosupercharged radials with 1,200 hp each

Performance

Maximum speed: 287 miles per hour

Cruise speed: 182 miles per hour

Range: 2,000 miles with 6,000 pounds bombload

Armament

Guns: 13 × .50 inch (12.7 mm) M2 Browning machine guns in nine positions (two in the Bendix chin turret, two on nose cheeks, two staggered waist guns, two in upper Sperry turret, two in Sperry ball turret in belly, two in the tail, and one firing upward from radio compartment behind bomb bay)

Bombs:
    Short range missions (400 miles): 8,000 pounds
    Long range missions (800 miles): 4,500 pounds

B-24 LIBERATOR

The first B-24 took to the air from its Consolidated Aircraft manufacture in San Diego in late 1939. Over the next six years, a total of 18,452 rolled off the assembly line in more than sixty variants, making it the most produced aircraft of World War II. One-third of these planes went to Allies of the United States with Great Britain receiving some of the earliest models. It was the Royal Air Force that christened the B-24 as the Liberator and the USAAF soon adopted the name as well.

B-24s were known for their difficult flying characteristics that resulted in a higher accident rate than the B-17. Many in the Air Force referred to the B-24 as "the widow maker." It also lacked overall comfort. The B-24 had a lack of interior crew member space and inferior heating. Gasoline fumes often filled the fuselage, requiring the opening of the bomb bay doors to clear the air.

Because of its design, the B-24 was forced to fly at a lower altitude than the B-17s, resulting in a higher rate of combat losses to flak. It was not considered as "rugged" as the B-17. Despite its flaws, most crews loved their B-24s and argued that the Liberator was superior to the Fortress.

General

Crew: 11 (pilot, copilot, navigator, bombardier, radio operator, nose turret, top turret, two waist gunners, ball turret, tail gunner)

Length: 67 feet 2 inches

Wingspan: 110 feet

Height: 17 feet 7.5 inches

Empty weight: 36,500 pounds

Gross weight: 55,000 pounds

Max takeoff weight: 65,000 pounds

Fuel capacity: 2,344 gallons

Powerplant: 4 × Pratt & Whitney R-1830-35 Twin Wasp, R-1830-41 or R-1830-65 14-cylinder two-row air-cooled turbosupercharged radial piston engines, 1,200 hp each

Performance

Maximum speed: 297 miles per hour at 25,000 feet

Cruise speed: 215 miles per hour

Range: 1,540 miles at 237 miles per hour and 25,000 feet with normal fuel and maximum internal bomb load

Armament

Guns: 10 × .50 caliber M2 Browning machine guns in four turrets and two waist positions

Bombs: Short range (400 mi): 8,000 pounds
  Long range (800 mi): 5,000 pounds
  Very long range (1,200 mi): 2,700 pounds

B-26 MARAUDER

The twin-engine medium bomber Martin B-26 Marauder took to the air in the late 1930s. A total of 5,288 in two dozen variants were produced during the war with most flying in the European Theater. Considered difficult and dangerous to fly, it earned the nicknames "B-Dash-Crash," "Flying Coffin," and "Martin Murderer" by its crews.

Despite its problems, it earned the record of the best return from mission rate than any other bomber in the war. One B-26, named Flak-Bait, survived 207 missions—more than any other American bomber in World War II. It completed 725 hours of combat time and returned twice on one engine, had its electrical system knocked out twice, and on another occasion lost its hydraulic system.

General:

Crew: 7 (two pilots, bombardier/radio operator, navigator/radio operator, three gunners)

Length: 58 feet 3 inches

Wingspan: 71 feet 0 inches

Height: 21 feet 6 inches

Empty weight: 24,000 pounds

Gross weight: 37,000 pounds

Powerplant: 2 × Pratt & Whitney R-2800-43 Double Wasp 18-cylinder radial piston engines,

Performance

Maximum speed: 287 miles per hour at 5,000 feet

Cruise speed: 216 miles per hour

Range: 1,150 miles with 3,000 pounds bombload and 1,153 gallons of fuel

Armament

Guns: 11 × .50 in (12.7 mm) M2 Browning machine guns. One in nose position, four in blisters on fuselage, two in dorsal turret, two in tail turret, two in waist positions

Bombs: 4,000 pounds

A-20 HAVOC

The Douglas Aircraft Company initially designed the A-20 for the French Air Force in 1936 as a medium bomber, fighter, and reconnaissance aircraft. After the fall of France, the A-20 continued as a part of the British Air Force and with the lend-lease program with the Soviet Union. By war's end 7,478 A-20s had been produced.

A-20s were some of the first planes flown by US pilots over Nazi-occupied Europe after the United States entered the war in 1941. On July 4, 1942, twelve A-20s from the 8th Air Force flew the first missions as a part of the Royal Air Force's attack against German airfields in Holland.

The versatile A-20, with its various models having the capacities of both bomber and fighter, was popular among its crews. It was known as "a pilot's airplane" for its durability and capability to survive extreme battle damage. However, the introduction of large numbers of B-17s and B-24s relegated the A-20 to a minor role in the overall air campaign.

General:

Crew: 3

Length: 47 feet 11.875 inches

Wingspan: 61 feet 3.5 inches

Empty weight: 16,031 pounds

Fuel capacity: 400 gallons, 300 gallons in an optional external tank, 676 gallons in four optional auxiliary tanks in the bomb bay

Powerplant: 2 × 14-cylinder air-cooled radial piston engines, 1,600 hp each

Performance

Maximum speed: 317 miles per hour at 10,700 feet, 325 miles per hour at 14,500 feet

Cruise speed: 280 miles per hour at 14,000 feet

Time to altitude: 10,000 feet in 8 minutes 48 seconds

Armament

Guns: six fixed forward firing 0.5 in (12.7 mm) Browning machine guns in the nose, two 0.5 in (12.7 mm) Browning machine guns in dorsal turret, one flexible 0.5 in (12.7 mm). Browning machine gun, mounted behind bomb bay. Bombs: 4,000 pounds

C-47

The C-47 was the workhorse of the USAAF and Allies with its capability to transport soldiers, drop paratroopers, tow gliders, haul cargo, and serve as a flying ambulance. Initially designed and fielded as a commercial airliner in 1935 by the Douglas Aircraft Company as the DC-3, it immediately dominated the industry. In 1939, the USAAF made its first orders and in January 1942 began full-scale acquisition with the DC-3 modified with a reinforced fuselage, stronger cabin floors, larger rear doors for loading cargo and dropping paratroopers, and more powerful engines. By war's end, plants in California and Oklahoma had turned out more than 10,000 of the versatile aircraft.

General

Crew: four (pilot, copilot, navigator, radio operator)

Capacity: 28 troops

Length: 63 feet 9 inches

Wingspan: 95 feet 6 inches

Height: 17 feet 0 inches

Empty weight: 18,135 pounds

Gross weight: 26,000 pounds

Powerplant: 2 × 14-cylinder air-cooled radial piston engines, 1,200 hp each

Performance

Maximum speed: 224 miles per hour at 10,000 feet range; 1,600 miles Ferry range: 3,600 miles

Service ceiling: 26,400 feet

Time to altitude: 10,000 feet in 9 minutes 30 seconds

Appendix II

German Aircraft

ME-109

The Messerschmitt Bf 109 first saw service with the German Luftwaffe in 1937 in the Spanish Civil War. Allied airmen commonly referred to the fighter as the ME-109. Manufactured by Messerschmitt AG, the ME-109 had an all-metal monocoque (structure supported by an external skin) construction with a closed canopy and retractable landing gear.

The ME-109 was one of the principal German fighters for the entire war. With adaptations and constant upgrades, the 109 matched any of the fighters flown by the Allies. A total of 33,984 ME-109s were produced, many by slave labor in Nazi concentration camps, before the end of the war making it the most produced fighter in history.

While no American amassed more than forty kills, German pilots had great success with the ME-109. Eric Hartmann in a ME-109 downed 352 Allied aircraft—345 Soviet and 7 American—to become history's most successful fighter pilot. Hartmann shot down his last plane on May 8, 1945, only hours before the end of the war. Imprisoned by the Soviets for ten years, he returned to Germany and helped form the West German Air Force. He died in 1993 at age seventy-one.

General

Crew: one (pilot)

Length: 29 feet 4 inches

Wingspan: 32 feet 7 inches

Empty weight: 4,954 pounds

Power plant: V-12 inverted liquid-cooled piston engine

Performance
Maximum speed: 320 miles per hour

Range: 547–711 miles

Combat range: 273–355 miles

Armament
Guns: 2 × 13 mm synchronized
  1 × 20 mm or
  1 × 30 mm
  2 × 20 mm MG 151/20 underwing cannon pods

Rockets: 2 × 21 cm

Bombs: 1 × 551 pound bomb or 4 × 110 pound bombs or 1 × 79 gallon drop tank

FW-190

The single-seat Focke-Wulf 190 joined the ME-109 to form the backbone of the German fighter force. Introduced in the late 1930s, it was considered equal or superior to Allied fighters early in the war. Its twin-row radial engine allowed it to lift a heavier load giving it more flexibility than the ME-109 to carry bombs and for ground attack. The FW-190 had greater firepower than the ME-109 and had superior maneuverability at low to medium altitudes. A total of 22,823 FW-190s were produced before the end of the war.

General:
Crew: one (pilot)

Length: 29 feet 4 inches

Wingspan: 34 feet 6 inches

Fuel capacity: 169 gallons

Powerplant: 1 × 14-cylinder air-cooled radial piston engine

Performance

Maximum speed: 404 miles per hour

Combat range: 250–310 miles

Rate of climb: 3,000 feet per minute

Armament

Guns: 2 × 13 mm (.51 in) synchronized
4 × 20 mm

Bombs: one bomb under fuselage or four bombs under wings

ME-262

The Messerschmitt 262 (Schwlabe or Swallow) was the first operational jet-powered fighter aircraft. Work on the ME-262 began before the outbreak of World War II, but design problems, engine defects, metallurgy, and lack of support from high level civilian and Luftwaffe officials delayed its deployment unit late1944.

More than 1,400 were built during the war but only 50 were ever approved for combat. This small number, however, accounted for shooting down a total of 542 Allied planes before the war ended. Superior to their propeller driven planes, the ME-262 was all but untouchable to the Allies unless it was on the ground, taking off, or landing. Although the ME-262 greatly influenced the future of fighter aircraft, it was too little, too late, to impact World War II overall.

General

Crew: one (pilot)

Length: 34 feet 9 inches

Wingspan: 41 feet 4 inches

Powerplant: 2 × axial-flow turbojet

Performance

Maximum speed: 560 miles per hour

Range: 650 miles

Service ceiling: 37,570 feet

Armament

Guns: 4 × 30 mm MI 108 cannon

Rockets: 24 × 55 mm (2.2 in) R4M rockets

Bombs: 2 × 550 pound bombs or 2 × 1,100 pound bombs

Appendix III

German Antiaircraft Defense

By definition, any projectile launched from the ground with the intention of downing enemy aircraft is a part of antiaircraft defense. The Germans referred to this effort as *flugabwehrkanone* (aircraft defense cannon) or flak. Its cornerstone was the 8.8 centimeter flak artillery gun known to the Americans as the 88. Shortly into the war the Americans began referring to all ground-launched missiles and shrapnel simply as "flak."

The 88 was developed in the 1930s and by the end of the war, the Third Reich had produced more than 20,000 of them. Usually deployed in a square formation of four guns, fire was controlled by a control data center. This complex (for its time) device required a five-man crew and combined a four-meter optical range finder with a mechanical computer that transferred azimuth and elevation to the guns. Ammunition came with time-delayed or barometric fuses to fill the sky with shrapnel.

In addition to their use against aircraft, 88s were effective in a direct fire mode against ground targets including infantry and tanks, using a ZF 20-E telescopic sight. The 88 became the most recognized Nazi weapon of the war to both American air and infantrymen.

Bibliography

PRIMARY

The US War Department, US Forces, European Theater, Military Intelligence Service (MIS) Escape and Evasion Section (MIS-X) and Interview Section, Collection and Administrative Branch Records Group 498 of the National Archives contains the individual debriefings and interviews conducted with each evader.

Information about Operation Halyard and evaders in Yugoslavia is located at the US Air Force War College Library, Maxwell AFB, Alabama. It is filed under 15th Air Force Air Crew Rescue Unit, July 1944–June 1945, 670.614.1.

BOOKS

Ankeny, Susan Tate. *The Girl and the Bombardier: A True Story of Rescue and Resistance in Nazi-Occupied France*. Clarksville, TN: Diversion Press, 2020.

Astor, Gerald. *The Mighty Eighth: The Air War in Europe as Told by the Men Who Fought It*. New York: Dutton, 1997.

Avriett, Carole E. and George W. Starks. *Coffin Corner Boys: One Bomber, Ten Men, and Their Harrowing Escape from Nazi-Occupied France*. Washington, D.C.: Regnery, 2018.

Bennett, Col. George Floyd. *Shot Down! Escape and Evasion*. Morgantown, WV: Mediaworks, 1992.

Bodson, Herman. *Downed Airmen and Evasion of Capture: The Role of Local Resistance Networks in World War II*. Jefferson, NC: McFarland & Co., 2005.

Bowen, Wayne H. *Spain During World War II*. Colombia: University of Missouri Press, 2006.

Bowman, Martin W. *Clash of Eagles: USAAF 8th Air Force Bombers Versus the Luftwaffe in World War II*. South Yorkshire, UK, 2007.

Brome, Vincent. *The Way Back: The Story of Pat O'Leary*. New York: W. W. Norton, 1957.

Burg, Maclyn P. and Thomas J. Pressly, editors. *The Great War at Home and Abroad: The World War I Letters of W. Stull Holt*. Manhattan, KS: Sunflower University Press, 1998.

Caiden, Martin. *Black Thursday*. New York: E. P. Dutton, 1960.

Caine, Philip D. *Aircraft Down! Evading Capture in WW II Europe*. Washington, D. C.: Potomac Books, 2005.

Cosgrove, Edmund. *The Evaders*. Markham, Ontario: Simon and Schuster of Canada, 1976.

Craven, Wesley Frank and James Lea Cate. *The Army Air Force in World War II*. Chicago: U. S. Air Force History Office, University of Chicago Press, 1948.

Culler, Dan. *Prisoner of the Swiss: A World War II Airman's Story*. Havertown, PA: Casemate, 2017.

Davies, Peter. *France and the Second World War: Occupation, Collaboration, and Resistance*. London: Routledge, 2000.

Dear, Ian. *Escape and Evasion: Prisoner of War Breakouts and the Routes to Safety*. London: Arms and Armour Press, 1997.

Eisner, Peter. *The Freedom Line: The Brave Men and Women Who Rescued Allied Airmen From the Nazis During World War II*. New York: Perennial, 2005.

Ethell, Jeffery and Alfred Price. *The German Jets in Combat*. London: Jane's Publishing, 1979.

Foot, M. R. D. and J. M. Langley. *MI9—Escape and Evasion*. Boston: Little, Brown, and Co., 1980.

Freeman, Gregory A. *The Forgotten 500: The Untold Story of the Men Who Risked All for the Greatest Rescue Mission of World War II*. New York: NAL Caliber, 2007.

Froom, Phil. *Evasion and Escape Devices Produced by MI9, MIS-X, and SOE in World War II*. Atglen, PA: Schiffer Publishing, 2015.

Green, William. *Warplanes of the Third Reich*. New York: Galahad Books, 1970.

Hemingway-Douglass, Reanne. *The Shelburne Escape Line: Secret Rescues of Allied Aviators by the French Underground, the British Royal Navy, and London's MI-9*. Anacortes, WA: Cave Art Press, 2014.

Horning, Art. *In the Steps of a Flying Boot*. New York: Carlton Press, 1994.

Janes, Keith. *Express Delivery*. Leicester, UK: Troubadour, 2019.

———. *They Came from Burgundy: A Study of the Bourgogne Escape Line*. Leicester, UK: Troubadour, 2017.

Katsaros, John. *Code Burgundy: The Long Escape*. Norwalk, CT: Oakford Media, 2008.

Kurapovna, Macia. *Shadows of the Mountain: The Allies, the Resistance, and the Rivalries that Doomed WWII Yugoslavia*. New York: Wiley, 2009.

Lavender, Emerson and Norman Sheffe. *The Evaders*. Toronto: McGraw Hill, 1992.

Meyerowitz, Seth. *The Lost Airman: A True Story of Escape and Evasion from Nazi-Occupied France*. New York: Dutton Caliber, 2016.

Middlebrook, Martin. *The Schweinfurt-Regensburg Mission: The American Raids on 17 August 1943*. Barnsley, South Yorkshire, UK: Pen and Sword, 2012.

Moore, Bob. *Resistance in Western Europe*. Oxford, UK: Berg Publishers, 2000.

Neave, Airey. *Little Cyclone*. London: Biteback, 2016.

Nichol, John and Tony Rennell. *Home Run: Escape from Nazi Europe*. New York: Penguin, 2007.

Nijboer, Donald. *Flak in World War II*. Mechanicsburg, PA: Stackpole Books, 2018.

Ottis, Sherri Greene. *Silent Heroes: Downed Airmen and the French Underground*. Lexington: University of Kentucky Press, 2001.

Prince, Cathryn J. *Shot from the Sky: American POWs in Switzerland*. Annapolis, MD: Naval Institute Press, 2016.

Prosser, David G. *Journey Underground*. New York: Dutton, 1945.

Roberts, Walter R. *Tito, Mihailovich, and the Allies 1941–1945*. New Brunswick, NJ: Rutgers University Press, 1973.

Schaffer, Ronald. *Wings of Judgement: American Bombing in World War II*. New York: Oxford University Press, 1985.

Shoemaker, Lloyd R. *The Escape Factory: The Story of MIS-X*. New York: St. Martin's, 1990.

Smith, Larry. *Trouble*. Canneaut Lake, PA: Page Publishers, 2018.

Snyder, Steve. *Shot Down: The True Story of Pilot Howard Snyder and the Crew of the B-17 Susan Ruth*. Seal Beach, CA: Sea Breeze Publishing, 2015.

Tanner, Stephen. *Refuge from the Reich: American Airmen and Switzerland During World War II*. Boston: Da Capo Press, 2001.

Todorovich, Boris J. *Last Words: A Memoir of World War II and Yugoslav Tragedy*. New York: Walker & Co., 1989.

Tudor, Malcom. *Prisoners and Partisans: Escape and Evasion in World War II Italy*. Newton, Powys, UK: Emilia Publishing, 2016.

Warmbrunn, Werner. *The Dutch Under German Occupation*. Palo Alto, CA: Stanford University Press, 1963.

Watts, George. *The Comet Connection: Escape from Hitler's Europe*. Lexington: University of Kentucky, 1990.

DOCUMENTS

Press Clippings: A Partial Collection of Press Clippings Compiled by the National Committee of American Airmen to Aid General Mihailovich and the Serbian People. Chicago: 1946.

Press Clippings: A Partial Collection of Press Clippings Compiled by the National Committee of American Airmen to Aid General Mihailovich and the Serbian People. Book II. Chicago: 1946.

PERIODICALS

Bubenzer, Gus. "Shot Down in Occupied France: Memories of World War II." *Laurels*, Fall, 1988.

Douglas, Jim. "Underground Escape." *Boeing News*, June 1944.

Jibilian, Arthur. "I Was There: Rescuer in Yugoslavia." *America in World War II*, April 2008.

Kahn, Jim. "A UW History Professor's Little-Known Story of Heroism at War." *University of Washington Magazine*, March, 2013.

Kelly, Lt. Cdr. Richard M. "Behind Enemy Lines Series: Halyard Mission." *Blue Book Magazine*, August, 1946.

Lyons, Chuck. "MIS-X's Shadowy Secrets: Aiding Allied POW Escapes." *WW II History*, December 2015.

Mears, Dwight S. "To Intern or Not to Intern? Neutral States and the Application of International Law to United States Airmen in World War II," *Journal of the History of International Law*, vol. 15, 2013.

Reynolds, Michael. "Massacre at Malmedy During the Battle of the Bulge." *World War II Magazine*, February 2003.

WORLD WIDE WEB
www.afhra.af.mil
www.ww2escapelines.co.uk
www.airmen.dk
www.b17flyingfortress.de
www.americanairmuseum.com
www.b17flyingfortress.de
www.8af.org
www.evasioncomete.org

Index

The photo insert pages are indicated by *p1, p2, p3*, etc.

268; Laux on, 246–47; saving, of evaders, in, 253; searches in, 250
Germany, escape routes through, *p2*
Germany, evasion from, 81, 254
Geron, Alva, 167
Gestapo: French Resistance and, 221–22; against helpers, retaliation by, 96, 244, 251; helpers curtailed by, 96–97; lines infiltrated by, 216
Gibraltar, 8, 158, *p3*; American Consulate in, 279–80; escape routes to, *p2*; Williams, J., crossing to, 155–56. *See also* Britain
Giles, Robert C., 99
Gill, Tony P., 179
Glaze, Ivan E., 97
Glennan, Thomas J., 30–31
Glover, Fred W., 145–46
Gochnour, Walter R., 238
Godlewski, Agaton J., 238
Goetsch, Daniel H., 89
Goicoechea, Florentino, 36
Gooch, Carl H., 303
Goodwin, Norman C., 180
Gordon, Richard J., 93–95
Gorglione, Louis P., 254
Grauerholz, Lawrence E., 116
Green, Earl W., 129
Greene, Frank W., 117
Grose, Richard L., 208
Grubb, Ernest O., 92
Grumbles, James A., 56–57, 154
Guerisse, Albert (Patrick Albert O'Leary), 28
guidelines, evade and escape, 15–16
guides, on Pyrenees, 27, 141–42; Basque, 36, 144; Dedee, 36–37; Glover on, 145–46; Goicoechea, 36; Olsen on, 261; paying, 144, 152–53

guns, aircraft: on A-20, 318; on B-17, 314; on B-24, 315; on B-26, 317; on FW-190, 323; on ME-109, 322; on ME-262, 323–24

Halyard (operation). *See* Yugoslavia
Hamblin, Oscar K., 50
Hamby, Jesse M., 55–56
Hammock, Clifford, 249
Hanes, Horace A., 209
Hargrove, Walter, 104–5; in France, 106–8; intelligence provided by, 108–11
Harper, Flamm D., 220
Hartin, Forrest D., 3, 18; appendix D of, 9–11; in France, 4–8, 12; in Spain, 8, 12
Hartmann, Eric, 321
Havoc. *See* A-20 Havoc
Hawes, Harry A., 91, 277
Hawkins, William C., 95–96
hay, hiding in, 99, 188
Hegg, John B., Jr., 297–98
Heinke, Melvin L., 57
Heldman, Henry M., 160–61
Helen (Romanian queen), 195
helpers, 26–27, 72; admiration expressed for, 98–99; advice on, 69–71; AFEES for, 309–11; in Belgium, identity verified by, 89; bicycles provided by, 78, 85; bribes, bounties offered to, 96–98; of Carroll, 60–65; code words of, 98; Comet Line, 33–38, 153; disguise provided by, 61, 73–74, 103; Dutch, hiding by, 82–83; Dutch, MIS-X Holland office and, 302–7; evaders spotted by, 93; former, 309–11; gendarmes as, 69, 92, 214, 260; German retaliation against, 96,

Schowalter, Gilbert T., 216

Schraeder, Ivan L., 102, 142, 284

Schroeder, Norman C., 73, 90–91

Schweiker, Richard S., 280

Sciranko, Michael T., 239–41

Seidel, Herman I., 55

Seniawsky, Peter, 71–72

SERE. *See* Survival, Evasion, Resistance, and Escape

Shapiro, Morton B., 73

Sheahan, William G., 98–99

Sheehan, Robert E., 141–42

Shelburne Line: Donaldson escaping via, 45–46; establishment of, 43–44; French Resistance and, 41–44; helpers of, 41–46; Hoffman escaping via, 41–43; map of, *p1*; MI9 and, 44; Shevchik escaping via, 45; Vogel escaping via, 44–45

Sheppard, Meyles A., 132

Shevchik, Milton V., 45, 244

Shilliday, James G., 267

shoes, 70, 131; in appendix D, 128, 130; Arp on, 74; Biggs on, 75; Carroll on, 62; Pyrenees, crossing, and, 74, 76; Russell on, 212; Utley on, 123–24, 128, 130

Shows, Waldo W., 217–18

Shuster, William E., 279

Simon, Murray L., 117, 221, 278–79

slave labor, 321

Smith, Bert I., Jr., 163

Smith, Carl N., 153–54

Smith, Carl W., 115

Smith, Dorothy A., 222, 285, 307

Smith, Karl Clive, 207

Smith, Michael L., 96, 100

Smith, Robert E., 295–96

Smith, Russell M., 102

smuggled correspondence, of evaders, 287

Snedeker, James C., 237–38

Snyder, Edward R., 255

Snyder, Walter R., 135

Soignies, Belgium, 29

Soviet Union, 97, 193, 317, 321; Romania and, 196, 208; Yugoslavia and, 202, 209

Spain: airmen unprepared for, 158–60; Allies and, 157–58; Axis and, 157–58; Basques, 36, 144; Britain, Gibraltar, and, 158; Carroll crossing to, 67–68; civilians in, reception by, 157; Collins in, 25; Comet Line to, 33–39, 141, 144, 153, 216, *p1*; difficulties in, 157–59; escape routes through, *p2*; German agents in, 157, 159, 161–63; Hartin in, 8, 12; historical context of, 157–58; lines in, map of, *p1*; Madrid, 155–56; MIS-X on, 160–61; Olsen on, 261–62; Pat O'Leary Line to, 25–31, 141–42, 144, 216, *p1*; Patterson in, 35–36; police in, 157–63; Stakes on, 140–41; trains in, 68; Williams, J., on, 155–57. *See also* Gibraltar; Pyrenees, crossing

Spanish Civil War, 157, 321

Stairs, Donald C., 153

Stakes, Richard Arthur, 136; in France, 137–40; across Pyrenees, journey of, 140–41

Stanford, Lloyd A., 131

Stars and Stripes, 300

Stead Air Force Base, Nevada, 308–9

Stevens, H. V., 53

Stinnett, Myrle J., 119

Supreme Allied Commander, Europe. *See* Eisenhower, Dwight

Survival, Evasion, Resistance, and Escape (SERE), 309–11

About the Author

Michael Lee Lanning is the author of twenty-eight nonfiction books on military history, sports, and health. More than 1.1 million copies of his books are in print in fifteen countries, and editions have been translated into twelve languages. He has appeared on major television networks as well as the History Channel as an expert on the individual soldier on both sides of the Vietnam War.

The *New York Times Book Review* declared Lanning's *Vietnam 1969–1970: A Company Commander's Journal* to be "one of the most honest and horrifying accounts of a combat soldier's life to come out of the Vietnam War." The London *Sunday Times* devoted an entire page to review his book, *The Military 100: A Ranking of the Most Influential Military Leaders of All Time*. According to the *San Francisco Journal*, Lanning's *Inside the VC and NVA* is "a well-researched, groundbreaking work that fills a huge gap in the historiography of the Vietnam War."

A veteran of more than twenty years in the US Army, Lanning is a retired lieutenant colonel. During the Vietnam War he served as an infantry platoon leader, reconnaissance platoon leader, and an infantry company commander. In addition to having earned the Combat Infantryman's Badge and Bronze Star with "V" device with two oak leaf clusters, Lanning is Ranger-qualified and a senior parachutist.

Lanning, born in Sweetwater, Texas, earned a BS from Texas A&M University and an MS from East Texas State University. He currently resides in Lampasas, Texas.